The Reader's Digest Good Health Cookbooks

Meat Dishes

The Reader's Digest Good Health Cookbooks

MEAT DISHES

PUBLISHED BY THE READER'S DIGEST ASSOCIATION LIMITED LONDON SYDNEY CAPE TOWN

Contents

The Good Health Cookbooks

Dieting need not be dreary. Whatever diet you may follow, you can still enjoy the classic dishes. Often, all you need are alternative ingredients that suit the recipe and suit the requirements of your diet. This book gives you the recipes for those classic dishes from *The Cookery Year*. It also gives you those vital alternatives. It has, in fact, several features unique in cookery books. In the special "Alternatives" column on each page, we identify how high each recipe is in salt, sugar, fat, cholesterol and fibre. We also give the calorie count. We check if it is gluten-free and wholefood. Then we suggest how you could adapt the recipe to any diet you, your family, or your guests might want to follow.

We do not lay down what diet you should follow. That is your decision. The book assumes that you yourself know what you want to do and tries to help you to do it by making suggestions (not commands), some or all of which you may want to follow. Perhaps you have been told to cut down drastically on salt; perhaps you have been thinking for some time that you should eat a little less sugar; perhaps you have a friend coming to a meal who cannot eat gluten or who is avoiding food high in cholesterol. You do not have to buy a new cookbook for each diet. You do not have to produce alternative meals for every guest. With these books, you can simply adapt the existing recipes to suit your needs.

You will find that we make use of a few conventions. This is mainly in order to avoid constant repetition. **The asterisk** (*) is used as follows:

1) Salt* indicates that this item may be omitted for those on a low-salt diet; the salt level of the recipe as given in the "Alternatives" column is calculated on the assumption that this salt has been omitted and that any ingredients that sometimes contain salt and sometimes don't (e.g. tinned tomatoes) have been bought in their salt-free version.

2) Gluten-free* indicates that the recipe is free of gluten so long as gluten-free flour (or bread or breadcrumbs) is used where appropriate.

3) Wholefood* indicates that the recipe is wholefood if wholemeal flour (or bread or breadcrumbs), brown rice and unrefined sugar are used where appropriate.

The levels of salt, **sugar**, **fat**, **cholesterol** and **fibre** for each recipe are denoted by symbols in the "Alternatives" column:

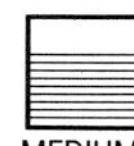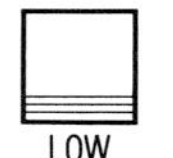

For definitions of what constitutes a high threshold level of any one of these, see under the appropriate diet on the following pages. Less than half this threshold level is considered low.

Calorie counts are given, firstly for the recipe as a whole and secondly as an indication of how many calories may be avoided as a result of following particular alternative suggestions.
Calories are automatically lost when either sugar or fat is significantly reduced. The calculations for calorie-

loss can be no more than approximate, and occasionally are omitted, as so many factors can vary: the fat level of fish and meat at different times of the year, the exact amount of fat trimmed off a cut of meat, or the amount of sugar that will make a dish acceptably sweet to a particular palate.

To convert calories to kilojoules, multiply the figure for calories by 4·18.

Cooking hints on when it is appropriate or helpful to use a pressure cooker, slow cooker, food processor, freezer or microwave are indicated by a tick, together with any further information required. With a microwave it is always essential that you also consult the manufacturer's instructions, as cooking times vary from cooker to cooker.

Measurements are expressed in both imperial and metric units. The figures are rounded up or down as necessary. As this is an international publication, we have borne in mind that teaspoons and tablespoons vary in capacity from country to country, but in any recipe where we have used these measurements, the dish should not be affected by such variations. For a check on the comparative values of these measures, consult the tables on the inside of the book's covers.

With practice you should find that the technique and alternatives recommended in this book will work with recipes from other books. In this way it becomes simple to adapt recipes so that they are both healthy and delicious. That is how it ought to be.

The Diets

Low-salt diet

Sodium is acknowledged to be a contributory factor in hypertension (high blood pressure) and thus in coronary heart disease and strokes; it can also be involved in some kidney disorders.

By far the most concentrated source of sodium is common salt (sodium chloride), and many processed foods contain a lot of added salt.

Diets which are very severely restricted in sodium are on occasion prescribed, but we are not concerned with them here. A certain minimum of both sodium and chloride is essential to good health, and the majority of salt-conscious people will simply want to cut out excessive consumption.

While setting an exact figure is very difficult, as the total level of salt in a meal depends on the combination of foods eaten, a target of 5 grams a day (generally considered to be not excessive) can usually be reached by cutting down on cooking or table salt as well as on monosodium glutamate. Foods such as salted or cured pork products and most cheeses should be eaten only in small quantities. Then the sodium occurring naturally in meat and fish, even in sodium-rich shellfish, need not be avoided.

It is important to check the labels on tins. Some tomatoes, for instance, are canned with added salt, others not. Egg whites and dried fruit are also relatively high in sodium and should not be overindulged in.

Salt substitutes are available but we do not specify them: they do not taste like salt and anyone suffering from heart or kidney disease should not take them without medical approval.

Many of those wishing to cut down on salt will also want to combine this with cutting down on fat. Therefore, for example, although double cream contains much less sodium than single cream or milk does, we do not advocate replacing milk with double cream.

Salt is used to to mean both common salt (sodium chloride) and sodium in general. Where the level of salt in the recipe is given, this takes into account sodium occurring naturally in the ingredients; in the list of ingredients, salt refers, as usual, to the sodium chloride commonly used for seasoning.

The salt content of a recipe is taken to be high if it contains the equivalent of more than 2 egg whites or $\frac{1}{2}$ pint (300 ml) of milk per person.

Low-sugar diet

Sugar is "empty calories": it provides no nutrients, but concentrated calories for a very little weight of food.

Sugar is the first thing to go if you are on a calorie-controlled diet. It is also known to encourage tooth decay; and high consumption, especially of refined sugar, has been correlated with certain diseases.

Refined sugar is pure sucrose, the form of sugar which is the least desirable. Sugar occurs naturally in other forms – for example, fructose in fruit, lactose in milk, dextrose (glucose) and maltose. These do not always have the same harmful effect on the body as sucrose, and are not eaten in anything like the same sort of quantity.

A low-sugar diet, therefore, usually aims at cutting out as much refined sugar as possible. This can be done simply by using less of it and deliberately cultivating a less sweet tooth, or by replacing it to some extent with other forms of sugar. Honey, for instance (which is mainly fructose and glucose, with little sucrose) is sweeter than sugar so less of it is needed. In this way you can cut down on both sucrose and the total quantity of sugar. Molasses, although a form of sucrose, has a very strong taste and again a teaspoon of it can sometimes be used instead of a tablespoon or more of sugar.

In this book, when the level of sugar in a recipe is indicated, it takes into account both the general level of sugar, including all its various forms – sucrose, fructose, glucose etc. – as well as any added sugar specified in the recipe. In the list of ingredients, sugar refers to the added sugar which is virtually pure sucrose. The suggestions for decreasing the sugar content of a recipe almost always refer to sucrose.

We are not concerned here with sugar substitutes nor with special diabetic sweeteners and jams. We do not aim to preserve an ultra-sweet taste. What we aim to do is to cut down the amount of refined sugar and to make more use of fruit and of small quantities of honey and molasses. The results will be definitely less sweet but still delicious.

The sugar content of a recipe is taken to be high if it contains the equivalent of more than 1 tablespoon of sugar per person.

Low-fat and low-cholesterol diets

One of the most common reasons for eating less fat and cholesterol is that there appears to be an undisputed link between the presence of cholesterol in the blood and liability to heart attacks.

Populations who eat less fat have lower levels of heart disease, although their consumption of oil may be high, as in many Mediterranean countries. The exact link has not yet been established, and it appears that other foods, for example garlic, onions and polyunsaturated fat, as well as fibre, have the ability to lower blood cholesterol. However, more and more people are coming to the conclusion that cutting down on fats, especially saturated fats, cannot do them any harm. Certainly it will help calorie control: fat contains twice as many calories per ounce as protein or carbohydrate.

Whether you want to lose weight or reduce the risk of a heart attack, low-fat and low-cholesterol diets are similar in many ways. Both encourage cutting down on the saturated fats which contain cholesterol.

Saturated fats are usually of animal origin but not always: coconuts, for example, have a saturated fat content of 83%. Unsaturated fats are mainly of vegetable origin and are further divided into monounsaturated and polyunsaturated fats. (These terms refer to the way in which their molecules are chemically bonded.) They are generally liquid at room temperature.

Monounsaturated fats (the most usual example is olive oil, which is 73% monounsaturated fat) have no effect on the level of cholesterol in the blood. Polyunsaturated fats can in fact, as stated above, actually lower the blood cholesterol level. There are a few foods which are very high in cholesterol relative to their fat content, notably shellfish, fish roes, and organ meats such as liver, kidney, brains and sweetbreads.

Those on a low-fat diet will want to cut down on all fats and oils. Those aiming at a low-cholesterol intake will want to eliminate as far as possible all saturated fats and will be cautious about eating shellfish and offal. This book shows you how to do either or both of these.

However the book does not purport to give a diet which actually lowers blood cholesterol. For instance, in the recipes olive oil is often specified. Those on such a diet will replace olive oil with safflower, soya or sunflower oils. Nor does this book attempt to give a fat-free diet. Such a diet should only be attempted under medical supervision, and even then it is bound to have a minimal fat content. Some fat is necessary in our diet, particularly linoleic acid, an essential fatty acid, which cannot be manufactured by the body: it is found in vegetable oils, particularly safflower oil.

Some particular foods that will be found useful in both low-fat and low-cholesterol diets are:

- skimmed milk, both liquid and dried
- low-fat cheese, particularly cottage cheese and low-fat curd cheese, such as quark or fromage blanc
- smetana (5–10% fat as opposed to 18% in sour cream)

For low-cholesterol diets:
- safflower, soya, sunflower and walnut oils
- (for frying over high heat): corn or peanut oils. It is, however, better to avoid frying over high heat as far as possible, since this changes the composition of the oils into something resembling saturated fat
- soft margarines with a high percentage of polyunsaturated oils (all margarines labelled "all vegetable" are virtually cholesterol-free)

The fat and cholesterol content of eggs is found only in the yolks, but in many cases yolks can be decreased or omitted, sometimes with a proportionate increase in the number of whites used.

The fat content of a recipe is taken to be high if it contains the equivalent of more than any 2 of the following per person:

$\frac{1}{2}$ oz (1 tablespoon) double cream or oil
$\frac{1}{4}$ oz (7 grams) butter, lard, suet or margarine
1 egg yolk
$\frac{1}{2}$ oz (10–15 grams) ham, bacon, pork or cheese

The above applies also to the cholesterol content of a recipe, except that unsaturated oils are freely allowed, and over $\frac{1}{2}$ an egg yolk is considered to be high.

Fibre

The importance of fibre in the diet is now widely recognised, and many people pursue a high-fibre diet.

Since one of the best and easiest ways of increasing fibre intake is to eat a slice or two of wholemeal bread with your meal, the recipes themselves have not (except in one or two cases) been modified to include more fibre. The original versions of the recipes are always based on fresh ingredients, including vegetables, fruit and nuts (most of which are high in fibre), and wholefood adaptations are available for almost all the recipes, thus helping to increase the fibre level.

Gluten-free diet

As coeliac sufferers are being identified more and more frequently, so the need for a gluten-free diet for them and for other gluten-sensitive patients is becoming widely recognised.

A gluten-free diet involves complete exclusion of gluten (a protein, found mainly in wheat but also, in a different form and to a lesser extent, in rye, barley and oats). Commercial gluten-free flour is available and can be used successfully for bread, and some pastry and cakes; if it is difficult to find or expensive to buy just for one recipe, there are other flours, many of which are familiar to those on wholefood diets, which are gluten-free. Chick pea flour, brown rice flour, cornflour, potato flour and soya flour are perhaps the best known.

All labels on tins and jars must be carefully read, as wheat flour is a common ingredient not just in the obvious breads, biscuits, cakes, pastries and many cereals, but in packet soups, baking powder, sausages, stock cubes, bottled sauces and baked beans as well as in some brands of mustard, ground white pepper, curry powder and cheap chocolate.

Gluten-free grains include rice, maize, millet and buckwheat. Cornflour, chick pea flour and split pea flour are all suitable for making white sauces. For soufflés, cornflour and potato flour (the latter is denser than wheat flour and half the amount given in the recipe is usually enough) can be used. Any of these will do for coating food which is to be fried. Millet flakes make a good gluten-free alternative to a breadcrumb coating.

As a gluten-free diet is often low in fibre, it is advisable to eat plenty of brown rice, other whole grains and potatoes. Pectin (available dried from specialist suppliers) can be used as a binding agent in doughs and batters; grated fresh apple can also sometimes be used.

Intolerance of gluten is often associated with an inability to digest fats, so that a low-fat diet may also need to be followed.

Wholefood diet

Since the recipes in this book are based firmly on fresh seasonal produce, they need little alteration to be acceptable to lovers of wholefood.

The main items to avoid are refined flour and sugar. Wholemeal flour and bread, and brown rice or sugar, can be used instead as desired. When buying brown sugar, look for the name of the country of origin on the packet. If this is not given, the sugar may be white sugar that has been coloured brown with caramel.

In the case of sugar, it may also be necessary to follow any suggestion given for reducing the total amount. A high level of even the comparatively unrefined brown sugar is not usually considered wholefood. Anything other than this will be covered in the Alternatives column. Where quantities or proportions are affected, as for instance in baking, this will also be covered.

CHILLED MULLIGATAWNY SOUP

Mulligatawny soup – a favourite among the British in India, and brought home by them – is a rich meat stock strongly flavoured with curry. This version transforms the traditional soup into a cool summer starter.

PREPARATION TIME: *20 min*
COOKING TIME: *30 min*
CHILLING TIME: *1½–2 hours*
INGREDIENTS *(for 6):*
1 onion
1 carrot
2 oz (50 g) unsalted butter
3 level tablespoons plain flour
2 level teaspoons curry powder
2½ pints (1½ litres) beef stock
2 tablespoons syrup drained from mango chutney
GARNISH:
Cauliflower florets

Peel and finely chop the onion and carrot. Melt the butter in a large pan over moderate heat and cook the vegetables until the onion is transparent. Sift the flour and curry powder together and stir into the vegetables. Continue cooking over moderate heat, stirring constantly, until the mixture is a deep brown colour. Gradually stir in the hot stock and bring the soup to the boil. Simmer over low heat for 30 minutes, then set aside to cool slightly.

Put the soup through a coarse sieve, or liquidise it for 1–2 minutes, then stir in the mango syrup. Chill for at least 1½ hours.

Before serving, remove any fat from the surface of the soup. Pour into bowls and garnish with tiny florets of raw cauliflower.

BEEF AND PRAWN SOUP

A soup from Malaysia, where it can be served either before the main curry course or as an accompaniment to it.

PREPARATION TIME: *30 min*
COOKING TIME: *2 hours*
INGREDIENTS *(for 4–6):*
1 lb (450 g) lean beef
3 onions
2 cloves garlic
Knob fresh ginger
¾ level teaspoon ground turmeric
1 level teaspoon ground coriander
8 oz (225 g) shelled prawns
3 level tablespoons ghee (page 99) or melted butter
*Salt**
1 tablespoon fresh lime or lemon juice

Put the beef in a pan with 2½ pints (1½ litres) cold water, 1 peeled and quartered onion, and 1 flattened clove of garlic. Bring to the boil, cover and simmer for 1 hour.

Peel and mince one onion and pound it with the remaining garlic, ginger, turmeric and coriander. Chop the prawns roughly and fry them in 2 tablespoons butter for 2 minutes. Add the pounded onion mixture and fry for 3–4 minutes.

Using a slotted spoon, lift out the onion and garlic from the soup. Add the prawn and onion mixture and continue simmering the soup until the beef is quite tender. Take out the beef, slice it thinly and return it to the soup. Season to taste with salt. Cut the remaining onion into thin rings and fry in the rest of the butter until crisp.

Stir the lime juice into the soup and sprinkle with the fried onion rings.

BEEF SATAY

These delicious little skewers with their peanut-flavoured sauce can be made with beef or chicken. In Malaysia and Indonesia they are sold from roadside stalls, but they are also simple to make at home.

PREPARATION TIME: *20 min*
STANDING TIME: *2 hours*
COOKING TIME: *20 min*
INGREDIENTS *(for 4–6):*
1½ lb (700 g) lean beef
1 tablespoon blanched almonds (page 96)
1 tablespoon sliced root ginger
1 level teaspoon ground coriander
1 level teaspoon ground turmeric
½ pint (300 ml) coconut milk (see below)
Salt and black pepper*
1 level teaspoon brown sugar
SATAY SAUCE:
PREPARATION TIME: *15 min*
COOKING TIME: *15 min*
INGREDIENTS:
2 onions
1–2 tablespoons peanut oil
3 oz (75 g) roasted peanuts
½ level teaspoon chili powder or cayenne
1 level teaspoon light brown sugar
*Salt**
1 tablespoon soya sauce
Juice of ½ lime

Pound the almonds, ginger, coriander and turmeric to a paste in a mortar and gradually dilute it with coconut milk. Cut the meat into bite-size pieces and sprinkle them with salt and ground pepper. Marinate the meat in the spiced coconut milk for 2 hours.

Peel and thinly slice one onion and fry in the hot peanut oil. Peel and finely chop the second onion and pound it with the peanuts and

CHILLED MULLIGATAWNY SOUP

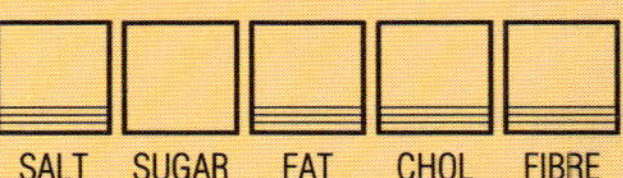

GLUTEN-FREE*   WHOLEFOOD*
TOTAL CALORIES: ABOUT 660

To reduce the **fat** level even further, the vegetables should be cooked in only 1½ oz (40 g) butter. Make sure the beef stock has been thoroughly skimmed of fat.
For minimal **cholesterol** level, replace the butter with vegetable margarine or oil; again, be sure to skim the stock thoroughly before using. (Calories lost: up to 230.)
A good **gluten-free** flour to use is potato flour: use only about 2 tablespoons. Check the label on your curry powder to make certain that it does not contain gluten.

Freezing: ✓ up to 3 months.
Microwave: ✓

BEEF AND PRAWN SOUP

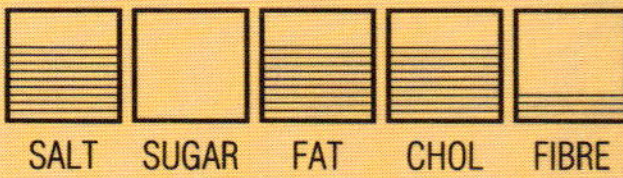

GLUTEN-FREE   WHOLEFOOD
TOTAL CALORIES: ABOUT 1830

The **salt** comes mainly from the prawns; to reduce the level, use a smaller proportion of prawns, or substitute monkfish. (Monkfish gives an interesting, if less authentic, flavour to the dish.)
The **fat** can be reduced to low by using only 2 teaspoons oil in which to cook the prawns. The **cholesterol**, like the salt, comes mainly from the prawns, which can be reduced or replaced as above. If this is done and if the

butter is replaced with vegetable margarine (or peanut oil, which would be authentic for this region's cuisine), the cholesterol level will be low. (Calories lost: up to 160.)

Pressure cooker: ☑
Microwave: ☑

BEEF SATAY

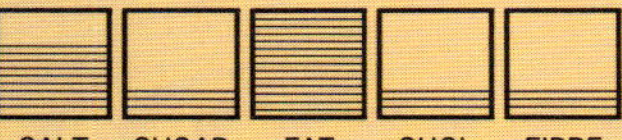

SALT SUGAR FAT CHOL FIBRE

GLUTEN FREE   WHOLEFOOD
TOTAL CALORIES: ABOUT 2980

Provided that the beef used is really lean, the method of cooking the beef itself is very healthy. The satay sauce adds some **salt**, mainly in the soya sauce. For a low-salt version reduce the soya sauce to 1 teaspoon or omit it entirely. The sauce also contributes a high **fat** level. To reduce this to medium, use only 2 teaspoons oil to soften the onions, adding a spoonful or two of stock if the mixture looks dry; cover tightly while cooking; and use only half the amount of peanuts. (Calories lost: up to 370.)

chili powder in a mortar or liquidiser. Add this paste to the pan and fry for a further 3 minutes, stirring continuously. Gradually dilute the mixture with ¼ pint (150 ml) warm water and stir in the sugar. Cook for a few minutes until the sauce has the consistency of single cream. Season to taste with salt, soya sauce and lime juice. Keep hot.

Remove the meat from the marinade and thread on to one end of bamboo skewers; sprinkle them with sugar and grill, turning and basting frequently with the marinade. Allow two skewers per person and serve with satay sauce.

COCONUT CREAM AND MILK
Fresh or desiccated coconut yields both cream and milk which are used in many soups and sauces.

Drill two or three holes at the top of the coconut and shake out the colourless liquid. Saw the coconut in half and scrape out the flesh. Shred it finely, pour over ¼ pint (150 ml) boiling water and leave for 20 minutes. Squeeze through cheesecloth to produce cream.

For coconut milk, put the squeezed coconut and ¼ pint (150 ml) cold water in a pan, and bring to the boil. Remove from the heat, leave for 20 minutes, then squeeze through cheesecloth again. Coconut cream and milk can also be made in a liquidiser.

DAUBE DE BOEUF

The French culinary term 'daube' describes a braising method of slowly cooking tougher cuts of meat, usually beef, in red wine stock. This cooking method, in a covered casserole, prevents the meat from shrinking.

PREPARATION TIME: *45 min*
COOKING TIME: *3 hours*
INGREDIENTS *(for 6):*
2 lb (900 g) lean stewing steak
4 oz (100 g) piece green streaky bacon
½ bottle red wine
1 lb (450 g) carrots
1 lb (450 g) onions
3 oz (75 g) butter
1–2 cloves garlic
Bouquet garni (page 99)
¾ pint (425 ml) beef stock
2 rounded tablespoons tomato purée
1 heaped tablespoon chopped parsley
Salt and black pepper*

Trim the fat from the beef and cut the meat into 1 in (2½ cm) pieces. Cut off the rind and dice the bacon. Put the meat and bacon in a large mixing bowl, pour over the red wine and leave to marinate for 3–4 hours.

Lift the meat from the marinade (the liquid will be used later). Peel or scrape the carrots and cut them into ¼ in (½ cm) slices; peel and finely slice the onions. Using half the butter, fry the beef and the bacon in a heavy frying pan until they are evenly brown. Lift out the beef and bacon, then fry the vegetables in the remainder of the butter. Peel and chop the garlic and add to the vegetables during frying.

Cover the bottom of a large casserole dish with half the vegetables, then add the beef and bacon and top with the remaining vegetables. Pour the marinade into the casserole and add the bouquet garni.

Rinse out the frying pan with the stock. Stir with a wooden spatula to loosen all sediment, and bring the stock to the boil. Stir in the tomato purée and pour this liquid over the contents in the casserole. Add the chopped parsley, cover with a lid and cook for 3 hours in the centre of an oven pre-heated to 300°F (160°C, mark 2). Check and if necessary correct the seasoning and remove the bouquet garni. Skim off as much fat as possible from the surface – this is more easily done if the casserole is allowed to cool and then re-heated.

Traditionally, this dish is served with creamed potatoes.

BEEF STEW WITH OLIVES

Shin or leg of beef is an inexpensive cut and excellent for stewing. The gelatinous part holding the nuggets of meat together adds a good texture to the sauce and prevents the meat becoming stringy during cooking.

PREPARATION TIME: *20 min*
COOKING TIME: *3¾ hours*
INGREDIENTS *(for 4–6):*
2½–3 lb (1–1½ kg) shin of beef
Seasoned flour (page 100)
1 large onion
1 large carrot
2 cloves garlic
Cooking oil
¼ pint (150 ml) red wine
1 pint (570 ml) beef stock
Bouquet garni (page 99)
1 teaspoon anchovy essence
Salt and black pepper*
4–6 oz (100–175 g) black or green olives
GARNISH:
Chopped parsley

Remove skin and any large lumps of fat from the beef. Cut the meat into 1–1½ in (2½–4 cm) chunks and coat with seasoned flour. Peel and finely slice the onion, carrot and garlic. Pour a thin layer of oil into a large frying pan; when hot, fry the meat and vegetables until brown. Transfer the contents of the pan to a casserole dish.

Pour the wine and a little stock into the frying pan. Boil these juices rapidly, scraping in all the residue. Pour into the casserole, adding enough stock to cover the meat. Tuck in the bouquet garni, stir in the anchovy essence and plenty of freshly ground pepper. Cover with a lid or foil. Simmer the casserole in the centre of an oven, pre-heated to 300°F (160°C, mark 2), for 2–3 hours or until the meat is tender.

Remove the cooked meat and vegetables to a shallow warm serving dish and sprinkle with a little salt. Boil the liquid in the casserole rapidly until it has reduced and thickened to a rich sauce. Remove the bouquet garni. Add the olives and simmer for 5 minutes. Correct seasoning if necessary. Pour some of the sauce over the meat and serve the remainder in a sauce boat.

Garnish the meat with parsley and surround with triangles of toast or boiled potatoes.

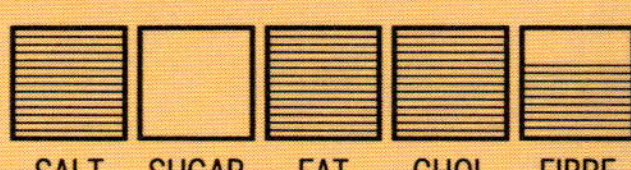

DAUBE DE BOEUF

GLUTEN-FREE   WHOLEFOOD
TOTAL CALORIES: ABOUT 4000

To reduce the **salt**, halve or omit the bacon. This brings the level down to medium-high, allowing for the amount of salt in the wine, the tomato purée and the beef itself.
For low **fat** and **cholesterol**, choose very lean beef, omit the bacon and brown the meat in a heavy pan lightly brushed with oil instead of butter. Ensure that the beef stock is well skimmed of fat. (Total calories lost: up to 1200.)

Pressure cooker: ☑
Slow cooker: ☑
Freezing: ☑ up to 2 months.

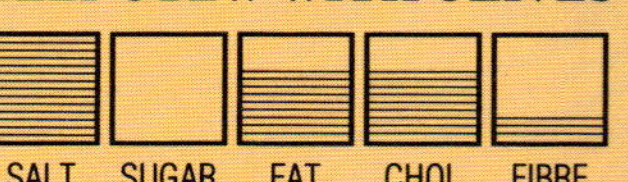

BEEF STEW WITH OLIVES

GLUTEN-FREE*   WHOLEFOOD*
TOTAL CALORIES: ABOUT 4980

Most of the **salt** comes from the olives, the rest from the anchovy essence and wine. To reduce the level of salt to medium, halve the amount of olives used.
This will also reduce the **fat** as olives average 11% oil. If, as well, the meat is browned in a heavy pan brushed lightly with oil, rather than in a thin layer of oil, and provided the beef is very lean, the dish will be low fat. (Calories lost: up to 200.)
The medium **cholesterol** level results from the generous portions. If smaller helpings are

served, with more vegetables, the cholesterol level (which comes entirely from the meat) will be low.

Pressure cooker: ☑
Slow cooker: ☑
Freezing: ☑ up to 4 months

MOUSSAKA

SALT SUGAR FAT CHOL FIBRE

GLUTEN-FREE* WHOLEFOOD*
TOTAL CALORIES: ABOUT 2730

The high **salt** level is mainly due to the salting of the aubergines. This step can perfectly well be omitted and the salt level thus reduced to low. Aubergines nowadays do not seem to have particularly bitter juices. Where salting does help is in reducing the need for so much oil, but this can be dealt with in another way (see below).

To reduce the **fat** level to low, choose very lean beef and instead of frying the aubergine slices, grill them for about 3 minutes on each side on a baking tin lightly brushed with oil. The onion can be softened in 2 teaspoons of oil, provided the pan is tightly covered and 1 tablespoon of stock or water is added after a minute or two. Use skim milk for the sauce, blending the flour, milk and egg instead of using the usual roux method, and omit the butter. The **cholesterol** level will now be moderate. (Calories lost: up to 1020.) Fat and cholesterol can be further reduced by having smaller helpings with plenty of salad.

Freezing: ☑ up to 4 months.
Microwave: ☑ for the mince.

MOUSSAKA

The aubergine, or egg plant, is the staple vegetable of the Middle East. It is the basic ingredient in moussaka, meaning aubergine casserole; the dish may also include minced beef or lamb.

PREPARATION TIME: *45 min*
COOKING TIME: *35–40 min*
INGREDIENTS *(for 4):*
4 aubergines
1 large onion
4–6 tablespoons olive oil
1 lb (450 g) lean minced beef
*1 level teaspoon salt**
2 rounded teaspoons tomato purée
¼ pint (150 ml) beef stock or water
Salt and black pepper
1 oz (25 g) unsalted butter
1 oz (25 g) plain flour
½ pint (300 ml) milk
1 egg

Peel and finely chop the onion; heat 1 tablespoon of the oil in a heavy-based pan and gently fry the onions for about 5 minutes, covering the pan with a lid. Add the minced beef and fry until brown and thoroughly sealed. Stir in the salt, tomato purée and stock; season to taste with freshly ground pepper. Bring this mixture to the boil, cover the pan with a lid and simmer gently for 30 minutes or until the meat is tender and the liquid is almost absorbed.

Meanwhile, peel and thinly slice the aubergines, arrange them in a layer on a plate and sprinkle generously with salt; let the aubergines stand for 30 minutes to draw out the bitter juices. Drain, rinse in cold water and pat thoroughly dry on absorbent kitchen paper. Fry the aubergine slices in the remaining oil until golden, then drain on absorbent

paper. Arrange a layer of aubergines in the bottom of a large buttered fireproof dish or casserole. Cover with a layer of the meat, another layer of aubergines and so on, until all is used up; finish with a layer of aubergines.

Melt the butter in a saucepan over low heat and stir in the flour. Cook gently for 1 minute, then gradually blend in the milk, stirring continuously. Bring this sauce to the boil, season with salt and freshly ground pepper and simmer for 1–2 minutes. Draw the pan off the heat and beat in the egg. Spoon this sauce over the moussaka; place in the centre of a pre-heated oven and bake at 350°F (180°C, mark 4) for 35–40 minutes or until bubbling hot and browned.

This is a rich and substantial meal, best served straight from the casserole. A tomato and onion salad could be served with it.

BEEF PAUPIETTES

Paupiettes are thin slices of meat, usually beef, which are stuffed with forcemeat and rolled into cork shapes which the French call *alouettes sans têtes* (larks without heads). The meat should be cut very thinly: ask the butcher to cut it on the bacon slicer.

PREPARATION TIME: *45 min*
COOKING TIME: *1½ hours*
INGREDIENTS *(for 4)*:
1½ lb (700 g) topside of beef, cut in thin slices
2 rounded teaspoons French mustard
Salt and black pepper*
STUFFING:
3 oz (75 g) green lean bacon
4 oz (100 g) cooked chicken or pork
1 shallot
1 large clove garlic
1½ oz (40 g) butter
2 oz (50 g) fine breadcrumbs
1 egg
1 level tablespoon chopped parsley
½ level teaspoon chopped thyme
2½ fluid oz (65 ml) brandy
SAUCE:
1 lb (450 g) mixed vegetables (onions, carrots, turnips, peas, green beans, parsnips)
1½ oz (40 g) beef dripping or lard
½ pint (300 ml) beef stock
¼ pint (150 ml) red wine
Beurre manié (page 83) made from 1 oz (25 g) flour, 1 oz (25 g) butter

Beat the beef slices wafer-thin between two pieces of waxed paper; each slice should measure about 4 in (10 cm) square. Spread a little mustard over each slice; season with salt and ground pepper.

Remove the rind and chop the bacon finely, together with the chicken or pork. Peel and finely chop the shallot and garlic. Melt the butter in a small frying pan over moderate heat and cook the shallot and garlic until soft and transparent.

In a mixing bowl, blend together the bacon, chicken, shallot and garlic. Add the bread-crumbs and the lightly beaten egg. Stir in the thyme and parsley, and season the stuffing with salt and pepper; add the brandy.

Spoon the stuffing equally on the beef slices; roll up each slice and tuck the ends over to keep the stuffing in place. Tie each pau-piette securely with fine string. Set the meat aside.

To make the sauce, peel and finely chop the onion, then brown it lightly over moderate heat in the lard or dripping. Wash and pre-pare the vegetables used, then chop them finely. Add these to the onion and cook for a few minutes to brown slightly. Spoon the vegetables into a large shallow casserole and put the paupiettes on top in a single layer. Pour the stock and wine into the pan in which the vegetables were fried, scraping up all the residue.

Pour the pan juices over the meat, cover the casserole with a lid and cook in the centre of the oven, pre-heated to 325°F (170°C, mark 3), for 1½ hours. Remove the lid after 20 minutes. Turn the meat over once during cooking.

Lift the paupiettes from the casserole, remove the string and arrange the meat on a warm serving dish. Surround them with the vegetables. Pour the cooking liquid into a small sauce-pan and boil rapidly to reduce the sauce by a third. Thicken the sauce with beurre manié, and heat it through. Spoon a little of the sauce over the meat and serve the rest in a sauce boat.

Serve with buttered noodles or creamed potatoes.

HUNGARIAN GOULASH

This internationally famous stew is usually made from beef, though pork, veal and chicken may also be used. Different regions of Hungary have their own favourite goulash recipes. Some use fresh tomatoes, others caraway seeds, garlic or mar-joram. But whatever else goes into a goulash, it always contains paprika.

PREPARATION TIME: *35 min*
COOKING TIME: *about 2 hours*
INGREDIENTS *(for 4)*:
1¼ lb (550 g) chuck steak
1 lb (450 g) onions
2 oz (50 g) lard
1½ pints (900 ml) beef stock or water
*Salt**
1 tin (2¼ oz, 60 g) tomato purée
3–4 level teaspoons paprika
2 level teaspoons caster sugar
2 level tablespoons plain flour
2½ fluid oz (65 ml) soured cream

Wipe the meat and trim off any fat and gristle. Cut it into 1½ in (4 cm) cubes. Peel and thinly slice the onions. Melt the lard in a deep, heavy-based sauté pan and fry the meat and onions over moderate heat until the onions are golden and the meat is sealed. Pour over the hot stock, season with salt and bring to simmering point.

Meanwhile, blend the tomato purée, paprika, sugar and flour in a small bowl until smooth. Stir in a few tablespoons of the simmering

BEEF PAUPIETTES

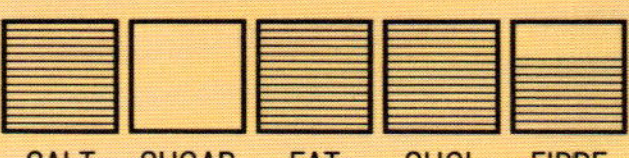

GLUTEN-FREE*   WHOLEFOOD*
TOTAL CALORIES: ABOUT 4200

For low **salt**, omit the bacon and use crumbs from bread made without salt.
To reduce **fat** and **cholesterol** to low, choose very lean meat; omit the bacon and soften the shallot and garlic in a pan lightly brushed with oil instead of butter. Soften the sauce vegetables in the same way, and thicken the dish by making a purée of some of them, rather than using beurre manié. (Calories lost: up to 1400.) Serve with plain rice or potatoes rather than buttered noodles. These steps will make the dish **gluten-free**, if there is no gluten in the mustard. Cooked millet makes a good substitute for breadcrumbs in the stuffing.

Pressure cooker: ☑
Slow cooker: ☑
Food processor: ☑ for the stuffing.
Freezing: ☑ up to 2 months.
Microwave: ☑

HUNGARIAN GOULASH

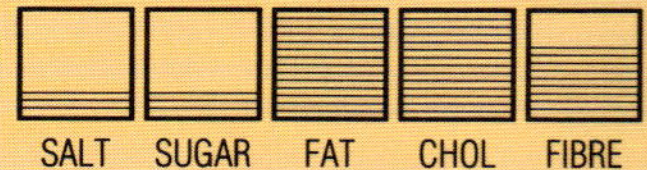

GLUTEN-FREE*   WHOLEFOOD*
TOTAL CALORIES: ABOUT 2870

The **salt** level is taken as low on the assumption that you have used unsalted tomato purée.
To reduce the levels of **fat** and **cholesterol** to low, choose very lean meat and brown it in a heavy pan lightly brushed with

oil, thus avoiding the lard. Replace the soured cream with smetana or cultured buttermilk. (Calories lost: up to 560.)

Pressure cooker: ☑
Slow cooker: ☑
Freezing: ☑ up to 4 months.
Microwave: ☑

STEAK AU POIVRE

| SALT | SUGAR | FAT | CHOL | FIBRE |

GLUTEN-FREE   WHOLEFOOD
TOTAL CALORIES: ABOUT 3640

To compensate for the lack of added **salt**, crumble a little dried tarragon or marjoram over the steak.
The lavish use of butter, oil and cream in this recipe makes it very rich indeed. To keep the peppery character but reduce **fat** and **cholesterol** to moderate (low if the steak is extremely lean), brush the steaks lightly with butter or oil before pressing in the peppercorns, then grill instead of frying for the same cooking time.
Transfer the steaks to a heated metal serving dish; warm the brandy and pour it over, set it alight immediately and pour over warmed smetana (or quark or fromage blanc thinned with a little skim milk). Be careful not to boil. (Calories lost: up to 960.)
Instead of the traditional brandy sauce, this is also good with a purée of watercress made by softening watercress for about 10 minutes in a little stock and then liquidising. It could be mixed with a little smetana or fromage blanc if you like.

liquid from the stew.

Draw the pan with the onions and meat from the heat and stir in the tomato mixture, blending thoroughly. Return to the heat and bring back to a simmer. Cover and leave the stew to cook over gentle heat for about 2 hours or until the meat is quite tender. Stir occasionally.

Just before serving, stir in the soured cream and adjust seasoning. Ribbon noodles are traditional with goulash, but boiled floury potatoes could be served instead.

STEAK AU POIVRE

A classic peppered steak is always prepared with whole, crushed peppercorns. It is traditionally served with brandy sauce and is ideal for cooking in a chafing dish at the table.

PREPARATION TIME: *15 min*
COOKING TIME: *15–20 min*
INGREDIENTS *(for 4):*
4 fillet or entrecôte steaks
2 tablespoons whole black
   peppercorns
2 oz (50 g) unsalted butter
1 tablespoon olive oil
2 tablespoons brandy
¼ pint (150 ml) double cream
Salt★

Wipe the steaks and trim off any fat and gristle. Crush the peppercorns coarsely in a mortar or on a wooden board with a rolling pin. With the fingers, press the crushed peppercorns into the surface of the meat on both sides.

Heat the butter and oil in a heavy-based pan; cook the steaks over high heat for 2 minutes, turning them once. This initial hot frying seals the juices and peppercorns in the meat; lower the heat and cook the steaks for 5 minutes for rare steaks, 8–10 minutes for medium-rare and 12 minutes for well-done steaks.

Lift the steaks from the pan on to a hot serving dish; add the brandy to the butter in the pan and set it alight when hot. Draw the pan off the heat and as soon as the flames have died down, gradually stir in the cream. Season the sauce with salt and pour it over the steaks. Freshly cooked broccoli and croquette potatoes, or a green salad, go well with these steaks.

Beef

BOEUF À LA JARDINIÈRE

Joints of beef, such as topside, silverside and brisket, are not tender enough to oven-roast successfully. They do, however, make excellent pot roasts, cooked with fresh vegetables (*à la jardinière*). Topside and silverside are lean joints, but brisket usually needs some of the fat trimmed off before being rolled and tied.

PREPARATION TIME: *25 min*
COOKING TIME: *2½–3 hours*
INGREDIENTS (*for 6*):

3 lb (1½ kg) rolled topside,
   silverside or brisket of beef
8 small onions
½ lb (225 g) small carrots
2 young turnips
2 oz (50 g) beef dripping
4 fluid oz (100 ml) dry red wine
2 bay leaves
½ level teaspoon mixed herbs
6 peppercorns
1 level teaspoon salt★
½ lb (225 g) young runner or
   French beans or fresh peas
1 lb (450 g) potatoes (optional)

Peel the onions, leaving them whole. Scrape or peel the carrots, and peel and quarter the turnips. Melt the dripping over high heat in a large heavy-based pan or flameproof casserole. Brown the meat quickly on all sides in the fat to seal in the juices. Add the onions and fry until golden. Put the carrots, turnips and wine into the pan, together with the bay leaves, mixed herbs, peppercorns and salt.

Cover the pan with a close-fitting lid or foil and simmer over low heat or in the centre of an oven pre-heated to 300°F (160°C, mark 2) for 2½–3 hours or until the meat is tender. If the liquid evaporates during cooking, add a little beef stock or water.

Top, tail and string the beans and cut them into 1 in (2½ cm) pieces. Alternatively, shell the peas. Cook them in lightly salted boiling water for 10 minutes or until just tender.

Remove the meat from the pan, carve it and arrange the slices on a hot serving dish. Surround the meat with the vegetables and garnish with the beans. Remove the bay leaves from the pan juices; skim off the fat or soak it off the surface with absorbent kitchen paper. Season the gravy to taste with salt and freshly ground pepper and pour it into a warm sauce boat.

Potatoes may be added to the meat for the last hour of cooking, or served separately.

STEAK DIANE

This famous dish originated in Australia where tender beef fillet is obligatory, but rump steak is equally suitable.

PREPARATION TIME: *20 min*
COOKING TIME: *10 min*
INGREDIENTS (*for 6*):
1½ lb (700 g) fillet or top rump of
   beef
1 small onion
2 level teaspoons caster sugar
1 large lemon
6 oz (175 g) unsalted butter
Worcestershire sauce
1 level tablespoon chopped parsley
4 tablespoons brandy

Trim the rump steak and cut it into six even pieces; beat them flat with a rolling pin until they are no more than ¼ in (½ cm) thick. Peel and finely chop the onion. Grate the lemon rind finely, squeeze out the juice and strain.

Melt 2 oz (50 g) of the butter in a large, heavy-based pan and fry the onion for about 5 minutes or until soft and transparent. Lift the onion on to a plate with a perforated spoon and keep warm. Fry two steaks at a time, over high heat for 1 minute only on each side. Lift out and keep hot.

Melt another 2 oz (50 g) of butter until foaming and fry two more steaks; repeat with the remaining meat. Return the onions to the pan, stir in the sugar, lemon rind and juice, add a few drops of Worcestershire sauce and the parsley. Cook lightly, then put in the steaks. Flame the steaks with warm brandy.

Serve the steaks with the onion and brandy poured over them. New potatoes and braised celery are suitable vegetables.

BOEUF À LA JARDINIÈRE

GLUTEN-FREE   WHOLEFOOD
TOTAL CALORIES: ABOUT 5570

The **salt** is only low if fresh beef is used. Silverside is extremely high in salt.
The exact **fat** content depends on the cut of meat. For low fat and **cholesterol** choose a lean cut, trim off all the visible fat carefully, and brown the meat in a heavy pan lightly brushed with oil; omit the dripping. (Calories lost: up to 550.)

Pressure cooker: ☑ (but you might need a little more liquid).

Freezing: ☑ up to 4 months.

STEAK DIANE

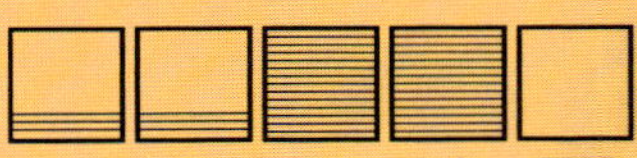

GLUTEN-FREE   WHOLEFOOD
TOTAL CALORIES: ABOUT 3680

To reduce both the **fat** and **cholesterol** levels of this recipe to low, soften the onions in a heavy pan, using only 2 teaspoons butter or oil. Choose very lean meat and either grill it, brushing it first with a little of the butter or oil from the pan in which the onions have been softened, or cook it in the same pan. Special pans for frying meat are available which need virtually no fat and give an attractive criss-cross pattern, as if the meat had been grilled. (Calories lost: up to 1200.)

TOURNEDOS EN CROÛTE

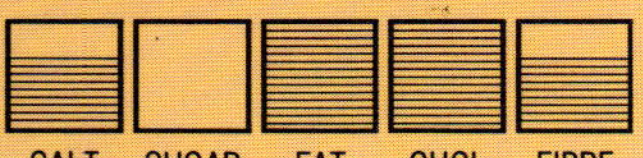

| SALT | SUGAR | FAT | CHOL | FIBRE |

TOTAL CALORIES: ABOUT 4580

The moderate **salt** level assumes that you have been able to buy (or make) a low-salt pâté. (See the recipe for liver pâté on page 67.)

To reduce **fat** and **cholesterol** to moderate, the puff pastry must be replaced by a dough much less rich in butter. Bought phyllo pastry makes a very good wrapping; yeast pastry and strudel pastry can also be used. Halve the amount of butter used for sealing, and fry the onion for the sauce in a pan very lightly brushed with butter or oil. Make your own pâté (see page 67) using a minimum of fat. (Calories lost: up to 850.)

Wholefood: strong wholemeal flour is very successful in both strudel and yeast pastry.

TOURNEDOS EN CROÛTE

The small, thick, round slices, or tournedos, cut from the fillet of beef are among the most expensive cuts of meat. But for a special occasion, tournedos can be encased in puff pastry, and a 4 oz (100 g) portion of meat will then be sufficient for each person.

PREPARATION TIME: *30 min*
COOKING TIME: *40 min*
INGREDIENTS *(for 6):*
6 tournedos
2 oz (50 g) unsalted butter
12–13 oz (about 350 g) prepared puff pastry
4 oz (100 g) pâté with mushrooms or truffles
1 egg
1 onion
4 fluid oz (100 ml) red wine
½ pint (300 ml) beef stock
Salt★ and black pepper
GARNISH:
Watercress

Trim any excess fat off the tournedos and wipe them with a damp cloth. Heat the butter in a heavy-based pan and brown the meat quickly on both sides to seal in the juices. Set aside to cool.

Roll out the puff pastry on a floured surface, to a rectangle, ⅛ in (¼ cm) thick. Divide the pastry into six equal squares, each large enough to wrap round a tournedos. Spread one side of each tournedos with pâté and place it, pâté side down, on a pastry square. Brush the edges of the pastry with cold water and draw them together over the meat to form a neat parcel. Seal the edges carefully.

Place the pastry parcels, with the seams underneath, on a wet baking tray. Lightly beat the egg and brush over the pastry. Make two or three slits in each parcel for the steam to escape, and decorate with leaves cut from the pastry trimmings. Brush with beaten egg.

Bake the tournedos in the centre of a pre-heated oven at 425°F (220°C, mark 7) for 15–20 minutes. At this point, the pastry should be well risen and golden brown and the meat will be rosy-pink in the middle. For well-done steaks, lower the heat to 350°F (180°C, mark 4) and cook for a further 10 minutes.

Make the sauce while the tournedos are cooking. Peel and finely chop the onion and fry until just coloured in the butter left in the pan. Add the wine and let it bubble over moderate heat for 2–3 minutes, stirring up the residue from the pan. Blend in the stock and simmer for a further 5 minutes. Season with salt and pepper.

Arrange the tournedos on a warm serving dish garnished with sprigs of watercress. Pour the sauce into a sauce boat and serve with potatoes and perhaps carrots or a salad.

SAUERBRATEN

This German farmhouse dish of spiced braised beef is marinated for 4–6 days to flavour and tenderise the meat. It is traditionally served with potato dumplings, but noodles or macaroni are less heavy alternatives and also go well.

PREPARATION TIME: *15 min*
COOKING TIME: *1½ hours*
INGREDIENTS *(for 4):*

2 lb (900 g) topside of beef
1 onion
4 peppercorns
1 clove
1 small bay leaf
Salt★ and black pepper
1 level teaspoon caster sugar
½ pint (300 ml) wine vinegar
2 oz (50 g) unsalted butter
1 piece breadcrust
2 rounded teaspoons cornflour

Wipe the meat with a clean cloth and trim off any fat. Tie the meat with thin string to maintain its round shape and put it in a large earthenware bowl. Peel and slice the onion, and add it to the meat, together with the peppercorns, clove, bay leaf, salt, freshly ground pepper and the sugar. Pour the vinegar mixed with ¾ pint (425 ml) of water over the meat and leave it to stand, covered, in a cold place for 4–6 days, turning it once a day in the marinade.

Lift the meat from the marinade and pat it thoroughly dry on absorbent paper. Melt the butter in a deep, heavy-based pan, add the meat and brown it quickly all over. Season to taste with salt and pour ½ pint (300 ml) of the strained marinade over the meat. Add the crust of bread (or, as in Germany, a piece of honey cake or gingerbread as well to give extra flavour). Cover the pan with a lid and simmer over low heat for 1½ hours or until the meat is tender. Add extra marinade if it becomes necessary.

Lift out the meat and keep it warm. Strain the gravy through a fine sieve, measure off ½ pint (300 ml) and top up with more marinade if necessary. Blend the cornflour with a little water and stir into the gravy; bring to the boil, stirring until smooth. Check and correct flavour and seasoning – the gravy should taste slightly sweet and sour.

Serve the meat cut into slices, with boiled noodles or macaroni; hand the gravy separately. Glazed carrots or a green vegetable such as broccoli would also be suitable.

CARBONNADES À LA FLAMANDE

This is an adaptation of a Belgian recipe for beef in beer. The ale gives the meat a distinctly nutty flavour, heightened by the garlic crust. The dish is best prepared in advance and later re-heated.

PREPARATION TIME: *55 min*
COOKING TIME: *2¾ hours*
INGREDIENTS *(for 6):*
3 lb (1½ kg) lean blade of beef
4 oz (100 g) dripping or unsalted butter
1 tablespoon olive oil
3 large onions
4 cloves garlic (optional)
Salt★ and black pepper
2 level tablespoons plain flour
1 level tablespoon soft brown sugar
½ pint (300 ml) strong beef stock
¾ pint (425 ml) brown ale
1 tablespoon wine vinegar
1 bouquet garni (page 99)
2 bay leaves
GARLIC CRUST:
½ lb (225 g) unsalted butter
3 cloves garlic
1 French loaf

Melt the dripping or butter, together with the oil, in a large sauté pan on top of the stove. Cut the beef into ½ in (1 cm) thick slices, about 3 in (7½ cm) long and 1½ in (4 cm) wide. Peel and finely slice the onions and crush the four cloves of garlic. Quickly brown the beef slices or carbonnades in the fat, drain and put to one side. Lower the heat and in the remaining fat cook the onions until golden, then add the garlic. Layer the onions and beef in a deep casserole, beginning with the onions and finishing with meat; salt and pepper each layer lightly.

SAUERBRATEN

GLUTEN-FREE★   WHOLEFOOD★
TOTAL CALORIES: ABOUT 3470

To reduce both **fat** and **cholesterol** to low, pick very lean beef (topside varies from 5%–12% fat) and brown it in a heavy pan lightly brushed with oil, omitting the butter. (Calories lost: up to 460.) If you have no **gluten-free** bread to hand, cut a floury potato into little pieces and add this instead. It will disintegrate and give body to the sauce, even when sieved. Serve with rice or potatoes instead of noodles or macaroni.

Pressure cooker: ☑

CARBONNADES À LA FLAMANDE

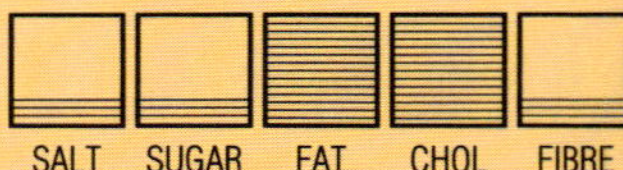

GLUTEN-FREE★   WHOLEFOOD★
TOTAL CALORIES: ABOUT 8220

Provided the beef is very lean, the total **fat** and **cholesterol** level of this recipe can be reduced to low. Brown the meat in a heavy pan lightly brushed with oil, and omit the dripping or butter and some of the oil: replace the garlic crust with potatoes mashed with skim milk and garlic. (Calories lost: up to 2610.) For a **gluten-free** dish, use a potato topping as suggested and instead of flour, thicken the casserole with 4 oz (100 g) split red lentils, added to the casserole for at least 30 minutes of the cooking time (and much longer if wished).

Wholefood: wholemeal French bread is quite good for this, but if it is unobtainable try the potato topping. A wholemeal scone dough, giving a cobbler topping, is also good.

Pressure cooker: ☑ but not the crust – this should be done in the oven.

Slow cooker: ☑ but not the crust – see above.

Freezing: ☑ up to 4 months (without the crust. Add this when reheating).

Microwave: ☑ but not the crust – see above.

STEAK TARTARE

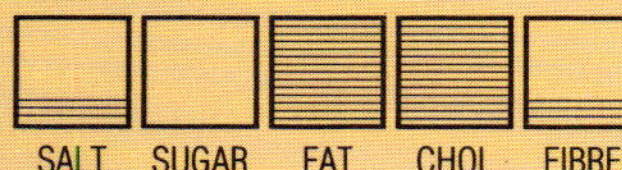

| SALT | SUGAR | FAT | CHOL | FIBRE |

GLUTEN-FREE   WHOLEFOOD
TOTAL CALORIES: ABOUT 2110

The high **fat** content comes mainly from the tartare sauce or mayonnaise, plus the egg yolks which also give a very high level of **cholesterol**. The meat itself can be as low as 5% fat if very lean, or as much as 20% or more. Instead of the high-fat sauce or mayonnaise, flavour smetana, quark or fromage blanc in the same way, with chopped tarragon, lemon juice and Tabasco, and mix it in with the meat. Instead of putting 1 egg yolk on each portion, 2 yolks can be beaten together and a little poured into the centre of a small onion ring on top of the meat. This will reduce both fat and cholesterol to low if the meat is really lean. (Calories lost: up to 400.)
If you are using bought tartare sauce or mayonnaise, check the ingredients to make sure it is **gluten-free** – wheat stabilisers, for instance, are often used.

Scrape up the juices in the pan in which the beef and onions were cooked, stir in the flour and sugar and increase the heat until the mixture forms a roux (page 83). Stir in a little of the stock until the mixture is smooth; bring to the boil. Add the remainder of the stock, the ale and the vinegar; bring back to the boil and simmer for a few minutes. Put the bouquet garni and bay leaves in the casserole and pour over the sauce to just cover the meat. Cover the casserole with a lid, and cook on a shelf low in the oven for 2½ hours, at 325°F (170°C, mark 3).

The flavour of the carbonnades is improved if the casserole is put aside at this stage and reheated the next day, before making the garlic crust.

For the garlic crust, melt the butter in a frying pan over low heat. Crush the three cloves of garlic and stir into the butter. Cut the French bread into ½ in (1 cm) thick slices and soak in the garlic butter, until this is completely absorbed. Put the bread on top of the carbonnades and cook the casserole in an oven pre-heated to 325°F (170°C, mark 3) for 30 minutes. The meat should then be thoroughly heated and the garlic crust should be crisp with a golden tinge.

Serve direct from the casserole. Cauliflower sprinkled with fried or toasted almonds could also be served.

STEAK TARTARE

This dish of raw steak, garnished with raw onions and egg yolk, is becoming increasingly popular. It is served with a number of finely chopped vegetables to which guests help themselves.

PREPARATION TIME: *15–20 min*
INGREDIENTS *(for 4):*
1 lb (450 g) fillet or rump steak
2 onions
1 cooked beetroot
4 tablespoons capers
1 large green or red pepper
2 tablespoons finely chopped parsley
¼ pint (150 ml) tartare sauce or mayonnaise (page 84)
1–2 level teaspoons made French mustard
Salt★ and black pepper
Tabasco sauce
4 egg yolks
GARNISH:
Grated horseradish

Peel and thinly slice the onions. Set four onion rings aside and chop the remainder finely. Peel and finely dice the beetroot. Chop the capers. Remove the stalk end and the seeds from the pepper and dice the flesh.

Make the tartare sauce or the mayonnaise (flavour the latter with mustard and a few drops of Tabasco sauce). Chill the sauce while assembling the dish.

Scrape the steak into fine thin shreds with a sharp knife or put it through the fine blade of a mincer. Season to taste with salt and freshly ground pepper, and shape the mixture into four flat rounds. Arrange them in the centre of a serving dish. Make a shallow hollow in the centre of each steak, put an onion ring round the depression and slip an egg yolk inside (the egg yolk may also be set in a half shell within the onion ring).

Arrange the chopped vegetables in small mounds round the steaks, and sprinkle the steaks and vegetables with finely grated horseradish. Serve the chilled sauce separately, with a tossed green salad and slices of buttered rye bread.

BOILED BEEF AND CARROTS

This is one of the classic dishes from the English kitchen. Carrots and onions are always cooked with the beef, which should, according to tradition, also be served with dumplings.

PREPARATION TIME: *30 min*
COOKING TIME: *3–3½ hours*
INGREDIENTS *(for 6):*

4 lb (1·8 kg) piece salt brisket
1 large onion
4 cloves
Bouquet garni (page 99)
6 peppercorns
2 bay leaves
1 rasher streaky bacon
10 small carrots
12 small onions
2 small turnips
¼ pint (150 ml) dry cider
½ level teaspoon dry mustard
½ level teaspoon ground cinnamon

DUMPLINGS:
PREPARATION TIME: *5 min*
COOKING TIME: *15 min*
INGREDIENTS *(8 dumplings):*
4 oz (100 g) suet crust pastry (half
    the quantity given for the steak
    and kidney pudding on page
    22)
Salt* and black pepper
Mixed herbs or chopped parsley or
    1 oz (25 g) grated cheese

Buy lean brisket; ask the butcher how long the meat has been in brine and soak it in cold water overnight if the meat has been brined for more than three days; otherwise soak for 30 minutes.

Put the brisket in a large saucepan; peel the large onion, stud it with the cloves and add to the beef, together with the bouquet garni, peppercorns, bay leaves and bacon. Cover with cold water, bring to the boil and after a few minutes remove the scum; keep the meat on the boil and continue skimming for about 10 minutes. Cover the pan with a lid and reduce the heat, then simmer for 1¾ hours. Remove from the heat and lift out the meat; strain the liquid into a basin.

When the liquid has cooled, remove the congealed fat from the surface. Peel the carrots and onions, and peel and coarsely slice the turnips. Arrange the vegetables in a deep pan, with the beef on top. Pour over enough strained liquid and the cider to cover. Sprinkle in the mustard and cinnamon, and cover the pan with a lid. Bring to the boil, then reduce the heat and simmer for 1 hour.

Make the pastry for the dumplings as described on page 22, adding the herbs or cheese to the dry mix. Divide the pastry into eight equal pieces and shape these into balls. Add them to the simmering beef for the last 20 minutes of cooking. Winter cabbage, cut into chunks, may also be added with the dumplings.

Arrange the piece of beef in the centre of a serving dish and surround with the vegetables; serve the liquid separately in a sauceboat. Serve with plain boiled potatoes.

MINCED COLLOPS

Collop Monday, the Monday before Lent, was the day on which all meats in the house had to be used up before fasting began. There are numerous recipes for collops. This one, from Scotland, uses beef.

PREPARATION TIME: *5 min*
COOKING TIME: *45–60 min*
INGREDIENTS *(for 4):*
1 lb (450 g) minced beef
2 onions
1 oz (25 g) dripping
Salt* and black pepper
½ pint (300 ml) water or beef stock
4 eggs

Peel and finely chop the onions. Melt the dripping in a heavy-based saucepan and fry the onions over low heat for about 5 minutes or until soft. Add the minced beef, cover with a lid and fry until the beef is browned and has separated into grains. Season to taste with salt and freshly ground pepper; pour over the water or stock until the meat is almost covered. Then put the lid on the pan and simmer the contents for 45 minutes. Stir occasionally and take the lid off the pan towards the end of the cooking time. When the meat is cooked, the liquid should have almost evaporated.

Poach the eggs in simmering salted water until just set. Spoon the meat on to slices of hot toast and top each portion with a poached egg. The minced collops could also be served with creamed potatoes instead of toast.

BOILED BEEF AND CARROTS

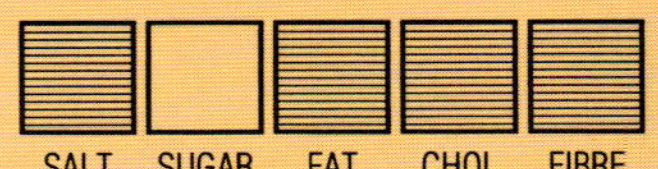

GLUTEN-FREE   WHOLEFOOD
TOTAL CALORIES: ABOUT 6655

The high **salt** content is of course unavoidable in salt meat such as brisket. The only way to reduce it is to soak the meat for as long as possible, but it will still be high in salt. You can avoid adding extra salt by omitting the bacon, but one rasher among six makes little difference.
The **fat** and **cholesterol** levels are also high in brisket. To reduce them to medium you could use silverside, although this is not traditional. Silverside is also high in salt but, when lean, much lower in fat than brisket. (Calories lost: up to 1400.)
Not all dry mustard is **gluten-free**: check the ingredients on the label.

Pressure cooker: ✓

MINCED COLLOPS

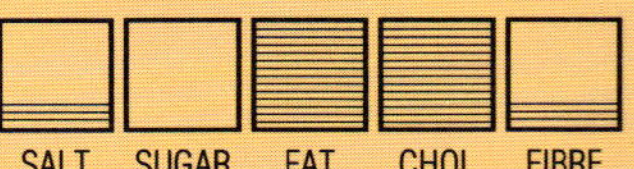

GLUTEN-FREE   WHOLEFOOD
TOTAL CALORIES: ABOUT 2120

The amount of **fat** will depend on the leanness of the beef chosen. Even lean mince will usually produce enough fat to brown itself in, if heated gently in a heavy pan until the fat runs. For low fat and **cholesterol** choose lean meat and cook it in its own fat, omitting the dripping; if you are using beef stock ensure it is well skimmed of fat; and omit the poached eggs, topping each serving instead with a whole mushroom, lightly poached for about 5 minutes in a little stock. (Calories lost: up to 1260.)

Pressure cooker: ☑ for the mince.

Freezing: ☑ up to 4 months for the mince (not the eggs).

Microwave: ☑

CHILI CON CARNE

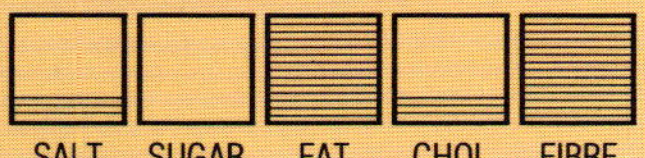

| SALT | SUGAR | FAT | CHOL | FIBRE |

GLUTEN-FREE   WHOLEFOOD
TOTAL CALORIES: ABOUT 2120

The low **salt** content assumes that the kidney beans and tomatoes have not had salt added. Check the labels on the tins, or use fresh tomatoes and dried beans.
For low **fat** choose really lean meat, and cook it in its own fat (see notes on the previous recipe). Soften the onions after the meat in the same fat, omitting the oil.
(Calories lost: up to 265.)
Cholesterol is already low, assuming that the meat is really lean.

Pressure cooker: ☑

Slow cooker: ☑

Freezing: ☑ up to 4 months

Microwave: ☑

CHILI CON CARNE

The Mexican national dish of beef and bean stew with chili is ideal on a cold winter's night. For an even spicier dish, a few cumin seeds may be added.

PREPARATION TIME: *30 min*
COOKING TIME: *2–2½ hours*
INGREDIENTS *(for 6)*:
1 lb (450 g) lean minced beef
12 oz (350 g) dried or 2 large tins
   red kidney beans
2 onions
2 tablespoons olive oil
14 or 16 oz (400 or 450 g) tin of
   tomatoes
2 level teaspoons chili powder or 1
   finely chopped chili pepper
Salt★
Cumin seeds (optional)

Soak beans in cold water overnight. Drain them and put in pan with plenty of fresh water (no salt). Bring to boil and keep boiling for 10 minutes. Lower heat, cover pan with lid and simmer for 1 hour. Peel and thinly slice onions.

Heat the oil in a flameproof dish over low heat and fry the onions until soft. Stir in the meat and continue frying, stirring occasionally, until the meat has browned. Blend in the drained kidney beans, add the tomatoes with their juice, and season to taste with chili, salt and crushed cumin seeds.

Cover the pan with a lid and cook on top of the stove or in the centre of a pre-heated oven, at 300°F (160°C, mark 2), for 1–1½ hours. Add a little water if the stew dries out during cooking.

Serve the stew straight from the dish, with crusty bread and a tossed green salad.

ROLLATINE DI MANZO AL FORNO

The name of this Italian dish means little beef rolls cooked in the oven. Wafer-thin slices of beef and ham are rolled round a savoury and sweet stuffing and cooked in wine.

PREPARATION TIME: *45 min*
COOKING TIME: *1 hour*
INGREDIENTS (*for 6*):
12 thin slices sirloin of beef, each 4 in by 3 in by ¼ in (10 cm by 7½ cm by ½ cm)
12 wafer-thin slices cooked ham
3 cloves garlic
12 thin slices salami
4 hardboiled eggs
5 oz (150 g) raisins
2 oz (50 g) grated Parmesan cheese
8 level tablespoons finely chopped parsley
½ level teaspoon grated nutmeg
½ level teaspoon oregano
Salt★ and black pepper
1 oz (25 g) unsalted butter
½ pint (300 ml) beef stock
½ pint (300 ml) dry white wine
4 bay leaves
6 cloves
2 tablespoons Marsala wine

Place each slice of beef between sheets of waxed or greaseproof paper and flatten it with a rolling pin. Cover the beef slices with ham, trimmed to fit, and spread with peeled and crushed garlic.

Finely chop the skinned salami, the hardboiled eggs and raisins, and put them in a bowl. Blend in the cheese, parsley, nutmeg and oregano, and season with salt and freshly ground pepper.

Divide this mixture equally over the beef and ham slices. Fold over the long sides to keep the stuffing in place and roll the slices up. Tie the parcels with fine string.

Place the rolls in a buttered ovenproof dish. Pour over the stock and wine and cook for 30 minutes in the centre of the oven, pre-heated to 375°F (190°C, mark 5). Add the bay leaves, cloves and Marsala, and cook for a further 30 minutes.

Serve the beef rolls with plainly boiled new potatoes and lightly cooked cauliflower or broccoli.

STEAK AND KIDNEY PUDDING

The traditional English beefsteak and kidney pudding is always served from the basin in which it was steamed. Have ready a white folded napkin or cloth to tie round the hot pudding basin before serving.

PREPARATION TIME: *30 min*
COOKING TIME: *3–4 hours*
INGREDIENTS (*for 4*):
1½ lb (700 g) lean stewing steak
¼ lb (100 g) ox kidney
1 onion
2 level tablespoons seasoned flour (page 100)
1 oz (25 g) butter
Salt★ and black pepper

SUET CRUST PASTRY:
PREPARATION TIME: *15 min*
RESTING TIME: *15 min*
INGREDIENTS:
8 oz (225 g) self-raising flour or 8 oz (225 g) plain flour and 3 level teaspoons baking powder
½ level teaspoon salt★
4 oz (100 g) shredded suet
¼ pint (150 ml) cold water (approx.)

To make the suet crust pastry, sift the flour and salt into a bowl (together with baking powder if plain flour is used). Add the suet – remove the skin from fresh suet, then grate or chop it finely with a little of the flour to prevent sticking – and mix thoroughly. Using a round-bladed knife, stir in the water to form a light, elastic dough. Turn the dough on to a lightly floured surface, and sprinkle it with a little flour. Knead the dough lightly with the fingertips and shape it into a ball. Put the dough on a plate and cover

ROLLATINE DI MANZO AL FORNO

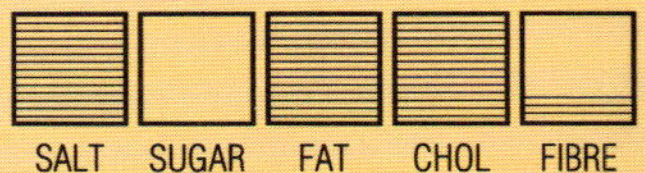

GLUTEN-FREE   WHOLEFOOD
TOTAL CALORIES: ABOUT 6210

The **salt** in this recipe comes mainly from the ham, salami and Parmesan and so is difficult to reduce, but using half quantities of salami and Parmesan would give a moderate to high salt level. Since salami average over 40% fat these measures would also help reduce **fat** and **cholesterol** levels. To keep these no more than moderate, also reduce the number of eggs to two (you can compensate by using double the amount of parsley) and choose lean ham. Make sure you buy very lean sirloin, which can have only a quarter of the fat of a less lean piece, and instead of buttering the oven dish, brush it lightly with oil. (Calories lost: up to 1000.)

Freezing: ☑ up to 2 months.
Microwave: ☑

STEAK AND KIDNEY PUDDING

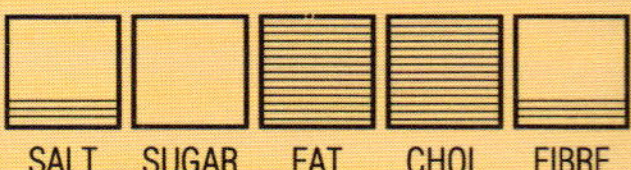

WHOLEFOOD★
TOTAL CALORIES: ABOUT 4490

Most of the **fat** in this recipe comes from the suet crust, and there is no way of reducing this without losing the traditional character of the dish. However, the fat can be reduced slightly by choosing very lean meat and using 3 onions in place of one: if you make a larger pudding the ratio of pastry to lean filling will fall.

Kidney, like most organ meats, is very high in **cholesterol** although not in fat. To reduce the level of cholesterol to moderate, use only half the amount the kidney and increase the steak proportionately.

Pressure cooker: ☑

Freezing: ☑ up to 3 months.

Microwave: ☑

HAMBURGERS WITH PIZZAIOLA SAUCE

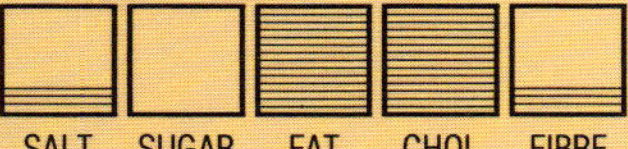

SALT	SUGAR	FAT	CHOL	FIBRE

GLUTEN-FREE   WHOLEFOOD
TOTAL CALORIES: ABOUT 3720

To reduce **fat** and **cholesterol** levels to low, choose very lean meat. Grill the hamburgers instead of cooking them in butter, using a baking sheet lightly brushed with oil (grilling them on a grid may result in the hamburgers breaking up slightly).

Freezing: ☑ up to 4 months.

Microwave: ☑ for the sauce. The hamburgers could be cooked in the microwave, but they will not brown.

with an inverted bowl; leave to rest for 10–15 minutes while the filling is prepared.

Trim away any fat or gristle from the beef, then cut it into ½ in (1 cm) pieces. Remove the core from the kidney (page 91) and cut it into ½ in (1 cm) pieces. Peel and finely chop the onion. Coat the steak and kidney with seasoned flour and mix with the onion.

Cut off a quarter of the prepared suet crust pastry and set it aside for the pudding top. Roll out the remainder to a circle, ½ in (1 cm) thick. Grease a 1½ pint (900 ml) pudding basin well, and fit the pastry to the bottom and sides, allowing it to overhang the edge of the basin by about ½ in (1 cm). Spoon the meat and onion mixture, with a seasoning of salt and freshly ground pepper, into the basin; pour over enough cold water to come three-quarters up the sides of the basin.

Roll out the remaining pastry to a circle to fit the top of the basin. Damp the edges of the suet crust lining, cover with the pastry top and pinch the edges of the lining and the lid tightly together to seal. Cover the top of the basin with double thickness of buttered greaseproof paper, folding in a wide pleat across the centre, to allow the pudding to rise; secure the paper tightly with string.

Put the basin in a saucepan and pour boiling water around it until it reaches one-third up the sides. Steam briskly for 3–4 hours, topping up with boiling water.

Serve the pudding, usually accompanied by boiled potatoes and Brussels sprouts.

HAMBURGERS WITH PIZZAIOLA SAUCE

One of the classics of the American kitchen – hamburgers – is here combined with a classic Italian tomato sauce.

PREPARATION TIME:
  Hamburgers 15 min; sauce 20 min
COOKING TIME:
  Hamburgers 6–10 min; sauce 35 min
INGREDIENTS *(for 4–6)*:
2 lb (900 g) lean sirloin or rump steak
1 oz (25 g) unsalted butter
Salt and black pepper*
SAUCE:
2 onions
2 cloves garlic
2 green peppers
2 teaspoons olive oil
2 oz (50 g) mushroom caps
14 or 16 oz (400 or 450 g) tin of tomatoes
2 level teaspoons oregano (or marjoram)
Chili sauce
Salt and black pepper*

Trim any fat from the steak, cut it into pieces and put through the mincer (coarse plate). Shape the mince into six or eight rounds, about 1½ in (4 cm) thick. Avoid overhandling as this makes them tough. Leave the hamburgers to rest while preparing the sauce.

Peel and mince the onions and garlic. Remove the stalks and seeds from the peppers and cut them crossways into thin slices. Heat the oil in a deep, heavy-based frying pan and, over a gentle heat, cook the onions and garlic until they are pale golden. Add the pepper slices and cook for a further 15 minutes. Wash or peel the mushrooms, chop them roughly and add to the pan together with the tomatoes and the oregano or marjoram. Cover and continue cooking for another 10 minutes. Season to taste with chili sauce, salt and freshly ground pepper. Keep warm while cooking the hamburgers.

Melt the butter in a heavy-based frying pan; fry rare hamburgers for 3 minutes on each side; for pink-rare hamburgers, add another minute each side; for medium, add 2 minutes. Sprinkle with salt and pepper.

Put the hamburgers on a hot serving dish and pour the sauce over them. Serve with coleslaw.

VICTORIANA DIABLE

Devilled sauces (strong and spicy) were popular in Victorian days. The sauce adds a different taste to left-over meat.

PREPARATION TIME: *5 min*
COOKING TIME: *35 min*
INGREDIENTS *(for 4)*:
8–10 slices cooked meat or poultry
1 tablespoon olive oil
2 onions
1 clove garlic
1 level tablespoon plain flour
1 level tablespoon Dijon mustard
1 tablespoon white wine vinegar
⅓ pint (200 ml) beef stock
2 level teaspoons soft brown sugar
¼ teaspoon Worcestershire sauce
1 teaspoon chopped capers
1 bay leaf
Salt★ and black pepper
3–4 level tablespoons browned breadcrumbs
1½ oz (40 g) unsalted melted butter

Heat the oil over medium heat, and cook the finely chopped onions and garlic until golden brown. Blend in the flour. Add mustard and vinegar, and gradually stir in the stock. Bring this sauce to boiling point and stir until thick and smooth. Add the sugar, Worcestershire sauce, capers and bay leaf and season with salt and pepper. Simmer for some 5–10 minutes, stirring frequently.

Put the sliced meat in a lightly buttered ovenproof dish. Pour over the sauce (first removing the bay leaf), sprinkle with the breadcrumbs and pour over the melted butter. Bake in the centre of a pre-heated oven at 375°F (190°C, mark 5) for about 20 minutes or until golden brown. Serve hot, with buttered rice.

BOEUF BOURGUIGNONNE

A hearty and satisfying stew, perfect for a dinner party on winter evening. Topside of beef can also be used.

PREPARATION TIME: *30 min*
COOKING TIME: *3 hours*
INGREDIENTS:
2 lb (900 g) top rump of beef, cut into 2 in (5 cm) cubes
4 oz (100 g) unsalted butter
1 tablespoon olive oil
1 onion
1 level tablespoon plain flour
3 tablespoons brandy
2 cloves garlic
Bouquet garni (page 99)
Salt★ and black pepper
1 bottle red wine
6 oz (175 g) streaky green bacon
20 baby onions
6 oz (175 g) mushrooms
Finely chopped parsley

Melt 3 oz (75 g) butter in a large, flameproof casserole dish, add the oil and then the meat. Cook over high heat until the meat is browned, then add the sliced onion. Cook until transparent, sprinkle over the flour and continue cooking for a few minutes. Pour over the warmed brandy and set it alight.

When the flames have died down, add the crushed garlic, the bouquet garni, salt and plenty of pepper. Pour over enough wine to cover the meat. Bring to simmering point, cover the casserole with a lid and cook in the centre of a pre-heated oven, at 300°F (160°C, mark 2), for 2 hours. The casserole can be cooked ahead of time to this stage, left to cool, and the fat skimmed off.

Meanwhile, fry the diced bacon in the remaining butter until crisp, add the small onions and cook until golden. Stir the contents of the pan into the casserole and continue cooking for a further 30 minutes. Add the sliced mushrooms and cook for another 15 minutes.

Remove the bouquet garni, sprinkle the casserole generously with parsley and serve straight from the pan. Plain boiled potatoes are all that are necessary with it.

SPICED BRISKET OF BEEF

This Irish dish is part of the traditional cold Christmas buffet. It also makes a perfect dish for summer, ideal for a buffet or a large dinner party. The beef should be left to steep in spices for 8 days before being cooked and pressed.

PREPARATION TIME: *20 min*
COOKING TIME: *4–5 hours*
INGREDIENTS *(for 8–10)*:
4 lb (1·8 kg) lean boned brisket of beef
10 oz (275 g) kitchen salt
2 shallots
3 bay leaves
1 level teaspoon potassium nitrate (saltpetre)
1 level teaspoon allspice
4 rounded tablespoons brown sugar
1 level teaspoon powdered cloves
1 level teaspoon powdered mace
½ level teaspoon crushed black peppercorns
½ level teaspoon chopped thyme

Wipe the boned, but not rolled, meat with a clean damp cloth and put it in a large bowl. Rub the meat well on all sides with 8 oz (225 g) of the salt. Cover the bowl

VICTORIANA DIABLE

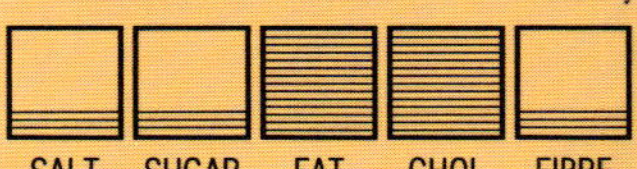

GLUTEN-FREE★   WHOLEFOOD★
TOTAL CALORIES: ABOUT 2070

For a very low **salt** level, use bread made without salt and choose a mustard which does not contain added salt. The cooked meat is assumed to be unsalted.
Provided that the cooked meat is lean (and the poultry, if used, skinned), this recipe will have a low **fat** and **cholesterol** level if the butter poured over it is omitted. (Calories lost: up to 340.)
It is assumed that the mustard is **gluten-free:** check that it contains no wheat. If gluten-free bread is not readily available, omit the breadcrumbs; cornflour or potato flour can be used for the sauce.

Microwave: ☑

BOEUF BOURGUIGNONNE

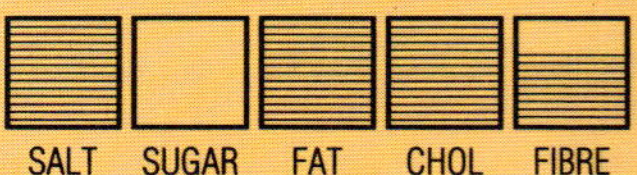

GLUTEN-FREE★   WHOLEFOOD★
TOTAL CALORIES: ABOUT 5050

Most of the **salt** is in the bacon, with a little in the wine and meat. For a low-salt dish, omit the bacon.
This will also make a considerable cut in the **fat**. For a low fat and **cholesterol** level, choose the leanest rump beef and brown it in a heavy pan lightly brushed with oil, omitting all the butter and most of the oil given. Add a few

spoonfuls of stock to prevent the meat sticking. Instead of frying the onions, add them directly to the pan, followed by the mushrooms. (Calories lost: up to 1000.)

Potato flour and cornflour, both **gluten-free**, can be used for thickening the stew. If you are using potato flour you will probably need only half a tablespoon.

Pressure cooker: ☑
Slow cooker: ☑
Freezing: ☑ up to 2 months.
Microwave: ☑

SPICED BRISKET OF BEEF

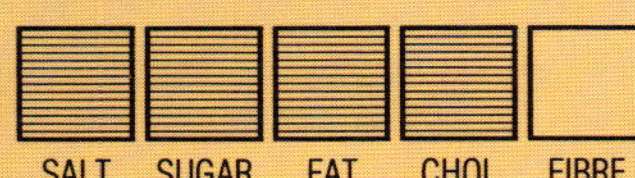

SALT SUGAR FAT CHOL FIBRE

GLUTEN-FREE
TOTAL CALORIES: ABOUT 6640

The **salt** and **sugar** content of this dish cannot really be reduced: both are necessary parts of the curing mixture. As it stands, the **fat** and **cholesterol** content is also high, since brisket is naturally about 20% fat (including all its visible fat). A dish with moderate levels of both can be achieved if lean silverside, which has less fat than brisket, is used. Trim the joint of all visible fat before cooking: there will be enough unseen fat left within the meat to keep it moist. (Calories lost: up to 900.)

Pressure cooker: ☑

with cheesecloth and leave for 24 hours in the lower part of the refrigerator or in a cool place.

Peel and finely chop the shallots and the bay leaves. Put these in a bowl with the remainder of the salt and the rest of the ingredients and mix together. Each day, rub this mixture well into the salted meat, pouring off any liquid that may have formed. All the spicing mixture should have been absorbed after 7 days.

Roll the spiced meat neatly and tie it securely with fine string. Put it in a heavy-based pan and cover with warm water. Simmer, covered, over low heat for 4–5 hours. Let the meat cool in the liquid, then lift it out. Place it between two plates with a heavy weight on top and leave it to press for 8 hours.

Serve the spiced brisket cold, sliced and accompanied by baked potatoes, a selection of salads and pickled beetroot and gherkins.

CHATEAUBRIAND STEAK

This famous dish is named after the 18th-century French writer, Chateaubriand. It cannot be served for less than two persons, as it is a double fillet steak cut from the thick end of the fillet.

PREPARATION TIME: *5 min*
COOKING TIME: *8–10 min*
INGREDIENTS *(for 2)*:
12–14 oz (350–400 g) thick fillet steak
½ oz (10 g) melted butter
Salt⋆ and black pepper
GARNISH:
Watercress
Maître d'hôtel butter (page 95)

Trim the fillet and if necessary flatten it slightly. It should be 1½–2 in (4–5 cm) thick. Brush one side with melted butter and season with freshly ground pepper. Do not add salt as this will extract the juices.

Put the steak, buttered and seasoned side up, under a hot grill and cook under high heat to brown the surface and seal in the juices. Turn the steak over, brush with the remaining melted butter and season with pepper. Turn the heat down and grill the steak for a further 4–5 minutes, turning it once only. The steak should be cooked through, but remain rosy-pink inside.

Lift the steak on to a board and carve it, at a slight angle, into six even slices. Remove the sliced steak, in one movement, on to a warm serving dish and garnish with sprigs of watercress and slices of maître d'hôtel butter.

Traditionally, a chateaubriand steak is served with a sauce Béarnaise (page 84) and with château potatoes (peeled po-tatoes shaped into small ovals, coated with melted butter and cooked, covered, for 30–35 minutes, shaking occasionally). A tossed green salad makes an excellent side dish.

BEEF WITH GREEN PEAS

Topside of beef is rather tough and is usually stewed or braised. It can, however, be made into a succulent joint by pot-roasting it slowly in a casserole with a tightly fitting lid.

PREPARATION TIME: *10 min*
COOKING TIME: *2–2½ hours*
INGREDIENTS *(for 6)*:
2½–3 lb (1–1½ kg) lean topside of beef
Salt⋆ and black pepper
2 oz (50 g) unsalted butter
1½ lb (700 g) fresh green peas

Wipe the meat with a damp cloth and season with freshly ground pepper. Melt the butter in a heavy-based frying pan over high heat and brown the beef in it on all sides to seal in the juices.

Put the meat in an ovenproof casserole into which it will fit fairly closely. Shell the peas and put them round the sides of the beef, and pour the butter from the pan over the meat. Cover the casserole with a lid and cook in the centre of a pre-heated oven at 325°F (170°C, mark 3) for 2 hours. At this stage the meat will be rare; allow another 30 minutes for well-done meat.

Lift out the beef, carve into thin slices and arrange them on a warmed serving dish, surrounded by the peas. Boiled new potatoes sprinkled generously with chopped mint or parsley are ideal for this dish.

BOEUF À LA MODE EN GELÉE

Most classic recipes for cold jellied beef use the expensive fillet, but topside, poached slowly to a near-jelly consistency, makes an excellent alternative. The dish, ideal for buffet entertaining, should be prepared a day in advance.

PREPARATION TIME: *30 min*
COOKING TIME: *4½–5 hours*
INGREDIENTS *(for 6–8)*:
3 lb (1½ kg) topside or top rump of beef
¼ lb (100 g) pork fat
1 calf's foot
½ pint (300 ml) dry red wine
2 cloves garlic
Salt⋆ and black pepper
1–2 tablespoons beef dripping
2 tablespoons brandy
2 shallots
2 bay leaves
½ pint (300 ml) beef stock or water
15 small onions
10 young carrots

Order the meat in advance and preferably larded with the pork fat. Have the calf's foot chopped into pieces. If the meat is not larded, cut the pork fat into strips, narrow enough to go through the eye of a larding needle, and long enough to be threaded through the meat. Pull the fat strips through the meat and trim them off at each end.

Put the meat in a deep bowl, pour over the wine and marinate for about 4 hours, turning the meat frequently.

Peel the garlic, cut it into small strips and push them into the meat with the point of a knife. Season with salt and pepper.

Bring a large pan of salted

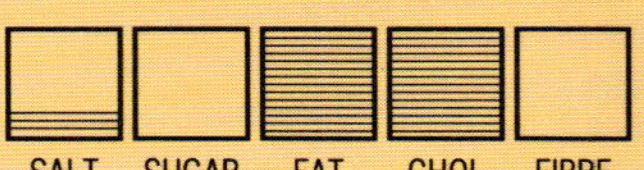

CHATEAUBRIAND STEAK

SALT · SUGAR · FAT · CHOL · FIBRE

GLUTEN-FREE · WHOLEFOOD
TOTAL CALORIES: ABOUT 1620

The fat level of steak varies hugely depending on how lean the meat is and how carefully visible fat is trimmed off. If a very lean steak is chosen, and no butter is served with it, the **fat** and **cholesterol** levels of this recipe will be moderate, even though the portions given here are generous. The only way to reduce fat still further is to reduce the portions, apart from using only a light brushing of butter on the meat before grilling. (Calories lost: up to 565.)

As an alternative to serving with the traditional high-fat Béarnaise sauce, mix smetana, quark, fromage blanc or thick low-fat yogurt with herbs and lemon juice to serve with the steak. (Further calories lost: up to 1000.)

BEEF WITH GREEN PEAS

SALT · SUGAR · FAT · CHOL · FIBRE

GLUTEN-FREE · WHOLEFOOD
TOTAL CALORIES: ABOUT 5250

This is already, by most standards quite a healthy dish. The **fat** and **cholesterol** can be reduced further, to low, if you choose the leanest possible joint (topside averages only 5% fat when lean, but about 12% if both lean and fat) and brown it in a heavy pan brushed lightly with oil, omitting the butter. (Calories lost: up to 450.)

BOEUF À LA MODE EN GELÉE

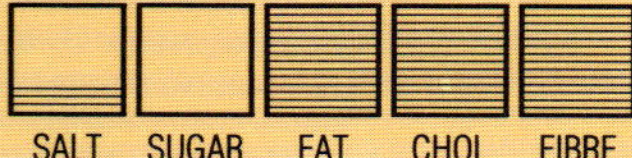

GLUTEN-FREE   WHOLEFOOD
TOTAL CALORIES: ABOUT 5740

The **fat** and **cholesterol** levels of this recipe can be reduced to low simply by choosing a very lean piece of meat and omitting the larding with pork fat. The meat can also be browned in a heavy pan lightly brushed with oil, using less fat than the beef dripping specified. Be careful to skim all possible fat from the chilled cooked meat and jelly. (Calories lost: up to 1000.)

water to the boil and blanch the calf's foot pieces for 10 minutes. Drain and set aside.

Melt half the dripping in a heavy-based deep pan or flame-proof dish over high heat, and brown the meat all over to seal in the juices. Reduce the heat. Pour the brandy over the meat, let it warm through slightly, then set it alight. When the flames have died down, add the calf's foot pieces.

Peel and finely chop the shallots and add them, with the bay leaves, to the pan. Heat the stock or water in a separate pan, blend in the wine and pour it over the meat. Bring this liquid to boiling

point, cover the pan tightly with foil and the lid. Cook in the centre of a pre-heated oven, at 300°F (160°C, mark 2), for 3 hours.

Meanwhile, peel the onions, leaving them whole. Wash and scrape the carrots and split them in half lengthways. Heat the remaining dripping in a small pan and lightly brown the vegetables. Add them to the meat after 3 hours' cooking and simmer for a further 1–1½ hours.

Lift the meat on to a dish and remove the vegetables with a perforated spoon. Let the liquid cool, then strain it through cheesecloth into a bowl. Leave

the liquid in the refrigerator overnight to set to a jelly.

The next day, carefully scrape the surface fat from the jelly with a spoon dipped in hot water. Cut the meat into neat thin slices and arrange them in a deep serving dish together with the carrots and onions. Melt the jelly in a saucepan over low heat, then pour it carefully over the meat and vegetables. Leave the dish in a cool place to allow the jelly to re-set.

Serve the jellied beef with a selection of salads, such as a crisp green salad tossed in a French dressing (page 85), a tomato salad and a cold potato salad.

Veal

OSSO BUCO

Italy is the homeland of this appetising, inexpensive stew of veal with marrow. The tradition-al Milanese garnish – known as *gremolata* – adds a colourful look to the finished dish.

PREPARATION TIME: *30 min*
COOKING TIME: *1¾–2 hours*
INGREDIENTS *(for 6):*
2½ lb (1 kg) shin of veal
Seasoned flour (page 100)
3 carrots
2 sticks celery
1 onion
2 cloves garlic
2 oz (50 g) butter
8 fluid oz (225 ml) dry white wine
8 fluid oz (225 ml) chicken or veal stock
14 or 16 oz (400 or 450 g) tin of tomatoes
Salt and black pepper*
Caster sugar
1 sprig fresh or ½ teaspoon dried rosemary
GARNISH:
4 tablespoons finely chopped parsley
Finely grated rind of 2 large lemons
2–3 cloves finely chopped garlic

Ask the butcher to saw the veal into pieces, about 1½ in (4 cm) thick. Wash and dry the meat and remove any chips of bone. Coat the veal pieces with seasoned flour. Clean the vegetables and chop them finely.

Melt the butter in a heavy-based pan, large enough to take all the meat in one layer. Brown the meat and the vegetables. When the meat has taken colour, stand each piece upright to prevent the marrow falling out during cook-ing. Pour over the wine and stock and add the tomatoes with their juice. Season to taste with salt, freshly ground pepper and sugar. Then add the rosemary. Simmer,

covered, over low heat for 1½ hours, or until the meat is tender.

While the veal is cooking, mix the ingredients for the garnish.

Pour the sauce over the meat and sprinkle with the garnish. The marrow is usually left in the bones, but it can also be extracted and spread on toast. In Italy, osso buco is traditionally served with a saffron-flavoured risotto (risotto alla milanese), but plain boiled rice also makes an appropriate accompaniment.

VITELLO TONNATO

In Italy, this cold terrine of veal in tuna fish sauce is a stand-by for hot summer days. The classic version uses boiled veal, but in some regions the meat is roasted instead. It should be made the day before and left to chill overnight.

PREPARATION TIME: *30 min*
COOKING TIME: *1¾ hours*
INGREDIENTS *(for 6):*
2½ lb (1 kg) leg or loin of veal
1 carrot
1 onion
1 stick celery
4 peppercorns
*1 level teaspoon salt**
3–3½ oz (75–90 g) tin of tuna fish
4 anchovy fillets
¼ pint (150 ml) olive oil
2 egg yolks
Black pepper
1½ tablespoons lemon juice
GARNISH:
Capers
Gherkins
Fresh tarragon (if available)

Ask the butcher to bone the meat, tie it in a neat roll and include the bones with the order.

Scrape and wash the carrot and peel the onion; quarter both.

The low **salt** level assumes that there is no added salt in the tomatoes or the stock. Veal is a little higher in sodium than some meat, but the total level can still be under 200 mg per portion in this dish.
To reduce the **fat** and **cholesterol** content to low, brown the meat in a heavy pan brushed lightly with oil; omit the butter. (Calories lost: up to 450.)

Pressure cooker: ✓
Slow cooker: ✓
Freezing: ✓ up to 4 months.

The high **salt** content comes partly from the tuna, partly from the anchovies. Both can be rinsed in a sieve under running water to remove some of the salt, but will still remain permeated with it. You could use only half the amount of each, which will reduce the salt level to moderate, but it will take away some of the character of the dish.
The high level of **fat** is largely due to the oil. Again, it is characteristic of the dish, but you could reduce the oil to only 2 teaspoons (just enough to keep a little of the olive oil

flavour – use a strong virgin oil if you can) mashed with the fish, and complete the sauce using about ¼ pint (150 ml) of low-fat quark, fromage blanc or thick plain yogurt. If you choose tuna canned in brine rather than oil the total fat content will then be low. (Calories lost: up to 1300.) To reduce the **cholesterol** level to low, use one whole egg instead of the two yolks. (Calories lost: up to 90.)

Pressure cooker: ☑ for the veal (not the tuna sauce).

Slow cooker: ☑ for the veal (not the tuna sauce).

VEAL ESCALOPES WITH GINGER WINE

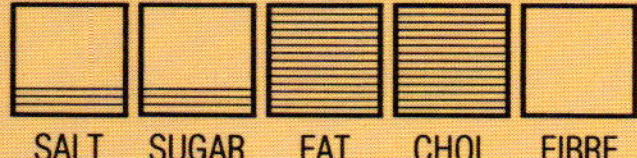

SALT	SUGAR	FAT	CHOL	FIBRE

GLUTEN-FREE★   WHOLEFOOD★
TOTAL CALORIES: ABOUT 1300

Veal is naturally very low in **fat** provided any visible fat is trimmed off. To minimise added fat and **cholesterol**, cook the escalopes in a non-stick pan lightly brushed with olive oil and omit the butter. Replace the double cream with 3 tablespoons of smetana, low-fat curd cheese or low-fat plain yogurt, but do not add until just about to serve and only heat gently; if it boils it will curdle.
With these changes, the fat and cholesterol content will be low, even using smetana, which contains considerably more fat than the other choices. (Calories lost: up to 560.)

Scrub and chop the celery. Put the meat into a large saucepan together with the bones. Add the vegetables, peppercorns, salt and enough water to cover the meat. Bring the water quickly to the boil, turn down the heat, cover the pan with a lid and simmer for about 1¾ hours, or until the meat is tender. Lift the meat carefully out of the pan and set aside to cool. Reduce the cooking liquid by fast boiling, strain through muslin and set aside.

To make the sauce, drain the tuna and anchovy and put in a bowl with 1 tablespoon of the oil. Mash with a fork until thoroughly mixed. Blend in the egg yolks and season with pepper. Rub this paste through a sieve into a small bowl. Stir in half the lemon juice, then add the remaining oil, little by little, beating well after each addition. When the sauce has become thick and shiny, add more lemon juice to taste. Stir in about 2 tablespoons of the veal liquid to give the sauce the consistency of thin cream.

Cut the cold meat into thin slices and arrange them in a terrine. Cover the meat completely with the sauce, then wrap the dish closely in foil and leave overnight to marinate.

Before serving, garnish the dish with capers, a few sliced gherkins or with a sprig of tarragon. Cold savoury rice or a tossed green salad could complement the meat.

VEAL ESCALOPES WITH GINGER WINE

These thin cuts from the veal fillet are usually served with a creamy sauce. This is frequently made from white wine or Marsala – the ginger wine in this recipe adds an unusual, slightly spicy flavour.

PREPARATION TIME: *10 min*
COOKING TIME: *15 min*
INGREDIENTS *(for 4):*
4 veal escalopes, each ¼ in (½ cm)
    thick and weighing about 3 oz
    (75 g)
Seasoned flour (page 100)
2 oz (50 g) unsalted butter
1 teaspoon olive oil
6 tablespoons ginger wine
2 teaspoons lemon juice
3 tablespoons double cream
Salt★ and black pepper
GARNISH:
4 lemon twists (page 97)
1 tablespoon chopped parsley

Cut off any fat from the escalopes and trim them into neat shapes. Dust them lightly with the seasoned flour. Heat the butter and oil in a heavy-based pan over moderate heat and fry the veal for 5–6 minutes, until golden brown on both sides. Lift the slices on to a serving dish and keep them warm while you are making the ginger wine sauce.

Add the ginger wine to the pan and bring it gently to the boil, scraping up the pan juices with a rubber spatula. Reduce the heat and simmer slowly for 5 minutes, or until the wine is syrupy. Stir in the lemon juice and the cream, and simmer for a further 2–3 minutes, or until the sauce has a pale coffee colour. Season to taste with salt and freshly ground pepper. Pour the sauce over the meat and garnish each escalope with a lemon twist sprinkled with chopped parsley.

Serve the escalopes with plain boiled potatoes and French beans. A plain green salad would also go well.

Veal

VEAL ROLLS WITH FRITTATA FILLING

A frittata is an Italian cross between an omelette and a pancake. It is a traditional filling for rolled veal and is first fried like thin pancakes and then spread over the meat. The frittatas can also be served as a garnish with veal escalopes.

PREPARATION TIME: *30 min*
COOKING TIME: *1½ hours*
INGREDIENTS *(for 4)*:

8 veal escalopes, about 3 oz (75 g) each
2 eggs
2 oz (50 g) chopped mortadella sausage or lean ham
1 heaped tablespoon chopped fresh parsley
1½–2 level tablespoons grated Parmesan cheese
3 oz (75 g) butter
4–6 oz (100–175 g) button mushrooms
1 onion
1½–2 tablespoons plain flour
¼ pint (150 ml) milk
¼–½ pint (150–300 ml) stock or bouillon
Salt★ and black pepper
Lemon juice
Dried mixed herbs

Beat the escalopes thin between sheets of greaseproof paper. Trim them neatly and set aside. Beat the eggs lightly and stir in the chopped sausage, the parsley and grated cheese.

Melt a little butter in a small omelette pan and, when hot, spoon in enough of the egg mixture to thinly cover the base of the pan. Cook the frittata until golden brown, then turn it and cook the other side. Cook the remaining mixture, to make eight frittatas in all.

Cover each escalope with a frittata, trimming these to the shape of the meat. Roll up each escalope and tie at intervals with fine string.

Trim the mushrooms and cut them in half if large. Peel the onion and slice it thinly. Melt the remaining butter in a heavy-based pan and fry the veal rolls over high heat until golden brown. Lift the rolls from the pan. Fry the mushrooms and onion in the remaining butter in the pan until soft, then draw the pan off the heat. Blend in enough flour to absorb all the fat, and gradually stir in the milk and ¼ pint (150 ml) of stock. Lower the heat and bring the sauce to simmering point, stirring continuously. Cook for about 5 minutes, then season with salt, pepper, lemon juice and dried herbs.

Add the veal rolls to the sauce, thinning it with a little more stock if necessary – the sauce should cover the rolls completely. Put a lid on the pan and simmer over low heat for about 1 hour or until the meat is tender.

Lift out the veal rolls, remove the string, and arrange them on a hot serving dish. Spoon a little of the sauce over the meat and serve the remainder in a sauce boat. Creamed potatoes and buttered broccoli or beans would be good vegetable dishes.

TERRINE DE CAMPAGNE

The French word 'terrine' originally meant an earthenware dish, but by extension it now also refers to the contents of the dish, whether fish, meat or poultry. This farmhouse-style terrine of calf liver and veal is a good choice for a picnic, lunch or supper. It should, like all other terrines, be served cold.

PREPARATION TIME: *20 min*
COOKING TIME: *2 hours*
INGREDIENTS *(for 6–8)*:
12 oz (350 g) thin rashers streaky bacon
12 oz (350 g) calf liver
1½ lb (700 g) minced veal
1 large onion
2 cloves garlic
1 heaped tablespoon tomato purée
¼ level teaspoon summer savory or sage
¼ level teaspoon oregano
4 oz (100 g) butter
¼ pint (150 ml) dry red wine
Salt★ and black pepper
4 bay leaves

Remove the rind and any gristle from the bacon and stretch the rashers with the flat blade of a knife. Line a 2 pint (1 litre) terrine or soufflé dish with the bacon, allowing the rashers to hang over the edges.

Clean the liver, removing any gristle, and put the meat through the coarse plate of a mincer. Peel the onion and chop it finely. Mix together the liver, onion and veal in a large bowl. Peel the garlic and crush it over the meat mixture. Stir in the tomato purée, savory and oregano. Melt the butter and stir into the terrine mixture together with enough wine to give a moist but not wet consistency.

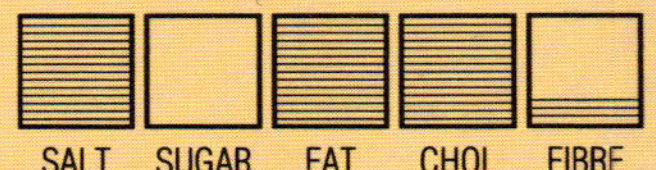

VEAL ROLLS WITH FRITTATA FILLING

GLUTEN-FREE★   WHOLEFOOD★
TOTAL CALORIES: ABOUT 2215

The high **salt** is a result of the combination of natural sodium from veal, the high salt level of cured meats like ham and mortadella, and the cheese. The best way of cutting down in this recipe is simply to use a little less of each of these three ingredients, as the portions are very generous. If you use only half quantities, and assuming there is no salt in the stock, the salt level will be moderate.
To reduce **fat** and **cholesterol** to moderate, choose lean ham instead of mortadella; cook the frittata in a pan lightly brushed with oil, rather than in butter; use the same method for cooking the veal rolls, mushrooms and onions; and use skim milk in the sauce. (Calories lost: up to 920.)

Freezing: ☑ up to 2 months.

TERRINE DE CAMPAGNE

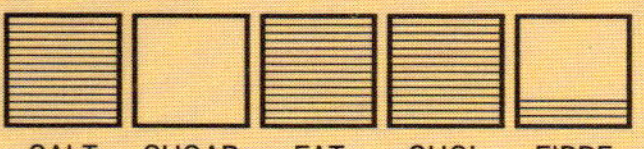

SALT SUGAR FAT CHOL FIBRE

GLUTEN-FREE   WHOLEFOOD
TOTAL CALORIES: ABOUT 4170

To avoid the high **salt** content of the large amount of streaky bacon, line the terrine dish with a double thickness of spinach leaves, previously dipped in simmering water for 30 seconds to soften them. If you also use unsalted tomato purée the overall salt level will be low. Leaving out the bacon will help to lower the **fat** level. You can also omit the butter, and although the resulting terrine will be far less rich, it will taste fresher. Make sure the terrine is very well sealed while cooking to prevent it drying out. (Calories lost: up to 2125.) These measures will reduce the fat level to low, but the **cholesterol** will still be high, since liver, like other organ meats, is very rich in cholesterol. Its other nutrients, such as iron, B vitamins and zinc, make it worth eating regularly, but not every day, especially if you are worried about the build-up of antibiotics and hormones, which do accumulate in the liver.

Food processor: ☑ for mincing the meat.
Freezing: ☑ up to 1 month.
Microwave: ☑.

Season to taste with salt and freshly ground pepper.

Spoon the mixture into the dish, over the bacon rashers. Arrange the bay leaves on top and fold over the bacon rashers. Cover the dish with a lid or tight-fitting foil. Cook the terrine for 2 hours on the middle shelf of an oven pre-heated to 350°F (180°C, mark 4).

When cooked, remove the lid from the dish, cover with fresh foil and a flat board which will fit neatly inside the terrine. Place a heavy weight on the board and leave overnight.

Serve straight from the terrine or turn out on to a serving dish and cut into wedges. Crusty bread and a tossed green salad make this terrine a substantial main course for lunch, or serve in smaller portions as a first course.

VEAL SCALOPPINE

Italian scaloppine are similar to French escalopes, but they are cut against the grain of the meat. Ask the butcher to beat the scaloppine flat and thin.

PREPARATION TIME: *15 min*
COOKING TIME: *30 min*
INGREDIENTS *(for 4):*
4 veal escalopes
Seasoned flour (page 100)
6 oz (175 g) unsalted butter
1 tablespoon olive oil
½ lb (225 g) button mushrooms
¼ pint (150 ml) Marsala or sweet
*   sherry*
½ pint (300 ml) chicken stock

Trim any fat and gristle from the scaloppine and coat them thoroughly with seasoned flour. Heat 2 oz (50 g) of the butter and the oil in a heavy-based pan and fry the meat over low heat for 3–4 minutes on each side, turning once. Lift the meat from the pan and keep it hot.

Pour all but one tablespoon of the hot fat from the pan. Trim and slice the mushrooms and add to the pan; cook over low heat, tossing the mushrooms until coated in the butter, then stir in the wine and stock. Bring this sauce to the boil and return the scaloppine to the pan. Cover with a lid, lower the heat and simmer gently for 15–20 minutes. Turn the meat once or twice so that it cooks evenly. Arrange the scaloppine and mushrooms on a serving dish and keep it hot. Boil the sauce rapidly until it has reduced by about one-third and has thickened slightly. Whisk in the remaining butter, remove the pan from the heat and pour the sauce over the veal.

Boiled rice or buttered pasta, and French beans or broccoli can be served with the scaloppine.

VEAL WITH TOMATOES

The shoulder of veal used in this recipe was formerly known as an oyster of veal. The joint, a boned cut from the top of the fore leg, is best cooked in a casserole.

PREPARATION TIME: *20 min*
COOKING TIME: *1½–2 hours*
INGREDIENTS *(for 6):*
2½ lb (1 kg) shoulder of veal
Salt★
2 oz (50 g) unsalted butter
1½ lb (700 g) tomatoes
2 onions
6–8 black peppercorns
Sprig tarragon (fresh or dried)

Wipe the meat with a damp cloth and tie it neatly with string to keep its shape during cooking. Season lightly with salt. Melt half the butter in a flameproof casserole over moderate heat, and brown the meat on all sides to seal in the juices.

Skin and roughly chop the tomatoes. Peel and finely chop the onions. Melt the remaining butter in a pan and fry the tomatoes and onions over moderate heat for 3–4 minutes. Grind the pepper into the tomato mixture, add the tarragon and pour it all over the meat in the casserole. Cover with a lid or foil and bake in the centre of a pre-heated oven at 300°F (160°C, mark 2) for 1½–2 hours.

Remove the string and serve the veal hot, cut into thick slices, with the tomato sauce spooned over. Plain boiled potatoes and a green vegetable would make this a substantial meal.

VEAL WITH ORANGE

This is reputed to have been Cromwell's favourite meal. It is prepared with a fruity forcemeat stuffing and sauce which add extra flavour to the meat.

PREPARATION TIME: *20 min*
COOKING TIME: *2½ hours*
INGREDIENTS *(for 6):*
4–5 lb (about 2 kg) breast of veal,
*   boned*
4 oz (100 g) fresh white
*   breadcrumbs*
2 oz (50 g) stoned raisins
2 oz (50 g) currants
2 oz (50 g) shredded beef suet
Salt★ and black pepper
Nutmeg
2 large oranges
1 large egg yolk (or 2 small ones)
2 oz (50 g) lard
1 oz (25 g) cornflour
Caster sugar
6 tablespoons claret

Prepare the forcemeat stuffing first by mixing the breadcrumbs, raisins, currants, suet and a pinch of salt, pepper and nutmeg together in a bowl. Finely grate the rind from the oranges and add to the stuffing, together with the lightly beaten egg yolk. Stir in enough cold water to bind the mixture.

Spread the stuffing over the boned veal, roll it up and tie with thin string at 1 in (2½ cm) intervals. Put the meat in a roasting tin, add the lard and roast the meat for 2½ hours in the centre of an oven, pre-heated to 400°F (200°C, mark 6). Baste occasionally and cover the meat with foil if it browns too quickly.

Put the meat on a serving dish and keep it hot in the oven. Skim all the fat from the juices in the

butter. Be sure to trim any visible fat from the veal, although it is generally low in fat. (Calories lost: up to 450.)

Pressure cooker: ☑
Freezing: ☑ up to 4 months.

VEAL WITH ORANGE

SALT SUGAR FAT CHOL FIBRE

GLUTEN-FREE *
WHOLEFOOD *
TOTAL CALORIES: ABOUT 7290

The high **salt** level is due not to any particularly salty ingredients, although bread has a substantial salt content; here, the intake is raised simply by the very generous amounts of meat per portion. A smaller helping, say not more than 5 oz (150 g) meat per person, and the use of unsalted bread, will give a moderate salt level. The low **sugar** level assumes that only a teaspoon or two of sugar is added to the sauce. As veal is basically lean, the **fat** and **cholesterol** content of this dish will be low if the suet is omitted from the stuffing and the meat roasted without adding fat. To avoid dryness, cover the roasting dish tightly throughout, removing the cover only 20 minutes before the end of cooking to allow the meat to brown. Again, a smaller portion will produce a drop in fat intake without being ungenerous. (Calories lost: up to 1040.)
Suet and lard are both disliked by **wholefood** lovers for their high saturated fat content; omitting them will make this dish wholefood.

Pressure cooker: ☑
Freezing: ☑ up to 4 months.

roasting tin and heat them in a small saucepan. Blend the cornflour with 1 tablespoon of cold water and add to the juices, stirring continuously until the sauce has thickened. Bring to the boil and season to taste with salt, freshly ground pepper, sugar and nutmeg. Stir in the claret and simmer the sauce gently. Remove the pith from the oranges and cut the flesh into small sections. Add these to the sauce and heat it through.

Cut the veal into thick slices and arrange them on a warmed serving dish; offer the sauce separately. An orange and chicory salad, sauté potatoes and button onions would go well with this joint.

**SCALOPPINE WITH ARTICHOKES
AND LEMON SAUCE**

For this easily prepared dish, choose small veal escalopes (*scaloppine*), ¼ in (½ cm) thick. Veal cutlets may be used instead but will require longer cooking. Be sure to buy *fonds* (bottoms) of artichokes, not the hearts.

PREPARATION TIME: *15 min*
COOKING TIME: *25 min*
INGREDIENTS (*for 4*):
8 veal escalopes, each about 2–
  3 oz (50–75 g)
Seasoned flour (page 100)
2 oz (50 g) butter
1 level tablespoon finely chopped
  shallot or onion
12 oz (350 g) tin artichoke
  bottoms
4 fluid oz (100 ml) dry white wine
½ pint (300 ml) chicken stock or
  bouillon
2 small lemons
¼ pint (150 ml) double cream
Salt★ and black pepper

Trim any fat from the escalopes and coat them in seasoned flour. Heat the butter in a heavy-based pan over medium heat and fry the escalopes for a few minutes, until golden brown, turning once. Add the shallots and artichoke bottoms, and pour over the wine. Bring the mixture to simmering point, and reduce the heat. Add sufficient stock or bouillon to cover the veal completely. Grate the rind from the lemons and set aside, and add the squeezed lemon juice to the sauce. Cover the pan with a lid and cook over low heat for 20 minutes or until the veal is tender.
  Stir in the cream and simmer the sauce for 5–6 minutes

more, uncovered, until the sauce has a creamy texture. Adjust seasoning with salt and freshly ground pepper.
  Arrange the escalopes in the centre of a warmed serving dish and surround with a border of buttered noodles or fluffy rice. Pour the sauce over the meat and top with a scattering of grated lemon rind.

VEAL CHOPS MAGYAR

Paprika is the most usual spicing in Hungarian dishes. It varies considerably in strength according to its origin, and the sauce should be tasted after being cooked for a while.

PREPARATION TIME: *20 min*
COOKING TIME: *1¼ hours*
INGREDIENTS (*for 4*):
4 large veal chops
Seasoned flour (page 100)
½ lb (225 g) mushrooms
1 onion
1 oz (25 g) butter
1 tablespoon oil
2–2½ tablespoons plain flour
½ pint (300 ml) milk
½ pint (300 ml) veal stock or
  chicken bouillon
Salt★
Juice of a small lemon
1 small tin (2¼ oz, 60 g) tomato
  concentrate
3–4 level teaspoons paprika
2 level teaspoons caster sugar
¼ pint (150 ml) single cream
GARNISH:
Rice
6–8 mushroom caps
Paprika
1 level tablespoon chopped parsley

Trim the fat off the chops and coat them with seasoned flour. Trim the mushrooms and, if large, cut

using butter. Cook the mushrooms and onions in a lightly greased heavy pan and use skim milk in the sauce. Replace the cream with smetana, low-fat curd cheese or plain yogurt, adding this only at the end of cooking (see notes on the previous recipe). (Calories lost: up to 550.)
A **gluten-free** flour such as brown rice flour, potato flour or split pea flour can be used in the sauce.

BAKED STUFFED SHOULDER OF VEAL

GLUTEN-FREE   WHOLEFOOD*
TOTAL CALORIES: ABOUT 4290

The high **salt** comes mainly from the bacon; omitting this will give the dish a low salt level provided the stock is unsalted and the butter is either unsalted or omitted.
Leaving out the bacon will also substantially reduce the **fat** content, which can be limited to low by omitting the butter (used to brown the bacon and so unnecessary if bacon isn't used), and using only half the amount of walnuts. This will also give low **cholesterol**, providing portions are not more than about 5 oz (150 g). (Calories lost: up to 850.)
Use brown rice to make this **wholefood**: it will need to cook for 20–25 minutes, even though it will continue to cook with the joint.

Pressure cooker: ☑ both for the stock and, later, for the meat.
Freezing: ☑ up to 2 months.

them into quarters or halves. Peel and thinly slice the onion. Heat the butter and oil in a flameproof casserole, pat the loose flour off the chops and fry them over high heat until golden brown, turning once. Remove the chops from the pan and fry the mushrooms and onion for a few minutes, until they are soft.

Remove the casserole from the heat and stir in sufficient flour to absorb the fat. Gradually blend in the milk and then the stock, stirring continuously. Bring to simmering point and cook for 3 minutes until the sauce has thickened. Season to taste with salt and lemon juice. Mix the tomato concentrate, paprika, sugar and cream together in a small bowl. Blend in 2 or 3 tablespoons of the hot sauce and pour the mixture back into the sauce, stirring thoroughly.

Return the veal chops to the casserole. They should be completely covered by the sauce, so add a little more stock if necessary. Cover the casserole with a lid and cook over low heat for 45 minutes or until the veal is tender, stirring from time to time to prevent sticking. Do not allow to reach boiling point or the sauce will separate.

Adjust seasoning and arrange the chops in the centre of a serving dish with the sauce spooned over them. Surround with a border of fluffy rice, garnished with the whole mushroom caps fried in a little butter. Set the mushrooms, dark side uppermost, on the rice and fill the centre of each with paprika. Sprinkle chopped parsley between the mushrooms.

BAKED STUFFED SHOULDER OF VEAL

This is one of the less expensive cuts of veal. It is braised rather than roasted, to preserve the juices. Make the stock the day before if possible, since it takes 3–4 hours to cook.

PREPARATION TIME: *35 min*
COOKING TIME: *1¾ hours*
INGREDIENTS *(for 6):*

3 lb (1½ kg) boned shoulder of veal
2 oz (50 g) butter
¼ pint (150 ml) dry white wine
¼–½ pint (150–300 ml) stock
STOCK:
1 large onion
2 carrots
1 stick celery
Bouquet garni (page 99)
STUFFING:
¾ pint (425 ml) stock

4 oz (100 g) long grain rice
Pinch saffron
4 oz (100 g) streaky bacon
1 bunch watercress
2 oz (50 g) shelled walnuts
1 lemon
Salt and freshly ground black pepper*
1 egg
GARNISH:
Watercress

Ask the butcher to bone the shoulder of veal and to include the chopped bones with the order. Put the bones, together with the cleaned and chopped stock vegetables, in a saucepan and cover with cold water. Add the bouquet garni and a good seasoning of salt and black pepper. Cook this stock for about 3 hours, strain and set aside.

With a sharp knife, open the cavities in the meat to make pockets for the stuffing. Cook the rice, with the saffron, in ¾ pint (425 ml) of the reserved stock for 12–14 minutes or until tender.

Meanwhile, cut the rind and gristle from the bacon rashers. Wash and chop the watercress, chop the walnuts finely and grate the rind from the lemon. Fry the bacon rashers in a little of the butter, over low heat, until crisp. Remove the bacon from the pan, drain and chop it.

Put the drained rice in a mixing bowl, and add the bacon fat from the pan, the bacon, watercress, walnuts and lemon rind. Season to taste. Bind the stuffing with the lightly beaten egg.

Spread the stuffing evenly into the pockets of the veal, roll up the joint and tie with string.

Brown the veal briskly in the remaining butter in a roasting tin. Pour over the wine and roast the veal in the centre of a pre-heated oven at 350°F (180°C, mark 4) for about 1½ hours. Baste frequently with the wine, adding a little stock if necessary.

Put the joint on a warm serving dish and remove the string. Add ¼ pint (150 ml) of stock to the roasting tin. Boil over high heat until the liquid is light brown and has reduced by about half. Pour the gravy into a warm sauce boat.

Serve the sliced veal garnished with sprigs of watercress. Roast potatoes go well with the meat; so do courgettes, plain or au gratin.

Veal

VEAL STUFFED WITH KIDNEYS

This makes an excellent and substantial main course dish for a formal picnic party.

PREPARATION TIME: *25 min*
COOKING TIME: *3 hours*
INGREDIENTS *(for 8–10):*
5 lb (2·3 kg) loin of veal
½ lb (225 g) calf kidneys
Salt and black pepper*
2 cloves garlic
2–3 sprigs marjoram or thyme
1 small onion
2 carrots
¼ pint (150 ml) dry white wine
GARNISH:
Watercress

Ask the butcher to bone the loin and to include the bone with the order. Trim the fat off the kidneys and remove the outer skin; snip out the cores with scissors. Lay the boned meat flat on a board and spread the kidneys over the cut side. Season with salt and freshly ground pepper. Peel and finely chop the garlic and herbs; sprinkle them over the kidneys. Carefully roll up the meat and tie it securely with string at 1–2 in (2½–5 cm) intervals.

Rub the outside of the meat thoroughly with salt and pepper, place it in a roasting tin, and surround with the veal bones. Peel and roughly chop the onion; scrape and finely chop the carrots. Arrange the vegetables round the meat. Heat the wine, with ¼ pint (150 ml) of water, in a small pan and pour over the meat. Cover the tin with foil or a lid and cook in the centre of the oven, preheated to 350°F (180°C, mark 4) for 2¼ hours. Turn the meat over half-way through cooking, and add more liquid if needed. Remove the covering for the last 30 minutes to brown the meat.

Lift the meat from the pan and set it aside to cool. Pour the pan juices, bones and vegetables into a pan and simmer over low heat for 45 minutes. Strain the liquid into a bowl and leave until cool. Let it set in the refrigerator and remove any fat on the top.

Serve the stuffed veal with cold chopped jelly, cos lettuce, sliced tomatoes, cucumber in soured cream, and new potatoes dressed in mayonnaise.

VEAL STUFFED WITH KIDNEYS

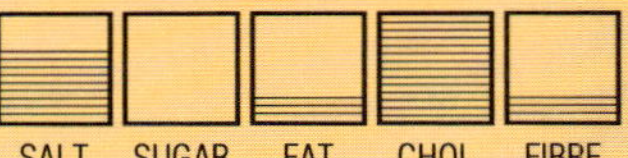

GLUTEN-FREE   WHOLEFOOD
TOTAL CALORIES: ABOUT 4400

The medium **salt** level is due to the generous portions of meat, plus the higher level naturally present in kidneys, so it cannot be reduced except by using only 6 oz (175 g) kidneys in the recipe, and serving smaller helpings.

The high **cholesterol** comes from the kidneys. You could replace them with a completely different stuffing, combining the herbs with, for instance, chopped mushrooms or leeks, or with boiled chestnuts. This would provide a dish low in both fat and cholesterol, assuming the veal is lean and all visible fat trimmed off it. (Calories lost: up to 200.)

Pressure cooker: ☑

NOISETTES OF LAMB SHREWSBURY

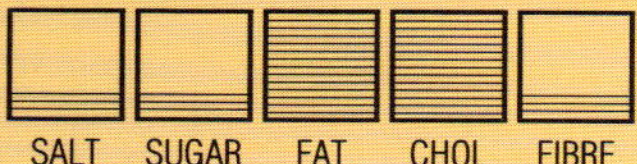

GLUTEN-FREE*   WHOLEFOOD*
TOTAL CALORIES: ABOUT 4170

The **sugar** content is due to the redcurrant jelly; to reduce it to very low, use only 1 tablespoon, or substitute jelly made with no added sugar, if you can find it.

The **fat** and **cholesterol** content will vary hugely depending on how lean the lamb is. Fatty lamb can have as much as 30% fat if both lean and fat are eaten; lean cuts can have as little as 9% – not extremely low, but acceptably so. Choose lean lamb and trim off all visible fat. Soften the sauce vegetables in a pan lightly brushed with oil, omitting the butter. Cover tightly, adding a few tablespoons of stock if necessary to prevent sticking. Cook the noisettes by grilling instead of frying, for the same length of time. All these changes will produce low fat and cholesterol levels. (Calories lost: up to 1000.)

Pressure cooker: ✓ for the sauce.
Freezing: ✓ up to 4 months.

NOISETTES OF LAMB SHREWSBURY

These little round fillets – or noisettes – are cut from the loin or best end of lamb. They are excellent as the main course for a dinner party, especially as the time-consuming sauce can be made well in advance.

PREPARATION TIME: *15–25 min*
COOKING TIME: *2 hours for sauce; 30 min for the noisettes*
INGREDIENTS *(for 4–6):*
8–12 noisettes of lamb
2½ oz (65 g) unsalted butter
1 tablespoon olive oil
SAUCE:
1 small carrot
1 small onion
2 sticks celery
1 oz (25 g) lean bacon
1½ oz (40 g) butter
Lamb trimmings
1 oz (25 g) plain flour
1 pint (570 ml) brown stock (page 81)
½ pint (300 ml) dry white or red wine
2 rounded teaspoons tomato purée
Bouquet garni (page 99)
1 sprig fresh or ½ teaspoon dried rosemary
Salt★ and black pepper
2–3 tablespoons redcurrant jelly

The noisettes, weighing 2–3 oz (50–75 g) each, can be cut from cutlets from the loin or from best end of neck; the latter are smaller, but have a more delicate flavour. Most butchers will prepare the noisettes on request, but ask for the trimmings to be included with the order. Alternatively, cut the piece of meat into single cutlets, remove the bone from each, and shape the meat into a neat round, about 2 in (5 cm) across. Tie

firmly with string.

Prepare the sauce first: scrape the carrot, peel the onion and scrub the celery; dice these vegetables. Cut the rind from the bacon and chop the flesh into small dice; blanch for a few minutes. Melt the butter in a heavy pan over moderate heat. Fry the diced vegetables, chopped lamb trimmings and bacon in this for 10 minutes. Remove the pan from the heat and stir in the flour; return the pan to a low heat and cook for a further 10 minutes, stirring continuously, until the mixture is light brown. Take the pan off the heat.

Bring the stock and wine to the boil in a separate pan; whisk this into the vegetable mixture. Stir in the tomato purée and add the bouquet garni (with fresh rosemary if used). Simmer the sauce, partly covered, over gentle heat for at least 2 hours, stirring occasionally to prevent sticking. Remove any scum from time to time. When the sauce is thick enough to coat the back of a spoon, remove it from the heat. Strain the sauce through a coarse sieve and remove any fat which rises to the top.

About 30 minutes before serving, re-heat the sauce gently, stir in the redcurrant jelly and powdered rosemary (if used); simmer until the jelly has melted. Season to taste and keep warm.

Heat the butter and oil in a heavy-based pan and cook the prepared noisettes over moderate heat for 4–6 minutes on each side, depending on the size. They should be well browned, and slightly pink inside.

Serve the noisettes with the thick, dark brown sauce poured over them. Boiled new potatoes and courgettes or green beans are suitable vegetables.

Lamb

LAMB AND LEMON SOUP

This Greek soup is a thick and meaty broth, and almost a meal in itself.

PREPARATION TIME: *15 min*
COOKING TIME: *3¼ hours*
INGREDIENTS *(for 6)*:
*2 lb (900 g) scrag of lamb,
    chopped*
2 carrots
1–2 turnips
2 onions
2 leeks
1 stick celery
1 sprig parsley
2 bay leaves
*½ teaspoon dried oregano or
    marjoram*
½ teaspoon dried thyme
2 oz (50 g) barley or rice
Salt★ and black pepper
Juice of a lemon
2 egg yolks
GARNISH:
1 lettuce heart

Trim as much fat as possible off the lamb, put the meat into a large saucepan with 2 pints (1·2 litres) of water and bring to the boil. Meanwhile, wash and scrape the carrots and turnips and chop them roughly; peel and roughly chop the onions. Trim the leeks and wash them under cold running water. Scrub the celery and chop this and the leeks roughly.

Remove any scum from the broth. Add the vegetables to the lamb, together with the herbs and barley (if using rice, add this 1 hour later). Season to taste with salt and freshly ground pepper. Cover the pan and simmer the broth for 2–2½ hours, or until the meat comes away from the bones.

Remove the bay leaves and parsley and lift out the meat.

Leave the soup to simmer while picking the meat off the bones. Chop up the lamb and return it to the pan.

Remove the broth from the heat and allow it to get cold (if possible leave overnight). Lift off the fat which has solidified in a layer on top of the broth. Bring the soup back to the boil and, just before serving, beat the lemon juice and the egg yolks together in a small bowl. Mix in 3 or 4 tablespoons of the hot broth and add this mixture to the pan; heat the broth through without allowing it to boil.

Serve the soup sprinkled with finely shredded lettuce heart.

CARRÉ D'AGNEAU DORDONNAISE

Walnuts and liver pâté are an integral part of many dishes from the Dordogne region of France. They are both used in this recipe, which transforms best end of lamb into a party dish.

PREPARATION TIME: *30 min*
COOKING TIME: *1¼ hours*
INGREDIENTS *(for 4–6)*:
2 best end necks of lamb
2–3 oz (50–75 g) shelled walnuts
½ small onion
4 oz (100 g) pâté de foie truffé
4 tablespoons fresh breadcrumbs
*2 tablespoons finely chopped
    parsley*
Salt★ and black pepper
Lemon juice
2 tablespoons cooking oil
4 fluid oz (100 ml) dry white wine
*1 level teaspoon powdered
    rosemary*

Order the best ends skinned and boned and ask the butcher to include the bones with the order.

Trim any excess fat off the meat before wiping it with a damp cloth. Chop the walnuts finely or put them through an electric grinder. Peel and grate the onion. Stir the pâté smooth, and beat in the walnuts and onion. Mix the breadcrumbs and parsley into the stuffing and season with salt, pepper and lemon juice.

Spread the underside of each best end with the stuffing. Roll the meat neatly and tie with string at 2 in (5 cm) intervals. Put the two meat rolls in an oiled roasting tin and brush them with oil. Cook in the centre of the oven pre-heated to 400°F (200°C, mark 6) for about 20 minutes, or until golden brown. Reduce the heat to 375°F (190°C, mark 5) and cook for a further 40–50 minutes, or until tender.

Meanwhile, put the lamb bones in a saucepan with salt and pepper. Cover with cold water, bring to the boil and simmer the stock for 30–40 minutes.

Remove the meat from the roasting tin, leave to cool and set slightly before removing the string. Put the meat back in the oven to keep warm. Carefully pour off the fat in the roasting tin and add the wine to the meat juices. Bring to the boil on top of the stove, add about ½ pint (300 ml) of strained stock and the rosemary. Cook this gravy over high heat until it has reduced slightly. Correct seasoning and strain the gravy into a warm sauce boat, preferably of the kind which separates the fat from the gravy.

Serve the lamb, cut into thick slices, on a warm serving dish. Sauté potatoes, Brussels sprouts and grilled tomatoes could be arranged round the lamb.

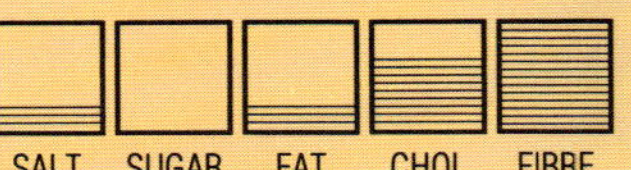

LAMB AND LEMON SOUP

GLUTEN-FREE★   WHOLEFOOD★
TOTAL CALORIES: ABOUT 3310

To ensure the low **fat** level, buy lean lamb and skim off all the fat after the soup has cooled. The **cholesterol** level is raised by the eggs: the egg and lemon mixture is very typical of Greek cooking, but you can perfectly well use 1 whole egg instead of the yolks. If the lamb is lean and the stock de-fatted as above, the cholesterol will be fairly low. To reduce it even further, leave out the eggs altogether, add a potato to the vegetables, and liquidise some of the cooked vegetables, stirring them back into the soup to give it a thicker consistency. (Calories lost: up to 500.) Rice is **gluten-free**, but barley does contain some gluten. For a **wholefood** dish, buy pot barley and brown rice. Short-grain rice is the kind typically used for this soup.

Pressure cooker: ☑
Freezing: ☑ up to 3 months.

CARRÉ D'AGNEAU DORDONNAISE

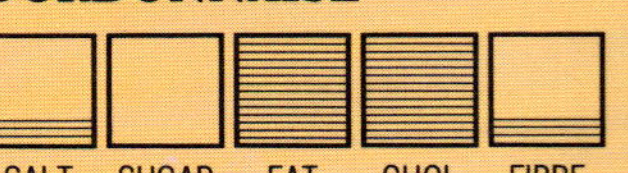

GLUTEN-FREE★   WHOLEFOOD★
TOTAL CALORIES: ABOUT 3410

The **fat** level will vary widely depending on the lamb (see notes on the previous recipes); but even if it is very lean, the dish will have a high fat content because of the pâté de foie and the walnuts. You can reduce

this level to medium by halving the amount of walnuts and using the low-fat version of the pâté on page 67. Also, avoid brushing the meat with oil before roasting, and cook it on a rack so that the fat drains off. Then pour the pan juices off (ideally into a fat-separating gravy boat with a lower spout for pouring off juice after the fat has risen to the surface) and allow to cool so that the fat separates, before adding the stock (also carefully skimmed of fat) to make the gravy. (Calories lost: up to 570.) The **cholesterol** level will remain high because it is naturally high in liver.
Gluten-free: check the ingredients on the label if you buy a pâté. The same applies to **wholefood**.

Pressure cooker: ☑ for the stock.
Food processor: ☑ for the stuffing.

DURHAM LAMB SQUAB PIE

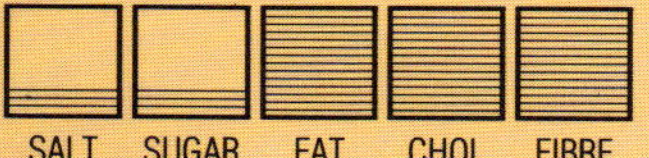

| SALT | SUGAR | FAT | CHOL | FIBRE |

GLUTEN-FREE   WHOLEFOOD
TOTAL CALORIES: ABOUT 4250

To reduce the **fat** and **cholesterol** levels to low, choose lean meat and brown it in a non-stick or heavy pan brushed lightly with oil, omitting the butter. Replace the remaining butter for greasing the pie dish with a bare smear of oil. Do not brush the potato layer with butter, but cover the casserole while it cooks so that it does not dry out. (Calories lost: up to 680.)

Freezing: ☑ up to 4 months.

DURHAM LAMB SQUAB PIE

Originally, this recipe probably contained squabs – or young pigeons – but, in the course of time, meat became the chief constituent of the pie. There are several variations of this English farmhouse dish; the following comes from Durham.

PREPARATION TIME: *30 min*
COOKING TIME: *1–1¼ hours*
INGREDIENTS *(for 4–6):*
8 lamb chops
2 lb (900 g) potatoes
1 large onion
3 cooking apples
3 oz (75 g) unsalted butter
1 heaped teaspoon brown sugar
Salt★ and black pepper
⅓ pint (200 ml) chicken stock

Peel and thinly slice the potatoes and cover with cold water. Trim excess fat from the lamb chops. Peel and finely chop the onion, and peel, core and chop the apples. Melt 2 oz (50 g) of the butter in a pan and fry the chops lightly on both sides. Remove them as soon as the blood starts to run. Fry the apples and onion in the fat for about 5 minutes.

Use half the remaining butter to grease the inside of a pie dish. Dry the sliced potatoes and line the base of the dish with half of them. Arrange the chops on the potato bed and spoon the apple and onion mixture over them. Sprinkle over the sugar, a little salt and a couple of twists of pepper from the mill. Cover with the rest of the potatoes and pour over the chicken stock. Melt the remaining butter and brush it over the potato layer. Put the dish on the middle shelf of an oven preheated to 350°F (180°C, mark 4) and cook for 1 hour or until the potatoes are tender and golden brown.

Serve straight from the casserole. Brussels sprouts tossed in soft brown sugar and allspice could be served with it.

LAMB IN RED WINE

A leg of lamb makes a good choice for a large gathering. Spices and wine give a fresh summer taste to succulent young lamb.

PREPARATION TIME: *15 min*
COOKING TIME: *1¾–2 hours*
INGREDIENTS (*for 6–8*):
4–5 lb (about 2 kg) leg of lamb
2 cloves garlic
¼ oz (5–10 g) lard
Salt★ and black pepper
Ground ginger
2 onions
2 carrots
2 oz (50 g) unsalted butter
3–4 sprigs of thyme
½ pint (300 ml) dry red wine

Wipe the lamb thoroughly with a damp cloth. Peel the garlic and cut each clove into three or four slivers. With the point of a sharp knife, make small incisions in the meat and press the garlic into these. Rub the skin with the lard, a little salt, freshly ground pepper and dust with ginger. Peel the onions and carrots and chop them roughly.

Melt the butter in a roasting pan, and quickly brown the meat over moderate heat to seal in the juices. Remove the meat from the pan and cook the onions and carrots for a few minutes in the butter until golden. Spoon the pan mixture into a large oven-proof dish, add the thyme and place the meat on top; cover with a lid or foil.

Roast the meat in the centre of an oven pre-heated to 425°F (220°C, mark 7) for 25 minutes, then pour over the wine and reduce the heat to 350°F (180°C, mark 4) for a further 1–1¼ hours. Baste two or three times with the wine.

Remove the joint and keep it warm on a serving dish in the oven. Strain the cooking juices and boil them briskly until they have reduced by about one-third. Remove any fat by drawing absorbent kitchen paper over the surface of this gravy. Heat through and correct seasoning.

Serve roast potatoes and young carrots, tossed in parsley, with the lamb. Pour the gravy into a sauceboat and serve it separately.

LAMB KEBABS

Skewered chunks of meat, or kebabs, are usually grilled over a charcoal fire.

PREPARATION TIME: *20 min*
COOKING TIME: *10 min*
INGREDIENTS (*for 4*):
1½ lb (700 g) boned shoulder of lamb
¼ level teaspoon green chili
1 in (2½ cm) piece root ginger
5 fluid oz (150 ml) plain yogurt
¼ level teaspoon ground coriander
¼ level teaspoon ground cumin
1 clove garlic
Juice of ½ lemon
1 level teaspoon salt★
GARNISH:
Lemon wedges
Mint

Trim any excess fat from the lamb, wipe with a damp cloth and cut it into 1 in (2½ cm) cubes. Chop the chili finely; peel the ginger until the green part just shows, and chop it roughly. Put the yogurt in a large bowl and stir in the coriander, cumin, chili and ginger. Peel the garlic and crush it into the yogurt before adding the lemon juice and salt. Mix the lamb into the yogurt and leave to marinate for at least 30 minutes.

Remove the lamb chunks from the marinade and thread them on to four steel skewers, 8–10 in (20–25 cm) long, packing the pieces closely together. Put the skewers under a hot grill or on a barbecue and cook, turning from time to time, for 8–10 minutes, or until browned on the outside and pink in the centre.

Arrange the lamb kebabs, on their skewers, on a bed of rice garnished with lemon wedges and sprigs of mint.

LAMB IN RED WINE

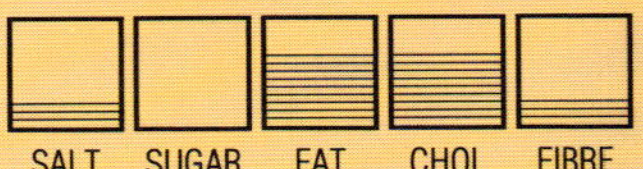

GLUTEN-FREE   WHOLEFOOD
TOTAL CALORIES: ABOUT 7550

To reduce the **fat** and **cholesterol** level of this dish to low, choose the leanest possible piece of lamb and trim off any visible fat. Omit rubbing with lard and bake the meat and vegetables without sealing them first, thus omitting the butter. To reduce the fat level further, pour the pan juices into a fat-separating gravy boat, which will have a spout set low down on one side. When the fat separates after cooling a little, the juice alone can be poured off via this spout to make the gravy. It is easier to do this before reducing the gravy by boiling. (Calories lost: up to 550.)

LAMB KEBABS

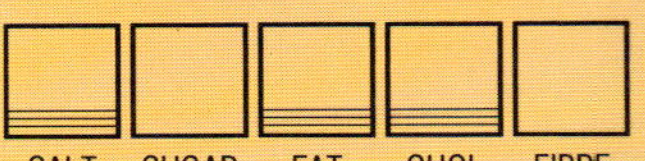

GLUTEN-FREE   WHOLEFOOD
TOTAL CALORIES: ABOUT 2115

This recipe needs no alteration to suit healthier eating, provided the lamb chosen is lean and is trimmed as the recipe suggests.

ORANGE-GLAZED LAMB ROAST

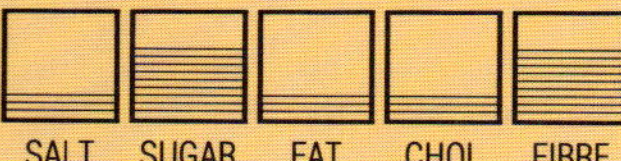

SALT   SUGAR   FAT   CHOL   FIBRE

GLUTEN-FREE*   WHOLEFOOD*
TOTAL CALORIES: ABOUT 7380

To reduce the amount of added **sugar** to low, mix the glaze ingredients with 1 tablespoon clear honey and smear this over the meat.

The low **fat** and **cholesterol** levels (and the calorie count) assume that you choose a very lean leg of lamb, trim off any visible fat and, after cooking, allow the pan juices to cool slightly so that you can pour off any fat before using them to make the gravy. Serve with unbuttered vegetables.

ORANGE-GLAZED LAMB ROAST

A fruit-flavoured glaze and stuffing transform a leg of lamb into a dish fit for a special occasion. Ask the butcher to bone the lamb, but not to roll it.

PREPARATION TIME: *20 min*
COOKING TIME: *2¼ hours*
INGREDIENTS *(for 6–8):*
4–4½ lb (1·8–2 kg) leg of lamb
  (boned)
1 large onion
Grated rind of 2 oranges
1 oz (25 g) butter
3 oz (75 g) fresh breadcrumbs
2 oz (50 g) sultanas
2 oz (50 g) raisins
2 oz (50 g) currants
½ level teaspoon dried rosemary
½ level teaspoon dried thyme
Salt★ and black pepper
Juice of an orange
GLAZE:
2 oz (50 g) soft brown sugar
Juice of half lemon
Juice of an orange
2 tablespoons Worcestershire
  sauce
SAUCE:
4 fluid oz (100 ml) red wine
½ pint (300 ml) beef bouillon
GARNISH:
Orange slices and watercress

Prepare the stuffing for the lamb first. Peel and finely chop the onion and grate the rind from two oranges. Melt the butter in a pan over medium heat and fry the onion for 3 minutes. Mix together in a bowl the breadcrumbs, sultanas, raisins, currants and the fried onion. Blend in the orange rind, rosemary and thyme and season to taste with salt and pepper. Bind the stuffing with the juice of one orange.

Wipe the meat with a damp cloth, and pack the stuffing into the lamb. Tie the joint into a neat shape, securing it with string. Put it in a greased baking tin.

Place the glaze ingredients in a small pan and cook over low heat for 1 minute, then spoon the glaze over the meat. Roast in the centre of a pre-heated oven, at 375°F (190°C, mark 5), for 2 hours, basting frequently.

Remove the joint to a warm serving dish and keep it hot. Stir into the pan the wine and bouillon for the sauce, and boil over high heat, scraping up all the residue from the glaze. Continue boiling briskly until the sauce has reduced and thickened slightly. Correct seasoning if necessary.

Serve the joint, having first removed the string, and garnish with thin orange twists (page 97) and with sprigs of watercress. Roast potatoes and buttered baby sprouts or salsify would go well with the joint.

Lamb

DOLMAS

In Turkey, one of the most popular main course dishes is fresh vine leaves stuffed with rice and minced lamb. Tinned vine leaves or young cabbage leaves make good substitutes.

PREPARATION TIME: *40 min*
COOKING TIME: *1 hour*
INGREDIENTS *(for 4–6):*
12 fresh vine or cabbage leaves or 6½ oz (185 g) tin of vine leaves
1 onion
4 oz (100 g) long grain rice
3 oz (75 g) butter
1½ pints (900 ml) white stock or water
1 lb (450 g) lean minced lamb
2 level teaspoons chopped fresh mint or parsley
1 level teaspoon powdered rosemary
Salt★ and black pepper
Juice of half lemon
5 fluid oz (150 ml) natural yogurt

Peel the onion and chop it finely. Melt 1 oz (25 g) of the butter in a large heavy-based pan and fry the onion and rice until lightly coloured. Add enough stock to cover the rice and cook over low heat until tender. Stir frequently and add more stock if necessary.

Leave the rice and onion to cool and set. Stir in the minced lamb, the mint or parsley and rosemary and mix thoroughly. Season to taste with salt and freshly ground pepper. Blanch the fresh vine or cabbage leaves for a few minutes in boiling water, then remove the coarse stalks. If using tinned vine leaves, unravel them carefully without breaking them.

Spread out the leaves and put a spoonful of the lamb and rice filling on each; fold the leaves over to make small, neat parcels. Pack them closely in layers in a flameproof casserole or sauté pan. Add enough stock to cover, and sprinkle with the lemon juice; dot with the remaining butter. Put a plate on top of the stuffed vine parcels to keep them under the liquid.

Cover the dish with a lid or foil and simmer over low heat for about 1 hour. Lift out the vine parcels with a perforated spoon and arrange them on a warm serving dish. Serve the yogurt in a separate bowl.

HARICOT LAMB CASSEROLE

This French country-style casserole is made from one of the least expensive cuts of meat, but has great appeal to both eye and palate. Ask the butcher to joint the lamb into single ribs.

PREPARATION TIME: *35 min*
COOKING TIME: *1¾ hours*
INGREDIENTS *(for 4–6):*
3 lb (1½ kg) middle neck of lamb
3 leeks
6 fresh or 14 or 16 oz (400 or 450 g) tin of tomatoes
½ lb (225 g) carrots
2 cloves garlic
2 tablespoons oil
1 tablespoon caster sugar
Salt★ and black pepper
1 heaped tablespoon plain flour
¾ pint (425 ml) stock or bouillon
1 bay leaf
½ level teaspoon powdered thyme
½ lb (225 g) French or runner beans

Pre-heat the oven to 450°F (230°C, mark 8). Trim the roots and coarse outer leaves off the leeks, wash them thoroughly and chop them roughly. Skin the tomatoes. Peel or scrape the carrots, but leave them whole, and peel the garlic cloves.

Heat the oil in a flameproof

DOLMAS

GLUTEN-FREE   WHOLEFOOD★
TOTAL CALORIES: ABOUT 2530

The **salt** level is only low if fresh leaves are used.
The **fat** level of this recipe will depend largely on the meat used. Buy lean lamb and mince it yourself. The amount of butter can be reduced by cooking the onion and rice in a heavy pan lightly brushed with oil rather than in melted butter, and by omitting the butter dotted on top of the casserole. Butter is not a traditional part of Middle Eastern recipes. Assuming the yogurt is low-fat, making these changes will produce a dish low in both fat and **cholesterol**. (Calories lost: up to 700.)

Freezing: ☑ up to 4 months.
Microwave: ☑

HARICOT LAMB CASSEROLE

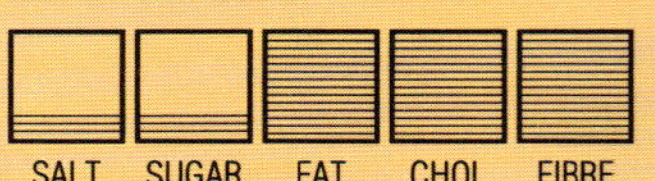

GLUTEN-FREE★   WHOLEFOOD★
TOTAL CALORIES: ABOUT 5570

The high **fat** level can be somewhat reduced by browning the meat in a non-stick pan or in a large heavy pan lightly brushed with oil. The middle neck is a fatty cut of lamb in most cases, and will quickly melt out enough to lubricate its own cooking. The remaining fat comes from the meat itself. As well as searching out the leanest piece you can

and trimming off the visible fat, cook the meat on a roasting rack so that the fat can drain off, and remove as much of the fat as possible before adding the leeks and other vegetables. This will give a low-fat dish. (Calories lost: up to 300.)
The high **cholesterol** level relates to the generous helpings: for low cholesterol, use not more than 6 oz (175 g) flesh per person.

Pressure cooker: ✓
Slow cooker: ✓
Freezing: ✓ up to 4 months.
Microwave: ✓

LAMB ARGENTEUIL

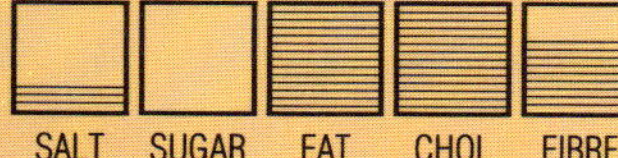

| SALT | SUGAR | FAT | CHOL | FIBRE |

GLUTEN-FREE *   WHOLEFOOD *
TOTAL CALORIES: ABOUT 4310

The **fat** and **cholesterol** levels can be reduced to low by the following measures: choose lean lamb, perhaps substituting leg for shoulder, which always has more fat, or using neck fillet; brown the meat in a non-stick pan brushed lightly with oil instead of using butter; replace the cream with low-fat curd cheese or thick yogurt, or with cultured buttermilk, making sure the dish does not boil after adding any of these or it will curdle. (Calories lost: up to 1000.)
This low cholesterol level assumes that each portion of meat (boned weight) does not exceed 5–6 oz (150–175 g).

Pressure cooker: ✓
Freezing: ✓ up to 4 months.
Microwave: ✓

casserole on top of the stove and quickly brown the lamb joints on both sides. Sprinkle with sugar, lower the heat and toss the contents until the sugar caramelises slightly. Season with salt and freshly ground pepper, and sprinkle in half the flour.

Place the casserole, uncovered, in the hot oven for 5 minutes. Turn the meat over, season again and sprinkle with the remaining flour. Bake for a further 5 minutes. Reduce the oven heat to 325°F (170°C, mark 3). Remove the casserole, lift out the meat, and lightly fry the leeks in the casserole on top of the stove. Add the stock and bring to the boil, scraping up any residue on the bottom of the casserole. Put in the meat, add the tomatoes, carrots, bay leaf, thyme and crushed garlic. Cover the casserole with a lid and bring to simmering point. The sauce should almost cover the meat; add a little more stock if you think it is necessary.

Return the casserole to the centre of the oven and cook for 1½ hours or until the meat is tender. Top and tail the beans, and string them if necessary. Cut them into ½ in (1 cm) pieces and cook in boiling salted water for 10 minutes, or until just tender. Drain, and add to the casserole and cook them in the sauce for a further 5 minutes.

Serve the lamb straight from the casserole, with potatoes baked in their jackets. No other vegetables are needed, but a green salad would go well with it.

LAMB ARGENTEUIL

In its classic form, this recipe uses asparagus from the district of Argenteuil in France.

PREPARATION TIME: *30 min*
COOKING TIME: *1 hour*
INGREDIENTS *(for 6)*:
2 lb (900 g) asparagus
2 lb (900 g) boned shoulder of lamb
4 small onions
2 oz (50 g) butter
1 heaped tablespoon seasoned flour (page 100)
¼ pint (150 ml) double cream
Salt★ and black pepper
Lemon juice

Wash and scrape the asparagus, but do not trim; tie in three or four bundles with soft tape and cook in a large pan of lightly salted water. When the asparagus is tender, after 15–20 minutes, drain well and set the cooking liquid aside. Cut off the asparagus tips about 3 in (7½ cm) down the stems. Put the tips aside and first liquidise, then sieve the stems to make a purée, discarding any tough or stringy parts.

Trim as much fat as possible off the lamb and cut the meat into 2 in (5 cm) pieces. Toss them in the seasoned flour to coat evenly. Peel and roughly chop the onions. Melt the butter in a deep frying or sauté pan, and cook the meat and onions until brown. Gradually blend in about ½ pint (300 ml) of the asparagus liquid, stirring continuously until the sauce is smooth and creamy. Simmer until the meat is tender (about 50 minutes), stirring occasionally and removing any fat which rises to the surface of the sauce. If the liquid evaporates too quickly, cover the pan with a lid.

When the meat is cooked, stir the asparagus purée and cream into the sauce. Season to taste with salt, freshly ground pepper and lemon juice. The sauce should be fairly thick.

Arrange the asparagus tips round the edge of a warm serving dish and spoon the meat and sauce into the centre. Boiled new potatoes are all that is needed with the meat.

Lamb

LANCASHIRE HOT POT

In Northern England, the 'hot pot' was a tall earthenware pot. Mutton chops were stood upright round the inside and the centre was filled with vegetables. It was usual, too, in the days when they were cheap, to put a layer of oysters beneath the potato crust.

PREPARATION TIME: *30 min*
COOKING TIME: *2–2½ hours*
INGREDIENTS *(for 4–6):*

2 lb (900 g) middle neck of lamb
Seasoned flour (page 100)
1 oz (25 g) dripping
1½ lb (700 g) potatoes
2 onions
6–8 carrots
2 sticks celery
1 leek
Salt★ and black pepper
¼ level teaspoon mixed herbs
GARNISH:
Chopped parsley

Wipe and bone the lamb. Put the bones in a saucepan and cover with cold water. Bring to the boil, and after a few minutes remove the scum; cover with a lid and let the bones simmer while the vegetables and meat are being prepared.

Trim away any fat and gristle, and cut the meat into small, even pieces. Roll them in seasoned flour, before frying in hot dripping until browned and sealed on all sides. Peel the potatoes and cut them into ¼ in (½ cm) thick slices. Put aside half the slices for the top and place the remainder in the base of a deep buttered casserole dish.

Peel and coarsely chop the onions. Scrape or peel the carrots and slice them thinly. Scrub the celery and chop it finely. Remove the outer coarse leaves and the root of the leek, wash it well and cut it across into thin slices. Mix all the vegetables together in a deep bowl, season with salt and pepper and sprinkle the herbs over them. Arrange layers of seasoned vegetables and meat in the casserole, beginning and ending with a layer of vegetables. Top with the remaining potato slices, arranging them neatly in overlapping circles. Strain the liquid from the bones and pour about ¾ pint (425 ml) of it into the casserole until it just reaches the upper potato layer. Cover with buttered greaseproof paper and a tight-fitting lid. Place in the centre of an oven pre-heated to 350°F (180°C, mark 4) and cook for 2–2½ hours.

About 30 minutes before serving, remove the lid and paper from the casserole. Brush the potatoes with a little melted dripping and sprinkle with coarse salt. Raise the oven heat to 400°F (200°C, mark 6) and return the uncovered casserole to the oven, placing it above the centre so that the potatoes will crisp and brown slightly.

Sprinkle with finely chopped parsley immediately before serving. The hot pot is a meal on its own, but is traditionally served with pickled red cabbage.

SUFFOLK STEW

This is one of those hearty, satisfying stews that requires nothing before it, and very little afterwards. Order the best end of lamb chined (page 89), and begin the preparations a day in advance.

PREPARATION TIME: *30 min*
COOKING TIME: *3 hours*
INGREDIENTS *(for 4–6):*
1 best end of lamb
2 oz (50 g) lentils
1 oz (25 g) haricot beans
1 oz (25 g) barley
2 large potatoes
1 large turnip
4 carrots
4 onions
2 bay leaves
½ level teaspoon salt★
½ level teaspoon black pepper
1 clove garlic
1 level teaspoon mixed herbs

Soak the lentils, haricot beans and barley in cold water overnight. The following day, peel and roughly chop all the vegetables; put them in a large saucepan. Trim any excess fat from the best end of lamb and cut the meat into single chops. Add these, together with the bay leaves, salt, pepper, crushed garlic and herbs to the vegetables.

Drain the lentils, haricot beans and barley, before adding them to the pan. Pour over 3 pints (1¾ litres) of water, cover the pan with a lid and bring to the boil. Simmer gently for 3 hours.

Spoon the stew into a warm serving dish. No other vegetables are necessary, but buttered hot muffins would make an unusual accompaniment to the stew.

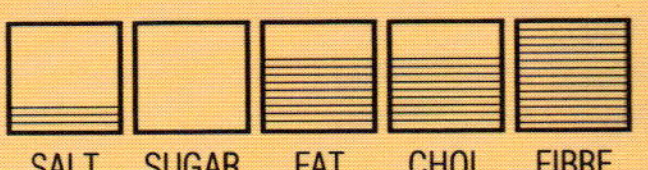

LANCASHIRE HOT POT

GLUTEN-FREE★   WHOLEFOOD★
TOTAL CALORIES: ABOUT 4340

The exact **fat** level depends on the cut of meat. Choose lean meat and trim off the fat carefully. In addition, for low fat and **cholesterol**, brown the meat in a non-stick pan in its own fat, which will soon melt out (if necessary, brush the pan lightly with oil). This avoids the need for dripping; do not, naturally, brush the potatoes with dripping near the end of cooking. (Calories lost: up to 300.)

Freezing: ✓ up to 4 months.

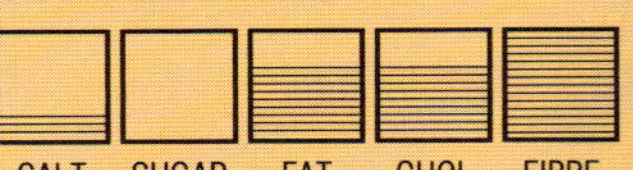

SUFFOLK STEW

WHOLEFOOD★
TOTAL CALORIES: ABOUT 3890

The exact **fat** and **cholesterol** levels depend on the meat chosen. To ensure this dish is low in both, buy the leanest piece of meat available and trim off any visible fat. Instead of serving with buttered muffins, try adding dumplings (see the recipe on page 20) to the top of the stew, or serve with lightly cooked sprouts.
For a completely **gluten-free** dish, replace the barley, which does contain some gluten, with rice, lentils or pre-soaked chick peas.
For a **wholefood** dish, use pot barley, or replace the barley with brown rice, lentils or chick peas as above.

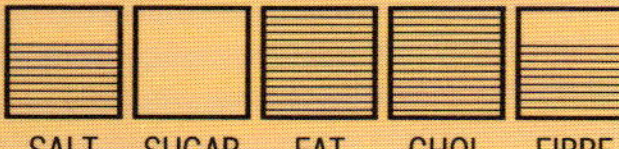

Pressure cooker: ☑
Slow cooker: ☑
Freezing: ☑ up to 4 months.

CROWN ROAST OF LAMB

SALT	SUGAR	FAT	CHOL	FIBRE

GLUTEN-FREE★   WHOLEFOOD★
TOTAL CALORIES: ABOUT 5330

The **salt** level can be reduced to low by using breadcrumbs from bread made without added salt, and ensuring that the pork is not cured or salted.

To reduce the **fat** and **cholesterol** levels, omit the pork from the stuffing and brown the stuffing ingredients in a heavy pan brushed lightly with oil, not butter. No dripping need be used as even lean lamb carries plenty of fat. For an overall low fat and cholesterol dish, use very lean lamb, trim off all visible fat and skim the pan juices thoroughly before making gravy. (Calories lost: up to 1550.)

If wished, the loss of bulk in the stuffing due to leaving out the pork can be made up by including two extra onions and a chopped dessert apple.

Food processor: ☑ for the stuffing.

CROWN ROAST OF LAMB

The crown is formed by joining two best ends of lamb, and the hollow between them is stuffed with a savoury filling. The cutlet bones are frequently decorated with cutlet frills, but glazed onions make an unusual, and edible, garnish for this meat dish.

PREPARATION TIME: *45 min*
COOKING TIME: *2 hours*
INGREDIENTS *(for 6)*:
2 best ends of lamb (6 cutlets each)
2 oz (50 g) beef dripping
STUFFING:
½ lb (225 g) cranberries
¼ pint (150 ml) chicken stock
1 oz (25 g) caster sugar
1 onion
¼ lb (100 g) mushrooms
½ lb (225 g) belly pork
1 oz (25 g) butter
1 clove garlic
4 level tablespoons chopped parsley
1½ level teaspoons ground thyme
4 oz (100 g) fresh breadcrumbs
1 egg
Salt★ and black pepper
GARNISH:
Glazed onions

Ask the butcher to trim off any excess fat and to shape the best ends of lamb into a crown (page 89).

For the stuffing, put the cranberries, stock and sugar in a saucepan; if necessary, top up the stock with enough water to cover the fruit. Bring the cranberries to the boil and cook over high heat until they burst open, and the liquid has reduced to a thick sauce.

Peel and finely chop the onion, trim and coarsely chop the mush-

rooms, and mince the belly pork. Melt the butter in a pan and fry the onion until soft but not coloured. Add the peeled and crushed garlic and cook for 1 minute. Add the mushrooms, turning them in the butter until they are lightly coloured. In a bowl, combine the cranberries and the onion and mushroom mixture with the minced belly pork. Mix in the parsley, thyme and bread-crumbs. Beat the egg lightly and use to bind the stuffing. Season to taste with salt and freshly ground pepper.

Spoon the stuffing into the hollow crown. Wrap foil round the cutlet bones to protect them during roasting. Melt the drip-ping in a roasting pan and place the stuffed crown in it. Roast on a shelf low in a pre-heated oven at 375°F (190°C, mark 5), for 10 minutes. Reduce the heat to 350°F (180°C, mark 4) and con-tinue roasting. Allow 30 minutes to the pound (450 g), and baste frequently.

Remove the crown roast and keep it warm. Skim off as much fat as possible and boil the pan juices to make a gravy. Sweeten with red currant jelly or a tablespoon of cranberry sauce, and pour into a warm sauce boat.

Serve the crown roast with garlic potatoes and a chicory and orange salad. Spike a glazed onion on each cutlet bone.

NAVARIN OF LAMB

Navarin is a French cooking term applied exclusively to a casserole of lamb, or mutton, and young root vegetables.

PREPARATION TIME: *30 min*
COOKING TIME: *1¾ hours*
INGREDIENTS *(for 4):*
2 lb (900 g) best end neck of lamb
Seasoned flour (page 100)
1½ oz (40 g) dripping or vegetable oil
1 lb (450 g) young carrots
1 onion
¾ pint (425 ml) chicken or beef stock
1 tablespoon tomato purée
Salt★ and black pepper
Bouquet garni (page 99)
8 small button onions
8 small new potatoes
GARNISH:
Chopped parsley

Ask the butcher to cut the meat into single rib pieces. Trim fat from the meat and coat the pieces with the seasoned flour. Melt the fat in a large frying pan and add the meat. Fry as many ribs as possible at one time, turning them to brown evenly on both sides. Remove from the pan and put them in a large casserole. Scrape and thinly slice the carrots, and peel and roughly chop the onion. Add these to the casserole. Drain off most of the fat from the frying pan. Stir in 1 level tablespoon of the seasoned flour; cook over low heat for a few minutes to brown, then gradually stir in the hot stock. Add the tomato purée and bring the sauce to the boil.

Draw the pan off the heat and strain the sauce into the casserole; season with salt and freshly ground pepper. Add the bouquet garni. Cover the casserole with a lid and place in the centre of a pre-heated oven at 325°F (170°C, mark 3); cook for 1¼ hours.

Peel the button onions, leaving them whole. Put them in a saucepan and cover with cold water. Bring this to the boil, then drain the onions at once. Scrape the new potatoes and add, with the onions, to the casserole, placing them on top of the meat. Replace the lid and cook the casserole for a further 30 minutes or until the vegetables are tender.

Remove the bouquet garni from the casserole, sprinkle with chopped parsley and serve the lamb straight from the casserole.

to medium, especially if the dish is served with unbuttered vegetables. (Calories lost: up to 600.) The **cholesterol** will be moderate if the portions are reduced – the quantities given are generous.

Freezing: ☑ up to 4 months.
Microwave: ☑

ÉPIGRAMMES D'AGNEAU

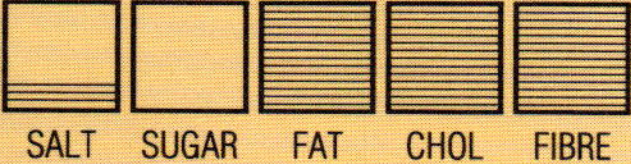

| SALT | SUGAR | FAT | CHOL | FIBRE |

GLUTEN-FREE*   WHOLEFOOD*
TOTAL CALORIES: ABOUT 6710

Breast of lamb is one of the fattiest meat cuts. Even if all visible fat is trimmed, the lean meat contains enough marbling to make it about 16% fat. However, this recipe allows you to remove more fat later. If you choose the leanest breast possible, trim it carefully both before and after cooking, the **fat** content will be medium – provided you grill, rather than fry, the breadcrumb-coated épigrammes at the last stage of cooking. This is in fact the more usual way of cooking épigrammes. Grill for about 10 minutes each side under a medium grill, thus eliminating the butter and oil. For a low **cholesterol** level, use only the egg white for coating the meat. (Calories lost: up to 600.)

Pressure cooker: ☑ for the first stage of cooking.

CORDERO A LA CHILINDRÓN

The mountain districts of Spain favour lamb as a festive dish: this version with pimento and tomatoes comes from Navarre.

PREPARATION TIME: *20 min*
COOKING TIME: *50 min*
INGREDIENTS (*for 6*):
2 lb (900 g) boned leg or shoulder
  of lamb
1 red pimento
Salt★ and black pepper
2 tablespoons olive oil
2 cloves garlic
1 onion
4 oz (100 g) cured ham
14–16 oz (400–450 g) tinned
  tomatoes

Put the pimento under a hot grill. Turn it frequently until charred all over, then rub the skin off under cold water. Remove the stalk and the seeds, and cut the flesh into narrow strips.

Finely chop the onion and garlic. Dice the ham. In Spain the ham used is mountain ham, chewy and full of taste.

Cut the lamb into 1½–2 in (4–5 cm) cubes, removing excess fat. Season to taste with salt and freshly ground black pepper. Heat the oil in a large, heavy-based pan and fry the garlic until golden. Add the onion, lamb and ham and cook over moderate heat for about 10 minutes or until the lamb is browned. Stir the chopped pimento and tomatoes, with their juice, into the pan.

Simmer the lamb, covered, over low heat for about 40 minutes or until tender.

Serve with buttered rice, crusty French bread and a tossed green side salad.

ÉPIGRAMMES D'AGNEAU

This is an unusual way of cooking breast of lamb. It is also an economical dish, for the stock can be used as the basis for the soup on page 38.

PREPARATION TIME: *30 min*
COOKING TIME: *2 hours*
STANDING TIME: *3 hours*
INGREDIENTS (*for 4–6*):
2 breasts of lamb, unboned and
  weighing about 3 lb (1½ kg)
1 onion
2 leeks
1–2 sticks celery
3–4 carrots
Bouquet garni (page 99)
2 level teaspoons salt★
6 peppercorns
1 large egg
2–3 oz (50–75 g) dry
  breadcrumbs
2 oz (50 g) unsalted butter
2 tablespoons corn oil
GARNISH:
Watercress sprigs
Lemon wedges

Peel and slice the onion. Cut the roots and coarse outer leaves from the leeks, wash them thoroughly under cold running water and chop them roughly. Scrub the celery and scrape or peel the carrots; chop both roughly.

Trim as much fat as possible from the breasts of lamb, and put them in a large pan, with the prepared vegetables, the bouquet garni, salt and peppercorns. Cover with cold water and bring to the boil. Remove any scum from the surface, then cover the pan with a lid and simmer gently for 1½ hours. Remove the meat from the pan, leave to cool slightly, then carefully pull out all the bones.

Lay the meat flat between two boards and place a heavy weight on top. Leave until quite cold, then trim off any remaining fat and cut the meat into 2 in (5 cm) squares. Dip the meat in the lightly beaten egg and coat evenly with the breadcrumbs. Set aside until the coating has hardened.

Heat the butter and oil in a heavy-based pan and fry the meat squares until crisp and golden on both sides, after about 20 minutes. Drain on crumpled absorbent kitchen paper.

Serve the épigrammes garnished with watercress and lemon wedges. Sauté potatoes and broccoli spears would go well with the épigrammes.

Lamb

LAMB À LA GRECQUE

Greek cooking is characterised by its use of spices and aubergines. Lamb is the meat most commonly used in Greece, but it is often lean and stringy and more suitable for casserole dishes than for roasting.

PREPARATION TIME: *1–1¼ hours*
COOKING TIME: *1¼ hours*
INGREDIENTS *(for 6):*
3 lb (1½ kg) boned shoulder of lamb
½ lb (225 g) aubergines
Salt and black pepper
4 tablespoons olive oil
4 oz (100 g) caster sugar
1 lb (450 g) apricots
2 large onions
14 or 16 oz (400 or 450 g) tin of tomatoes
6 oz (175 g) tin tomato paste
4 bay leaves
¼ level teaspoon crushed coriander seeds
¼ level teaspoon grated nutmeg
1 level tablespoon chopped parsley
Juice of a lemon
3 oz (75 g) unsalted butter
2 pints (1·2 litres) chicken stock
8 oz (225 g) long grain rice
GARNISH:
4 oz (100 g) stoned black olives
Orange peel

Remove the stalk ends and wipe the aubergines; cut them lengthways into ¼ in (½ cm) thick slices. Place the aubergine slices in a bowl and sprinkle them with 2 teaspoons salt, to draw out the excess water. Mix thoroughly, cover with a cloth and leave for 45 minutes. Wipe them dry.

Heat the olive oil in a heavy-based pan and fry the aubergine slices for just 1 minute until golden, then drain on absorbent kitchen paper.

Dissolve the sugar in a pan containing 8 fluid oz (225 ml) cold water. Boil this syrup for 10 minutes, and meanwhile halve and stone the apricots. Add the apricots to the syrup and poach for 5–15 minutes until tender.

Trim any excess fat from the lamb, cut the meat into 1 in (2½ cm) cubes and fry it over low heat in a dry sauté pan, turning it frequently, until the fat runs and the meat turns a light brown.

Peel and finely chop the onions, add them to the lamb and continue cooking until the onions are transparent. Add the chopped tomatoes with their juice, the tomato paste, bay leaves, coriander seeds, nutmeg, parsley, salt, pepper and lemon juice. Top up the apricot syrup with water to make ½ pint (300 ml), pour it over the lamb and bring to the boil.

Line the base of a large buttered casserole with the aubergine slices and spoon over the lamb mixture. Cover the casserole tightly with foil and the lid. Cook for 1 hour in the centre of an oven pre-heated to 350°F (180°C, mark 4). Remove the covering from the casserole, lay the apricots over the lamb and return the casserole to the oven.

Bring the stock and 6 pints (3½ litres) of water to the boil in a large saucepan. Add 2 teaspoons salt and the rice, stirring until the water returns to the boil. Cover the pan with a lid and boil the rice for 12–14 minutes or until just tender. Drain the rice through a sieve and rinse under hot water.

Melt the remaining butter in a saucepan and stir in the rice. Spoon the rice in a ring on to a warm serving dish and fill the centre with the lamb and aubergines. Garnish the rice with black olives, and apricots, and narrow strips of orange peel.

Serve with a lettuce and tomato salad tossed in an oil and orange juice dressing.

LAMB À LA GRECQUE

GLUTEN-FREE   WHOLEFOOD
TOTAL CALORIES: ABOUT 7430

To reduce the **salt** level to low, do not salt the aubergines. The main advantage of salting them is that they then absorb less fat when fried, but if they are cooked as suggested below this does not arise. Ensure the tinned tomatoes and tomato paste have no added salt.
To eliminate added **sugar**, using fresh apricots (or apricots canned in unsweetened juice), bake them, covered, in a medium oven with a few tablespoons of water or juice for about 30 minutes, until just tender. Halve, stone and use as garnish as suggested. (Calories lost: up to 440.)
Alternatively, for a sweeter taste (but still eliminating added sugar), use dried apricots, about half the quantity or a little less; soak them in water for an hour or two and then bake them as above.
For low **fat** and **cholesterol**, buy lean meat (leg or neck fillet are leaner than shoulder of lamb) and trim off all visible fat. Instead of frying the aubergine slices, grill them on a baking sheet lightly brushed with oil for about 4 minutes on each side. (Calories lost: up to 1000.)
Do not butter the cooked rice, but stir in a few tablespoons of chopped fresh herbs.

Freezing: ✓ up to 4 months (the lamb stew only, not the rice or apricots).

RILLETTES OF PORK

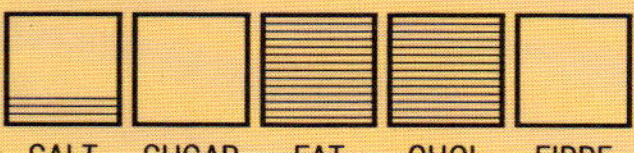

| SALT | SUGAR | FAT | CHOL | FIBRE |

GLUTEN-FREE   WHOLEFOOD
TOTAL CALORIES: ABOUT 5045

The high **fat** and **cholesterol** levels are of course due to the amount of pork fat needed. A lot of this drains out anyway through the sieve; to ensure as much as possible is lost, reheat the mixture very gently to melt any fat that may have cooled and solidified and let this drip through. The purpose of adding the fat back to the rillettes is to preserve them. Nowadays, with refrigeration, this is not necessary, so simply cover them when chilling. The fat and cholesterol will now be moderately, rather than astronomically, high.

Pressure cooker: ☑

Food processor: ☑ if you wish, but remember that rillettes should not have too smooth a texture.

Freezing: ☑ up to 1 month.

RILLETTES OF PORK

In France, most country towns have their own versions of rillettes – a coarse-textured terrine of pork and pork fat. It makes a pleasant change from smooth pâtés and is inexpensive to make.

PREPARATION TIME: *30 min*
COOKING TIME: *4 hours*
INGREDIENTS *(for 6):*
2 lb (900 g) belly pork
¾ lb (350 g) pork fat
Salt★ and black pepper
1 clove garlic
1 bay leaf
1 sprig parsley
1 sprig thyme or rosemary

Order the belly pork boned and with the rind taken off. Wipe the meat with a damp cloth and cut it into narrow strips. Dice the pork fat finely and season the meat and fat with salt, freshly ground pepper and the peeled crushed garlic. Pack the meat and fat into a casserole or terrine. Push the herbs down into the centre of the meat and pour about ¼ pint (150 ml) of water over it. Cover the casserole with a lid or foil.

Bake for 4 hours in the centre of the oven pre-heated to 275°F (140°C, mark 1). Stir the contents of the casserole occasionally to prevent a crusty top forming. When the meat is tender, turn the contents of the casserole into a sieve placed over a mixing bowl; leave until the fat has dripped through the sieve and into the bowl. Remove the herbs and shred the meat with two forks or put it in a liquidiser for a few moments to make a coarse purée. Adjust seasoning if necessary.

Pack the meat into one large earthenware pot, or several small ones. Pour enough liquid fat over the jar to cover the meat by ¼ in (½ cm). Leave in a refrigerator until the fat on the surface has set solid.

Serve the terrine with crusty French bread for a first course and with a watercress salad for a cold snack.

BARBECUED SPARERIBS

This is a substantial first course, prepared in the Chinese style – in this case, baked in a sauce. The racks of pork spareribs should be cut into 12 individual ribs for easy eating with the fingers.

PREPARATION TIME: *15 min*
COOKING TIME: *45 min*
INGREDIENTS *(for 4)*:
12 single pork spareribs
4 tablespoons clear honey
3 tablespoons soya sauce
3 tablespoons tomato ketchup
Tabasco sauce
1 small clove garlic
Dry mustard
Paprika
Salt★ and black pepper
Juice of 1 small orange
4 tablespoons wine vinegar

Grill the ribs for 10–15 minutes under a pre-heated grill until they are brown, turning them several times. Arrange them in a single layer in a large roasting pan and pour in the pan juices.

Put the honey, soya sauce, tomato ketchup and a few drops of Tabasco sauce into a bowl; peel the garlic; crush it with the side of a knife and add it to the bowl. Season to taste with the dry mustard, paprika, salt and freshly ground pepper, then add the orange juice and wine vinegar. Mix, then pour over the spareribs.

Cook, uncovered, in the centre of a pre-heated oven at 350°F (180°C, mark 4) for 30 minutes. Serve the ribs piping hot in the sauce. Provide a finger bowl for each guest.

SWEET AND SOUR PORK

Served the Chinese way, with three or four other dishes, this would be enough for six or eight people. On its own, with rice, it will serve four.

PREPARATION TIME: *5–6 min*
COOKING TIME: *8 min*
INGREDIENTS *(for 4)*:
2 lb (900 g) lean pork (boned)
2 level tablespoons cornflour
8 tablespoons vegetable oil
2½ tablespoons soya sauce
1 green pepper
SAUCE:
1 level tablespoon cornflour
2 level tablespoons caster sugar
2 tablespoons white wine vinegar
2 tablespoons fresh orange juice
1½ tablespoons soya sauce
1½ level tablespoons tomato purée
1½ tablespoons pale sherry

Mix all the sauce ingredients, with 6 tablespoons of water, in a bowl. Blend until smooth. Cut the pork into ½–¾ in (1–2 cm) cubes and toss them in cornflour.

Heat 6 tablespoons of oil in a frying pan, and fry the pork cubes over high heat for 4–5 minutes, turning them often until nearly brown. Pour off all the oil, add the soya sauce and mix with the pork, over low heat, for 1 minute.

Heat the remaining oil in a separate pan, and add the green pepper, cut into strips, 1 in (2½ cm) long by ½ in (1 cm) wide. Stir-fry in the oil for 1½ minutes, over moderate heat. Reduce the heat, stir the sauce and pour it over the pepper. Stir continuously until the sauce thickens and becomes translucent.

Add the pork cubes and turn them in the sauce for 1 minute. Serve with plain boiled rice.

SPARERIBS IN MARSALA

To many people, spareribs of pork are synonymous with Chinese cooking. This recipe, however, imparts a different flavour to spareribs.

PREPARATION TIME: *40 min*
COOKING TIME: *45 min*
INGREDIENTS *(for 6)*:
6 sparerib chops of pork
3 tablespoons olive oil
2 cloves garlic
2 heaped tablespoons parsley
1 level teaspoon ground fennel
Salt★ and black pepper
¼ pint (150 ml) fresh orange juice
¼ pint (150 ml) chicken stock
3 tablespoons Marsala wine
GARNISH:
Orange and watercress

Ask the butcher to cut the meat into single rib portions. Trim away as much fat from the ribs as possible, and heat the oil in a heavy-based pan. Peel and crush the cloves of garlic and rub over the ribs; chop the parsley finely and mix with the fennel; rub into the ribs. Put the ribs in the pan, pepper each well, and cook on both sides until pale brown. Pour over the orange juice and stock, add the Marsala, and correct seasoning.

Cook the spareribs on the middle shelf of an oven pre-heated to 350°F (180°C, mark 4) for 45 minutes.

Lift out the ribs and arrange them on a bed of noodles or rice. Skim the fat off the juices and pour these over the meat. Garnish with slices of orange and small bunches of watercress. Broccoli spears or cauliflower au gratin could also be served.

BARBECUED SPARERIBS

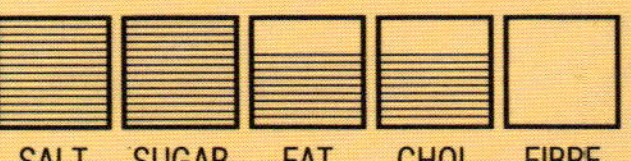

GLUTEN-FREE★   WHOLEFOOD★
TOTAL CALORIES: ABOUT 2270

Soya sauce and tomato ketchup are both very high in **salt**. To reduce the level to low, use only 2 teaspoons of each, or replace the ketchup with tomato purée (tinned without added salt). The high level of added **sugar** comes partly from the honey and partly from the ketchup, with its typical 23% sugar level. Using tomato purée instead will eliminate the added sugar, and the honey can be reduced to about 1 tablespoon. If you omit the ketchup, you may like to add a little extra lemon juice and vinegar to the flavouring. (Calories lost: up to 200.)
For low **fat** and **cholesterol** levels, choose very lean ribs and trim off visible fat. (Calories lost: up to 900.)
This dish is **gluten-free** and **wholefood** if there is no wheat or additives in the soya sauce or ketchup; check the labels.

SWEET AND SOUR PORK

GLUTEN-FREE★   WHOLEFOOD★
TOTAL CALORIES: ABOUT 3770

To reduce the **salt** level to low, omit the soya sauce and use salt-free tomato purée.
As the amount of **sugar** added in this recipe is generous, adding only 2 teaspoons will give enough sweetness for most tastes and reduces the sugar level to medium. (Calories lost: up to 50.)

To reduce **fat** to low choose very lean pork and sauté it in a non-stick pan merely brushed with oil, tossing constantly. (Calories lost: up to 500.) This is **gluten-free** and **wholefood** on the assumption that the soya sauce contains no wheat or additives. Tamari is a Japanese soya product and should contain no wheat.

Freezing: ☑ up to 1 month.

SPARERIBS IN MARSALA

SALT	SUGAR	FAT	CHOL	FIBRE

GLUTEN-FREE   WHOLEFOOD
TOTAL CALORIES: ABOUT 3615

For low **fat** and **cholesterol**, choose lean pork chops and trim the fat carefully; omit the olive oil and brown the meat in a heavy or non-stick pan, heating it gently to allow its own fat to run. (Calories lost: up to 400.)

PORK WITH PISTACHIO NUTS

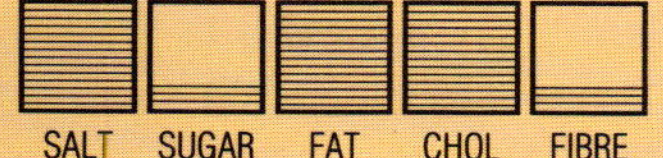

SALT	SUGAR	FAT	CHOL	FIBRE

GLUTEN-FREE
TOTAL CALORIES: ABOUT 5510

There is no way to reduce the high **salt** level which is inherent in the method of curing. The **fat** and **cholesterol** levels are not very malleable either. About all you can do is avoid eating the fat and jelly, which would give a medium fat and cholesterol intake.

PORK WITH PISTACHIO NUTS

A loin of pork is particularly suitable as a main dish for a cold buffet. Leave it to season for two or three days in saltpetre, which gives a pink glow to cold pork. If saltpetre is unobtainable, green uncooked bacon rashers placed down the middle of the joint can be used to impart a similar flavour and colour.

PREPARATION TIME: *20 min*
COOKING TIME: *2½ hours*
INGREDIENTS *(for 8–10):*
4–5 lb (1·8–2·3 kg) loin of pork
¼ teaspoon saltpetre
1 rounded tablespoon salt
1 level tablespoon brown sugar
1 oz (25 g) pistachio nuts
Black pepper
¼ pint (150 ml) dry white wine

Buy the pork two or three days before it is wanted and ask the butcher to bone and skin the joint, and to include the bones and the skin with the order. Mix together the saltpetre, salt and brown sugar; rub it into the pork, particularly on the boned side. Place the pork, boned side down, in a deep dish and leave in a refrigerator for two days.

Before cooking, pat the meat dry with a clean cloth. Make small incisions with a sharp knife in the fat and press in the shelled pistachio nuts. Sprinkle the meat with plenty of freshly ground black pepper; roll it neatly and tie securely with string.

For the cooking, use a deep, ovenproof pot into which the meat fits snugly with the bones and skin tucked round the sides. Pour the wine and ¾ pint (425 ml) of water over it. Add a little more water if the meat does not fit tightly into the dish. Cook, uncovered, in an oven pre-heated to 350°F (180°C, mark 4) for 30 minutes until the fat has coloured. Then cover with a double layer of foil; reduce the temperature to 300°F (160°C, mark 2) and continue cooking in the oven for a further 2 hours.

When the pork is cooked, remove the bones and skin and leave the meat to cool in the juice, which will set to a jelly. Remove the jelly when set and chop it up finely. Scrape the fat from the top of the meat and put into a serving jar. Carve the cold pork into ¼ in (½ cm) thick slices and arrange them on a dish garnished with the chopped jelly.

Serve with wholemeal bread and the jar of pork fat. The pistachio nuts give the pork a distinctive flavour and an attractive appearance – green and purple against the pink and white of the pork. A green salad, tossed in a French dressing (page 85), would go well with the cold pork.

SPARERIBS OF PORK IN CIDER

With the onset of cool autumn weather, casseroles give a warm and welcoming glow to the evening meal. Lean spareribs or shoulder chops of pork are ideal for this easily prepared dish; veal chops may also be cooked in the same way.

PREPARATION TIME: *30 min*
COOKING TIME: *45 min*
INGREDIENTS *(for 6)*:
6 sparerib chops
½ lb (225 g) mushrooms
1 large onion
3 oz (75 g) butter
1 level teaspoon dried savory
Salt and black pepper*
¼–⅓ pint (150–200 ml) dry cider
*4–6 oz (100–175 g) Cheddar
   cheese*
*6 tablespoons toasted
   breadcrumbs*
GARNISH:
Parsley sprigs

Wipe and trim the mushrooms, set six or seven caps aside and slice the remainder thinly. Peel the onion and chop it finely. Grease a shallow ovenproof dish with a little of the butter and arrange the sliced mushrooms over the base. Scatter the onion and savory over the mushrooms, and season with salt and pepper.

Trim most of the fat off the chops and lay them on top of the vegetables. Pour over enough cider to come just level with the meat, and push the mushroom caps, dark side uppermost, between the chops.

Grate the cheese and mix it with the breadcrumbs. Spread this mixture evenly over the chops and the mushroom caps, and dot with the remaining butter. Bake in the centre of a preheated oven at 400°F (200°C, mark 6) for 45 minutes, or until the chops are tender and the topping crisp and brown.

Serve the spareribs straight from the dish and garnish each mushroom cap with a small sprig of parsley. Runner beans and jacket potatoes dressed with soured cream and chopped chives go well with this dish.

ROAST LOIN OF PORK

The Scandinavians celebrate Christmas joyously. From December 13th, St. Lucia's Day, until well into the New Year, the tables are laden with traditional Christmas fare, including this popular loin of pork which has a crisp crackling.

PREPARATION TIME: *15 min*
COOKING TIME: *3¼ hours*
INGREDIENTS *(for 8)*:
6 lb (2·7 kg) loin of pork
2 oz (50 g) dripping or butter
Coarse salt
6 cloves
12 small bay leaves

Have the loin deeply scored into ½ in (1 cm) wide strips. For a really crisp crackling place the joint, skin side down, in a roasting pan and pour in boiling water to a depth of 1 in (2½ cm). Set the pan just below centre of an oven preheated to 450°F (230°C, mark 8). Cook for 15 minutes. Remove the pan, pour off the liquid and set aside for basting.

Grease the pan with dripping and rub the skin of the loin with salt. Insert the cloves and bay leaves in the score marks. Roast the pork, skin side up, at 350°F (180°C, mark 4), at 30 minutes to the pound (450 g). Baste every 30 minutes.

Serve the loin of pork garnished with roasted half apples filled with red currant jelly. Traditionally, the Christmas joint is served with roast potatoes and long-cooked red cabbage.

HOCK WITH CIDER AND RAISINS

Bacon, cooked with dried peas or beans, is one of the oldest known English dishes, dating back to the 14th century. The following is a 20th-century version of the medieval recipe.

PREPARATION TIME: *20 min*
COOKING TIME: *2½ hours*
INGREDIENTS *(for 6)*:
*2–2½ lb (about 1 kg) hock or
   shoulder of gammon*
*½ lb (225 g) split peas, lentils or
   chick peas*
1 small onion
2 tablespoons chopped celery
1½ oz (40 g) butter
1½ oz (40 g) plain flour
½ pint (300 ml) dry cider
2 oz (50 g) stoneless raisins
¼ pint (150 ml) gammon stock
2 teaspoons Demerara sugar
2 tablespoons chopped parsley

Wash the hock and place it in a large bowl, together with the peas or lentils. Cover with cold water and leave to soak for 8 hours or overnight. Drain the meat and peas, put them in a large heavy-based pan and cover with fresh cold water. Bring to the boil, then lower the heat and cover the pan with a lid. Simmer for 1½ hours or until the hock is tender.

Lift the meat from the pan and set it aside to cool slightly. Leave

SPARERIBS OF PORK IN CIDER

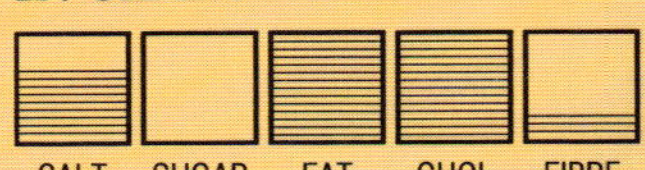

GLUTEN-FREE*   WHOLEFOOD*
TOTAL CALORIES: ABOUT 4820

The added **salt** comes mainly from the cheese and breadcrumbs. Either use bread made without salt, or replace the crumbs with rolled oats or rolled millet flakes; if you also halve the amount of cheese the salt count will be low. Reducing the cheese also lowers both the **fat** and **cholesterol** levels. However, the fat level depends on how lean the chops are. If they are really lean and well trimmed of fat, and if you grease the dish with only a brush of oil and do not dot the casserole with butter, the fat level will be low. (Calories lost: up to 1000.) The cholesterol will be medium to high, depending on the size of each serving.
Vegetables served with it can be dressed with smetana or thick low-fat yogurt in place of soured cream.

Freezing: ☑ up to 2 months.

ROAST LOIN OF PORK

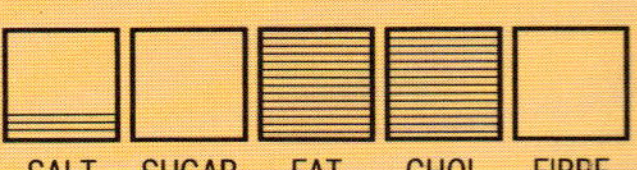

GLUTEN-FREE   WHOLEFOOD
TOTAL CALORIES: ABOUT 6760

The dripping or butter can be omitted and the joint roasted on a rack; however this dish will remain high in both **fat** and **cholesterol** unless you are prepared to sacrifice the crackling. This involves taking a bit of trouble, but you can remove the skin alone from the joint, trim off all the fat layer underneath, then lay the skin back over the top and fasten it on with skewers, scoring it as in the recipe. Do not baste while cooking. This should reduce fat and cholesterol to medium. (Calories lost: up to 520.)

HOCK WITH CIDER AND RAISINS

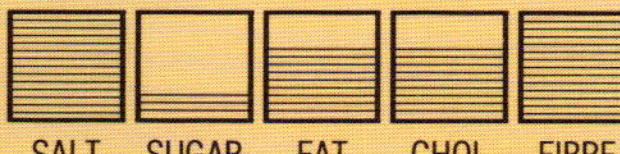

GLUTEN-FREE *
TOTAL CALORIES: ABOUT 4700

The high **salt** level is inherent in the bacon, which is cured with a high salt mixture. Soaking, as described in the recipe, will remove some salt, but the level will remain high. The **fat** content of gammon can be very low if you choose a lean joint and remove all visible fat. For low levels in the dish itself, omit the sauce-making stage of the recipe and add the celery, onion and cider to the empty pan. Cook them together gently to make a thin sauce, without adding the gammon stock which will be extremely salty. You can then thicken the sauce, either by stirring in some smetana, or fromage blanc just before serving, or by liquidising the sauce with enough of the pulses to make a smooth, thick texture (or you can combine the two methods). The **cholesterol** will also be low. (Calories lost: up to 500.) This method is **gluten-free**. No bacon dishes are **wholefood** because of the nitrates used in curing. However this recipe, and the ones that follow, could be adapted to other meats if you choose something less salty.

the peas to cook for a further 30–40 minutes or until quite tender. Skin the hock carefully while still warm, and cut the meat into 1 in (2½ cm) cubes, discarding the fat.

Peel and finely chop the onion, and prepare the celery. Melt the butter in a heavy-based pan over moderate heat, and fry the onion and celery for a few minutes until soft. Remove the pan from the heat and stir in the flour until it has absorbed all the butter. Gradually stir in the cider to make a smooth sauce. Return the pan to the heat and bring the sauce to simmering point, stirring continuously. Mix in the raisins, and add enough gammon stock to make a creamy sauce. Blend in the sugar and continue cooking and stirring over low heat for a further 10 minutes.

Add the cubed hock to the cider sauce, heating it through thoroughly and stirring occasionally. Drain the peas or lentils thoroughly and toss them in a little butter and parsley. Spoon the meat and sauce into the centre of a warmed serving dish and surround with a border of the peas or lentils.

GAMMON STEAKS IN MADEIRA SAUCE

English or sweet-cured gammon is ideal for this easily made appetising dish. Danish gammon can also be used, but it should first be soaked for 1 hour in cold water to reduce the salt content.

PREPARATION TIME: *20 min*
COOKING TIME: *20–25 min*
INGREDIENTS (*for 4*):
4 gammon steaks, each ½–¾ in (1–2 cm) thick
4–6 oz (100–175 g) mushrooms
1 large onion
4 large tomatoes
2 oz (50 g) butter or lard
¼ level teaspoon dried basil
¼ level teaspoon dried marjoram
2 fluid oz (50 ml) Madeira or sweet sherry
4 fluid oz (100 ml) ham stock or bouillon
Salt and black pepper*
1 teaspoon caster sugar
Lemon juice

Cut the rind off the steaks and snip the fat (page 90). Wipe the mushrooms, remove the stalks and chop them roughly, leaving the caps whole. Peel and thinly slice the onion; skin the tomatoes and chop them roughly.

Heat the butter or lard in a heavy-based pan over moderate heat until it stops bubbling. Fry the gammon steaks until golden on both sides, after about 8 minutes, turning once only. Remove the gammon from the pan and keep hot in the oven.

Fry the onion, mushroom caps and stalks lightly in the pan juices until softened; add the tomatoes, the basil and marjoram. Cover the pan with a lid or kitchen foil and simmer for about 5 minutes, shaking the pan occasionally.

Return the gammon steaks to the pan and add the Madeira or sherry, with enough stock to almost cover the meat. Season to taste with salt, freshly ground pepper, sugar and lemon juice. Cover the pan again and continue cooking over low heat for 10 minutes or until the gammon is tender.

Arrange the steaks on a hot serving dish with the sauce poured over them. Baby sprouts, tossed in butter, and creamed potatoes or fluffy boiled rice, to mop up the sauce, would be suitable with the gammon.

BAKED FOREHOCK OF BACON

Forehock is one of the most economical bacon joints, ideal for a family meal and providing plenty of left-over meat to serve cold or in sandwiches. The joint here is served with peaches; for a dinner party, middle cut of gammon could replace the bacon.

PREPARATION TIME: *20 min*
COOKING TIME: *2–2¼ hours*
INGREDIENTS (*for 8*):
4 lb (1·8 kg) boned, rolled forehock of bacon
8 peppercorns
3 cloves
Bouquet garni (page 99)
2–3 oz (50–75 g) Demerara sugar
¼ pint (150 ml) medium dry cider or unsweetened apple juice
4 peaches
3 oz (75 g) unsalted butter
1½ oz (40 g) honey or dark brown sugar
Cinnamon

Soak the bacon in cold water overnight. The next day, put the joint in a large pan with enough cold water to cover it completely. Add the peppercorns, cloves and bouquet garni. Bring to the boil over moderate heat, remove any scum from the surface, and cover the pan with a lid. Reduce the heat, and simmer the bacon for 1¼ hours.

Lift the meat from the pan, leave it to cool and set, then remove all the string. Cut away the rind with a sharp knife, score the fat in a diamond pattern, at ½ in (1 cm) intervals, and press the Demerara sugar firmly all over the fat. Put the joint in a roasting tin, heat the cider or apple juice and pour it over the meat, basting it without disturbing the sugar.

Skin the peaches (the skins will slip off easily if the peaches are covered with boiling water and left for 1 minute), cut them in half and remove the stones, and enlarge the cavities slightly with a pointed teaspoon. Blend the butter, honey (or sugar) and a pinch of cinnamon until creamy. Spoon this mixture into the peach halves.

Bake the joint in the centre of a pre-heated oven, set at 350°F (180°C, mark 4), for ½ hour, basting frequently with the juice. Place the peaches round the joint and raise the temperature to 400°F (200°C, mark 6) and bake for a further 15 minutes, or until the top of the joint is golden and shiny.

Serve the joint whole or sliced, garnished with the peaches. Plain boiled potatoes and a tossed green salad, or carrots, would make good vegetable dishes for the bacon.

GAMMON IN PUFF PASTRY

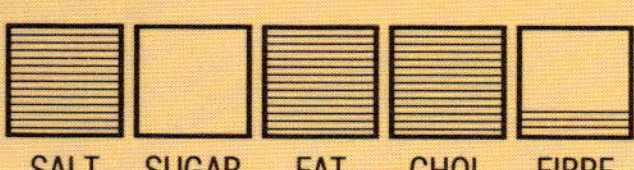

SALT SUGAR FAT CHOL FIBRE

TOTAL CALORIES: ABOUT 7150

As with the previous recipes, the **salt** level of gammon is inherently high.

The **fat** and **cholesterol** content is mainly in the puff pastry. Minimise the fat in the meat by choosing a lean joint and trimming the skin and fat thoroughly. If you like, although it is fiddly, remove first the skin and then the fat; then replace the skin before cooking, keeping it in place with skewers. For low fat and cholesterol, replace the puff pastry with yeast pastry or phyllo pastry; use egg white only for sealing and glazing the pastry. This last step reduces the cholesterol but has little effect on the overall fat. To keep the fat level low, if you are using phyllo pastry do not brush each layer with oil as is generally done. (Calories lost: up to 1000.)

GAMMON IN PUFF PASTRY

An inexpensive joint of bacon looks impressive and serves more people when encased in puff pastry which keeps the meat moist. It makes a good lunch or supper dish, but preparations should begin the day before.

PREPARATION TIME: *30 min*
COOKING TIME: *2¾ hours*
INGREDIENTS *(for 6)*:
4 lb (1·8 kg) gammon hock
1 large bay leaf
12 peppercorns
1 blade mace
4–6 parsley stalks
2 sprigs thyme
1 small onion
1 lb (450 g) prepared puff pastry
1 egg

Ask the butcher to bone part of the hock, leaving the end bone in to make carving easier.

Soak the gammon for 2 hours in cold water. Drain it and put it in a large saucepan. Cover with fresh cold water and add the bay leaf, peppercorns, mace, parsley stalks, thyme and onion. Bring to the boil, turn down the heat, then cover the pan with a lid and simmer for 20 minutes to each 1 lb (450 g). Remove the pan from the heat and let the gammon cool overnight in the cooking liquid.

Remove the gammon from the liquid and carefully pull off the skin. Roll out the puff pastry to an oblong shape, ⅛ in (¼ cm) thick, and put the gammon in the centre. Brush the pastry edges with some of the lightly beaten egg; wrap the pastry over the gammon, and press the edges together to enclose the meat. Seal the edges, pleating the pastry round the bone. Brush with egg.

Cover the bone with a piece of foil to keep it white while cooking. Use the pastry trimmings to decorate the casing, and carefully lift the gammon on to a wet baking tray; brush the pastry with the remaining egg.

Bake the gammon for 20 minutes in the centre of an oven preheated to 450°F (230°C, mark 8); lower the heat to 350°F (180°C, mark 4) and continue cooking for a further 30 minutes. Cover the joint with buttered greaseproof paper as soon as the pastry is golden.

Serve the joint hot or cold. A savoury rice salad, new potatoes and lettuce with green peas are appropriate side dishes for the gammon.

GRATIN OF HAM

The Morvan district of Burgundy is famous for its cured hams. These are often served with a cream sauce, as in the following recipe. York ham is more readily available in Britain and makes a delicious substitute.

PREPARATION TIME: *15 min*
COOKING TIME: *45 min*
INGREDIENTS *(for 6)*:
12 slices quality cooked ham, about 1½ lb (700 g)
¼ lb (100 g) button mushrooms
1 oz (25 g) butter
1 onion
3 shallots
4 fluid oz (100 ml) dry white wine
8–10 oz (225–275 g) tinned tomatoes
½ pint (300 ml) double cream
Salt★ and black pepper
1 oz (25 g) grated Parmesan cheese

Arrange the slices of ham, overlapping each other, in a large, shallow flameproof dish.

Trim the mushrooms and slice them thinly. Melt the butter in a small frying pan and cook the mushrooms for about 8 minutes over low heat. Spoon them, with the butter, over the ham. Peel and finely chop the onion and shallots and put them in a small pan with the wine. Bring to the boil and continue boiling over high heat until the wine has reduced to about 1½ tablespoons.

Chop the tomatoes roughly and add to the onions. Cover the pan with a lid and simmer over low heat for 10 minutes. Rub the onion and tomato mixture through a fine sieve, and put the resulting purée in a clean pan.

Blend the cream into the purée and bring this sauce to the boil. Season to taste with salt and freshly ground pepper. Pour the sauce over the ham and mushrooms and sprinkle the cheese on top. Bake the ham gratin near the top of the oven, pre-heated to 450°F (230°C, mark 8) for 10 minutes or until brown on top.

Serve the gratin while still bubbling, with boiled and buttered rice and a green salad.

PORK AND SPINACH PÂTÉ

This light, colourful pâté can be served hot or cold.

PREPARATION TIME: *20 min*
COOKING TIME: *1 hour 20 min*
INGREDIENTS *(for 8–10)*:
2 lb (900 g) spinach
2 lb (900 g) minced shoulder of pork
1 tablespoon salt★
1 teaspoon freshly ground black pepper
1 bay leaf
¼ teaspoon ground cloves
¼ teaspoon mace

Wash the spinach well. Bring 1 pint (570 ml) of water to a boil in a large pot. Add the spinach, return to a boil, and cook only until the spinach has wilted, about 5 minutes. Drain and chop the spinach coarsely. Squeeze a small amount of spinach at a time in your hands to extract as much water as possible. Add the minced pork and all seasonings and stir until well blended.

Put this mixture into a 2½–3 pint (1½–1¾ litres) terrine or bread pan, cover with a piece of buttered paper, and bake at 375°F (190°C, mark 5) for 1¼ hours. Do not overcook, or it will become dry. Slice and serve hot or cold.

GAMMON WITH APRICOT STUFFING

Baked stuffed hams and gammons are often credited to American cookery, but this recipe originated in the Cotswolds centuries ago. The American glazed crust is a great improvement on the English flour and water crust.

PREPARATION TIME: *15–20 min*
COOKING TIME: *2¼ hours*
INGREDIENTS *(for 10–12)*:
6 lb (2·7 kg) piece of gammon (boned)
⅓ pint (200 ml) red wine
2 bay leaves
½ lb (225 g) apricots
½ level teaspoon arrowroot (optional)
Cloves
2–3 heaped tablespoons Demerara sugar

Ask the butcher to bone and roll the gammon, leaving plenty of room for the stuffing. Put the meat in a large basin, add the wine and bay leaves and leave to marinate for at least 6 hours; turn the meat frequently.

Wash and dry the apricots, cut them in half and remove the stones. Lift the meat from the marinade, and put the wine and bay leaves in a saucepan. Add the apricots and bring to the boil over low heat. Simmer for about 10 minutes or until the apricots are soft and the wine has been absorbed. Remove the bay leaves, and let the apricots cool slightly.

Pat the gammon thoroughly dry. Stuff as much of the apricot purée as possible into the gammon joint (any surplus can be made into a purée boiled up with extra wine and thickened with a

GRATIN OF HAM

GLUTEN-FREE
TOTAL CALORIES: ABOUT 5350

The high **salt** level, as in the previous recipes, is inherent in the ham.
The **fat** and **cholesterol** levels can be reduced to low by the following steps: choose lean ham and trim away the visible fat; cook the mushrooms in a pan lightly brushed with oil, omitting the butter; replace the cream with the same amount of low-fat thick yogurt, quark, fromage blanc or smetana, making sure that the dish does not then boil again but only heats through; halve the amount of added Parmesan cheese (this will also reduce the salt a little). (Calories lost: up to 1000.)

Microwave: ✓

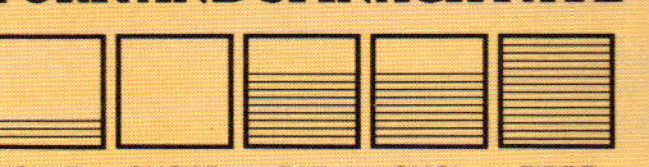

PORK AND SPINACH PÂTÉ

GLUTEN-FREE   WHOLEFOOD
TOTAL CALORIES: ABOUT 3000

The **fat** is given as medium, but in fact the level depends very much on the meat chosen. Ground meat often has a surprisingly high fat level, especially as pork is so pale that pale fat fails to show up clearly. For a low level, buy lean pork as a whole piece, checking that it has no visible fat, and mince it yourself. The **cholesterol** level cannot be reduced below medium.
To retain more vitamins and minerals in the spinach, cook it,

briefly, tightly covered, in just the water that clings to the leaves after it has been washed.

Food processor: 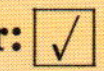 ✓

GAMMON WITH APRICOT STUFFING

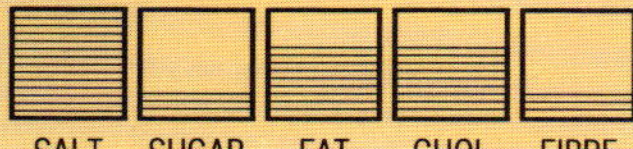

SALT SUGAR FAT CHOL FIBRE

GLUTEN-FREE
TOTAL CALORIES: ABOUT 8950

As with the gammon recipes on the previous pages, the **salt** level is inherently high and cannot be reduced except by eating smaller helpings.
The **fat** and **cholesterol** levels can be reduced to low if you choose lean gammon and remove both skin and fat before wrapping it in foil to cook; this method stops the meat from drying out. It also loses the crisp crust many people like, but if the cloves are inserted and the surface glazed as in the recipe, the flavour will be good. (Calories lost: up to 500.)

little arrowroot to make a sauce). Wrap the stuffed joint tightly in a double layer of foil, and make a slit in the centre of the foil for the steam to escape. Place on a baking tray and cook the gammon in the centre of the oven pre-heated to 350°F (180°C, mark 4) for 2 hours.

Remove the gammon from the oven, unwrap the foil and let the joint cool slightly. With a sharp knife, slit the skin lengthways and remove it entirely, leaving a layer of fat no more than ⅛ in (¼ cm) thick over the meat. Make shallow diagonal cuts, ¾ in (2 cm) apart, through the fat to form a pattern of diamond shapes, and insert a whole clove at each intersection. Pat the Demerara sugar firmly over the gammon and transfer it to a roasting tin.

Bake the joint in the oven, pre-heated to 425°F (220°C, mark 7), for about 15 minutes or until the sugar has melted and set to a golden brown glaze.

Serve the gammon hot or cold, cut into thin slices. Creamed spinach and buttered potatoes would be suitable for a hot joint, and salads for the cold meat.

CROWN OF PORK

This is an impressive and colourful main course for a large dinner party. The crown, which should be ordered in advance, is cut from a loin of pork and cannot be constructed from less than 12 cutlets. The crown should have the fat carefully trimmed off by the butcher, as it cannot crisp when filled with a stuffing.

PREPARATION TIME: *35 min*
COOKING TIME: *2½ hours*
INGREDIENTS *(for 10–12):*

1 crown of pork (12 cutlets)
Lard
1 bouillon cube
STUFFING:
1 large onion
3 oz (75 g) celery
6 oz (175 g) carrots
6 tinned pineapple rings
2 tablespoons corn oil
3 oz (75 g) cooked rice
3 tablespoons chopped fresh
 parsley
1 level teaspoon dried savory
1–2 level teaspoons paprika
3 oz (75 g) sultanas
Salt and black pepper*
Lemon juice
GARNISH:
6 tinned pineapple rings
Watercress

Prepare the stuffing first. Peel and finely chop the onion, celery and carrots. Finely chop six pineapple rings and set the juice aside.

Heat the oil in a pan over moderate heat and fry the onion and celery until just turning colour. Add the rice, carrots and parsley, together with the savory, paprika, pineapple and sultanas. Mix all the ingredients thoroughly and heat through. Season to taste with salt, freshly ground pepper and lemon juice. Set the stuffing aside to cool.

Stand the crown of pork in a greased roasting tin and cover the meat thoroughly with melted lard. Spoon the stuffing into the centre of the crown and cover it with a piece of foil. Wrap foil round each cutlet bone to prevent it charring. Roast the crown in the centre of a pre-heated oven, at 375°F (190°C, mark 5) for 2¼ hours or until amber-coloured juice runs out when a skewer is inserted in the meat. Lift out the crown and keep it warm on a serving dish in the oven.

Fry the pineapple rings for garnishing in the hot fat in the roasting tin for about 4 minutes or until golden brown on both sides. Slit through one side of each ring and arrange in a curling twist round the crown of pork.

Pour the fat carefully from the roasting tin and add the pineapple juice to the residue in the pan. Crumble the bouillon cube into the juices and bring the gravy to boiling point. Cook over high heat until the gravy is brown and has reduced slightly. Pour into a warm sauce boat.

Remove the foil from the tips of the cutlets and replace with paper frills. Garnish with small sprigs of watercress between the pineapple twists. Serve the crown with roast or sauté potatoes and with green beans.

PORK WITH LEMON

In Portugal, where this recipe comes from, pork is generally of inferior quality to the dairy-fed pigs in Britain. The Portuguese housewife cooks lean pork fillet in a spicy wine sauce.

PREPARATION TIME: *20 min*
COOKING TIME: *25–30 min*
INGREDIENTS *(for 4–6):*
2 lb (900 g) pork fillet
1 oz (25 g) lard
½ pint (300 ml) dry white wine
4 level teaspoons ground cumin
2 cloves garlic
Salt and black pepper*
6 slices lemon
2 level teaspoons ground coriander

Trim away any excess fat and the thin outer skin from the pork fillet, cut the meat into 1 in (2½ cm) cubes and pat dry on absorbent kitchen paper. Heat the lard in a large sauté pan and brown the meat, turning it continuously to prevent it sticking to the pan. Stir in just over half of the wine and add the cumin. Peel the garlic and crush it over the meat; season to taste with salt and freshly ground pepper. Bring the mixture to the boil, lower the heat and simmer for about 25 minutes or until tender. Add the remaining wine, cut the lemon slices into quarters and add them to the pan. Continue cooking, stirring until the sauce thickens slightly. Stir in the coriander.

Spoon the meat and the sauce on to a dish. Plain boiled rice is traditional with the pork.

CROWN OF PORK

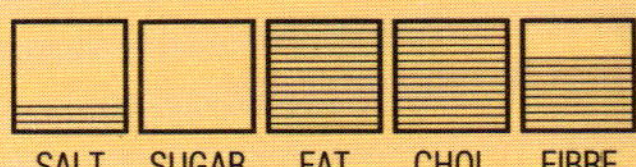

GLUTEN-FREE   WHOLEFOOD
TOTAL CALORIES: ABOUT 7590

It is assumed that the pineapple chosen has been tinned in juice alone with no added **sugar**. To reduce **fat** and **cholesterol** levels to low, choose the leanest meat possible, do not brush with lard, and cook the vegetables for the stuffing either in a non-stick pan, or in a few tablespoons of stock, omitting the oil. This last step affects the fat level only, not the cholesterol. (Calories lost: up to 800.)

Food processor: ☑ for the stuffing.

PORK WITH LEMON

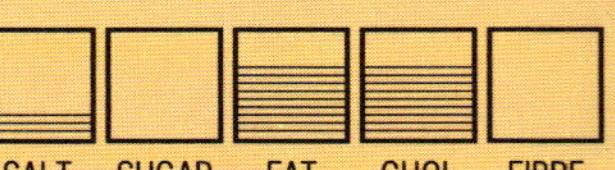

GLUTEN-FREE   WHOLEFOOD
TOTAL CALORIES: ABOUT 1730

The levels of **fat** and **cholesterol**, given here as moderate on average, can in fact be low if you choose very lean pork and trim off all visible fat. Brown the meat in a non-stick or heavy pan, brushed lightly with oil; omit the lard. (Calories lost: up to 260.)

Freezing: ☑ up to 2 months.
Microwave: ☑

PORK TENDERLOIN WITH MUSHROOMS

| SALT | SUGAR | FAT | CHOL | FIBRE |

GLUTEN-FREE   WHOLEFOOD
TOTAL CALORIES: ABOUT 2415

For low **fat** and **cholesterol**, check that the tenderloin, usually a lean cut, is in fact particularly so. Omit the oil from the marinade (for low fat only – it will not affect the cholesterol); soften the onion in a pan lightly brushed with oil, omitting the butter; when adding the pork, add also a few tablespoons of unsalted stock to moisten it instead of the butter; and replace the cream with quark, fromage blanc, thick low-fat yogurt or cultured buttermilk. Do not let the sauce boil after adding these. (Calories lost: up to 1270.)

Freezing: ✓ up to 2 months.

PORK TENDERLOIN WITH MUSHROOMS

The lean fillet or tenderloin of pork usually needs marinating or stuffing to give the meat extra flavour. It can be cooked whole, or cut into thick slices for a quick main course.

PREPARATION TIME: *30 min*
COOKING TIME: *15 min*
INGREDIENTS (*for 6*):
1½ lb (700 g) pork tenderloin
2 tablespoons oil
1 tablespoon lemon juice
Black pepper
1 small clove garlic (optional)
SAUCE:
6 oz (175 g) button mushrooms
1 onion
2 oz (50 g) unsalted butter
2 tablespoons dry sherry
¼ pint (150 ml) double cream

Trim away the thin skin, or sinew, and fat from the pork. Cut the meat crossways into 2 in (5 cm) thick slices. Lay the slices between two sheets of wet grease-proof paper and beat them flat with a rolling pin. Arrange the slices in a shallow dish. Measure the oil and lemon juice into a basin and season with black pepper. Skin and crush the garlic, and mix it into the oil and lemon juice. Spoon this marinade over the pork and leave for about 30 minutes.

Meanwhile, trim and thinly slice the mushrooms. Peel the onion and chop it finely. Melt the butter in a frying pan and gently fry the onion for 5 minutes until it is soft, but not brown. Add the mushrooms and fry for a few minutes. Lift the vegetables from the pan and keep them hot. Drain the pork pieces from the marinade and fry gently in the hot butter for 3–4 minutes, turning once. Transfer the pork to a hot serving dish and keep it warm.

Measure the sherry into the frying pan and heat briskly, stirring until it has reduced to 1 tablespoon. Return the onion and mushrooms to the pan and season with salt and freshly ground pepper. Stir in the cream. Heat gently, stirring until the sauce is almost boiling. Remove from the heat and pour the sauce over the pork. Serve surrounded by boiled or fried rice.

PORK NOISETTES WITH PRUNES

This is a speciality from Tours in the Loire district, where some of the finest French pork and wine are produced. It is an easily prepared dish, but the prunes – large Californian ones – should be soaked overnight.

PREPARATION TIME: *15 min*
COOKING TIME: *1 hour*
INGREDIENTS *(for 6)*:
6 slices pork fillet, each 1 in (2½ cm) thick, or 6 boned loin chops
1 lb (450 g) large prunes
½ bottle dry white wine
Seasoned flour (page 100)
2 oz (50 g) unsalted butter
1 heaped tablespoon red currant jelly
¾ pint (425 ml) double cream
Salt and black pepper*
Lemon juice

Leave the prunes in a bowl to soak in the wine overnight. Put the prunes and the wine in a pan and simmer, covered, for 20–30 minutes or until tender.

Trim any excess fat off the fillets or chops. Coat them with seasoned flour, shaking off any surplus. Melt the butter in a heavy-based pan and brown the meat lightly over gentle heat, turning it once only. Cover the pan with a lid and simmer the pork for 30 minutes.

When the meat is nearly done, pour the prune liquid into the pan. Increase the heat and boil rapidly for a few minutes until the liquid has reduced slightly. Lift the meat on to a warm serving dish and arrange the prunes round it. Keep the meat and prunes warm in the oven while making the sauce.

Stir the red currant jelly into the juices in the pan, and boil this sauce over high heat until it has the consistency of syrup. Gradually blend in the cream, stirring continuously until the sauce is smooth and thick. Season with salt, pepper and lemon juice.

Pour the sauce over the meat and serve at once. Traditionally, the noisettes are served with boiled potatoes only.

PORK COOKED IN MILK

The Italians frequently pot-roast meat and chicken in milk. For this recipe, choose boned leg of pork or, more economically, blade or the fore-end of a hand. It can be served hot or cold.

PREPARATION TIME: *10 min*
COOKING TIME: *2 hours*
INGREDIENTS *(for 6)*:
2½ lb (1 kg) boned rolled pork
Salt and black pepper*
1 clove garlic
12 coriander seeds
2 onions
2 slices cooked ham
1 tablespoon olive oil
1½ pints (900 ml) milk

Ask the butcher to bone the meat and to take the skin and part of the fat off the pork before rolling it. Wipe the meat with a clean damp cloth and rub it all over with salt and freshly ground pepper. Peel the garlic and cut it lengthways into small strips. Make small incisions in the meat with the point of a knife and push in the garlic strips and coriander seeds.

Peel and finely chop the onions; dice the ham. Heat the oil in a heavy-based pan or flame-proof dish into which the meat will fit closely. Fry the onions and ham in the oil for a few minutes until they begin to colour. Put in the meat and brown it lightly all over. In a separate pan, bring the milk to boiling point, then pour it over the pork so that it reaches ½ in (1 cm) over the meat.

Cook the pork, uncovered, over low heat (set the pan on an asbestos sheet), for about 1 hour. The milk should be kept barely at simmering point during cooking and will form a cobwebby skin which gradually turns pale golden brown. After 1 hour break the milk skin and turn the meat over, scraping all the skin from the sides into the bottom of the pan.

Continue cooking the meat slowly for a further 45 minutes, or until the milk has reduced to a cupful of thick sauce.

Lift the meat on to a serving dish and pour the sauce with the bits of onion and ham over it.

Serve the pork hot or cold, with boiled potatoes and a crisp green side salad.

PORK NOISETTES WITH PRUNES

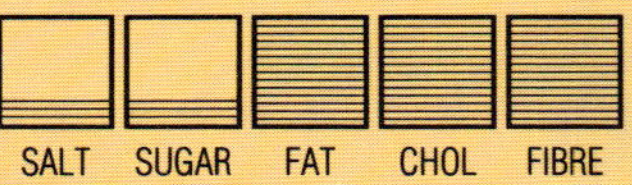

GLUTEN-FREE*   WHOLEFOOD*
TOTAL CALORIES: ABOUT 6570

Assuming that the pork fillet is quite lean, to reduce **fat** and **cholesterol** to low depends on browning the chops in a non-stick pan brushed lightly with oil instead of butter, and replacing the cream with the same amount of thick low-fat plain yogurt, cultured buttermilk or low-fat curd cheese. Take care the mixture does not boil after adding any of these or it will curdle: just warm through gently, stirring. If you want a thicker consistency, allow the sauce to cool a little so that any fat can be skimmed off, then add 1 tablespoon arrowroot which has been mixed to a smooth paste with a little water and continue with the recipe. (Calories lost: up to 1680.)

Freezing: ✓ up to 2 months.
Microwave: ✓

PORK COOKED IN MILK

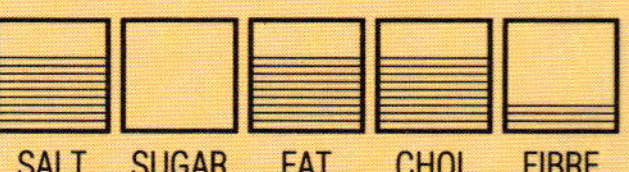

GLUTEN-FREE   WHOLEFOOD
TOTAL CALORIES: ABOUT 4265

No one ingredient in this recipe is high in **salt** (apart from the ham, but the amount per person is small), but the contributions made by the pork, ham and milk add up to a moderate level. Serving smaller portions, say 4–5 oz (100–150 g) of meat, combined with halving the amount of ham, will reduce this level to low.

It is not easy to find lean pork, but if you can, it will be low in fat. If you trim off all visible fat, use only 2 teaspoons of oil for preparing the filling and substitute skim milk, the total **fat** and **cholesterol** content will be low. However, skim milk tends to burn easily when boiled, and great care must be taken to ensure that it simmers very gently indeed, heating it slowly and stirring constantly while heating. The heavy pan and asbestos sheet specified will be of help. (Calories lost: up to 300.)

Slow cooker: ☑

ROAST PORK WITH APPLE AND NUT STUFFING

SALT	SUGAR	FAT	CHOL	FIBRE

GLUTEN-FREE *   WHOLEFOOD *
TOTAL CALORIES: ABOUT 6000

For very low **salt**, use bread made without salt for the crumbs.

For low **fat** and **cholesterol** levels, choose a lean piece of pork and trim it thoroughly of visible fat. Halve the amount of nuts (you could substitute lightly roasted hazel nuts, which have less fat); colour the onions in a pan brushed lightly with oil, omitting the butter; and do not brush the meat with oil (this last step does not affect the cholesterol level). As there will be no rind and fat to moisten the meat, cover the roasting dish in foil during the cooking. (Calories lost: up to 400.)

ROAST PORK WITH APPLE AND NUT STUFFING

Blade or shoulder of pork is a good joint for roasting, as the meat is tender and has plenty of rind for crisp crackling. When boned and stuffed it is easily carved even by the unskilled.

PREPARATION TIME: *20 min*
COOKING TIME: *2 hours*
INGREDIENTS (*for 6*):
3½ lb (1½ kg) blade of pork, boned
1 small onion
2 oz (50 g) cashew nuts or peanuts
2 oz (50 g) crustless bread
1 cooking apple
1 stick celery
2 teaspoons chopped parsley
1 oz (25 g) butter
Salt★ and black pepper
½ teaspoon dried summer savory
Lemon juice
2–3 tablespoons vegetable oil
¼ pint (150 ml) dry cider

Peel and finely chop the onion and roughly chop the nuts. Dice the bread; peel, core and dice the apple. Wash and finely chop the celery and parsley.

Melt the butter in a small pan over moderate heat and fry the onion and nuts until they are just turning colour. Add the bread, apple, celery, and parsley to the onion and nuts and continue cooking until the apple has softened. Season to taste with salt, pepper, summer savory and lemon juice.

Make sure that the rind of the joint is deeply scored (page 90). Open up the pocket and spread the stuffing evenly. Roll up the joint and tie securely with string at regular intervals.

Place the joint in an oiled roasting tin; brush the rind with oil and sprinkle generously with salt. Roast above the centre of an oven pre-heated to 400°F (200°C, mark 6) for 20–30 minutes, until the crackling is crisp and golden. Move the tin to a shelf just below the centre and reduce the temperature to 350°F (180°C, mark 4). Cook for a further 1½ hours or until the juice comes out amber-coloured when a skewer is pushed into the meat.

Put the joint on a serving plate and keep it warm. Leave the residue in the roasting tin to settle, then carefully skim or pour off the fat. Add the cider to the pan juices and bring to the boil over moderate heat, scraping in all the residue. When the gravy has coloured, season to taste and pour it into a warm sauce boat.

Roast potatoes and buttered cabbage or runner beans are ideal with this tasty joint.

Pork

PORK CHOPS WITH APPLE

Tart cooking apples are traditionally served with pork to counteract the fattiness of the meat. They appear as stuffings and sauces with roasts, and can also, as here, be used with oven-cooked chops.

PREPARATION TIME: *15 min*
COOKING TIME: *1 hour 10 min*
INGREDIENTS *(for 4)*:
4 thick pork chops
1–2 oz (25–50 g) unsalted butter
Salt★ and black pepper
3–4 large cooking apples
Juice of a lemon

Trim any excess fat from the chops, wipe them dry with a damp cloth, and put them in a buttered ovenproof dish. Season to taste with salt and freshly ground pepper. Peel, core and thinly slice the apples and arrange over the chops to cover them completely. Melt the remaining butter and brush some of it over the apple slices. Sprinkle with lemon juice and cover the dish closely with a lid or foil.

Cook the chops in the centre of a pre-heated oven, at 325°F (170°C, mark 3) for 1 hour. Remove the foil, brush the apples with the remaining butter and cook for a further 10 minutes, or until the apples are lightly browned but not dry, and the chops are tender.

Serve the chops from the cooking dish or on a warmed serving plate. Small new potatoes and braised chicory go well with the sharp apple taste.

FLAMED PORK FILLET WITH APRICOTS

This quick and easy dish is suitable for cooking in a chafing dish at the table, once all the ingredients have been prepared. Prunes may be used instead of apricots; they should be soaked in water for 3–4 hours.

PREPARATION TIME: *25 min*
COOKING TIME: *15 min*
INGREDIENTS *(for 4)*:
1¼ lb (550 g) pork fillet
Seasoned flour (page 100)
2 tablespoons dry sherry
4 oz (100 g) dried apricots
1 oz (25 g) unsalted butter
2 tablespoons brandy
2½ fluid oz (75 ml) soured cream
Salt★ and black pepper
Lemon juice

Put the apricots and the water in which they were soaking into a saucepan, add the sherry and cook over low heat for 15 minutes. Trim any fat off the pork fillet and remove the outer skin. Cut it into 1½ in (4 cm) thick slices or round medallions and toss them in the seasoned flour.

Heat the butter in a frying pan or chafing dish over medium heat and fry the pork on both sides until golden and tender, turning once only. Pour off any surplus fat. Heat the brandy, set it alight and pour it over the pork. Add the strained apricots and stir until the brandy flames have burnt out.

Mix the soured cream with the apricot liquid and pour it into the pan. Simmer for a few minutes, then season to taste with salt, freshly ground pepper and lemon juice. Serve with fluffy boiled rice.

PORK CHOPS WITH ALMONDS AND SHERRY

When a special main course is required at short notice, this dish may provide the solution. Choose large, thick pork chops, preferably with the kidneys still attached.

PREPARATION TIME: *10 min*
COOKING TIME: *20 min*
INGREDIENTS *(for 4)*:
4 pork chops
1 clove garlic
1 level teaspoon crushed dill seeds
1 tablespoon olive oil
1½ oz (40 g) unsalted butter
4 oz (100 g) flaked almonds
4 fluid oz (100 ml) dry sherry

Trim any excess fat off the chops, leaving ¼ in (½ cm) round the edge. Peel and crush the garlic and rub this and the dill seeds into both sides of each chop. Brush the chops all over with oil and put them under a hot grill, for 8 minutes to each side. Brush the chops again with oil when they are turned.

Meanwhile, melt the butter in a small pan and cook the almonds over low heat until they are straw-coloured. Pour in the sherry, boil until bubbling, and then reduce the heat to simmering point and continue cooking until the almonds turn a caramel colour.

Arrange the chops on a serving dish, with the sherry sauce and almonds poured over them. Creamed potatoes and Brussels sprouts with soured cream would be suitable vegetables.

PORK CHOPS WITH APPLE

GLUTEN-FREE   WHOLEFOOD
TOTAL CALORIES: ABOUT 2930

To restrict **fat** and **cholesterol** levels to low, grease the ovenproof dish by brushing it lightly with oil and omit the butter here and for brushing the apples. Make sure the pork is carefully trimmed of fat and the portions are not too large. You may still find that the juices at the bottom of the dish look fatty. If possible, skim them off, using a fat-separating gravy boat or a fat-skimming brush, before serving. (Calories lost: up to 400.)

Microwave: ✓ but may need final browning under grill.

FLAMED PORK FILLET WITH APRICOTS

GLUTEN-FREE★   WHOLEFOOD★
TOTAL CALORIES: ABOUT 2500

For low **fat** and **cholesterol** levels, choose very lean pork, trimming off any visible fat; brown the pork in a heavy or non-stick pan brushed lightly with oil, omitting the butter; and replace the soured cream with smetana or cultured buttermilk. Smetana has between a quarter and half as much fat as soured cream; buttermilk only a quarter. (Calories lost: up to 300.)

PORK CHOPS WITH ALMONDS AND SHERRY

| SALT | SUGAR | FAT | CHOL | FIBRE |

GLUTEN-FREE WHOLEFOOD
TOTAL CALORIES: ABOUT 3340

For low **fat** and **cholesterol** levels choose lean pork; trim off all visible fat; grill the chops without brushing with oil (this step affects the fat level only); and colour the almonds in only 1 teaspoon of oil in a heavy pan, omitting the butter. As almonds are roughly half oil (though do not contain cholesterol), the amount can be reduced to half or even a quarter, reducing the amount of sherry to match, so that the sauce remains the same but in less quantity. (Calories lost: up to 240.)

TENDERLOIN OF PORK

| SALT | SUGAR | FAT | CHOL | FIBRE |

GLUTEN-FREE* WHOLEFOOD*
TOTAL CALORIES: ABOUT 4175

For low **fat** and **cholesterol** levels, choose a very lean fillet and brown the stuffed meat in a heavy or non-stick pan brushed lightly with oil, omitting the butter; omit the melted butter added to the stuffing. For even lower levels, use only white of egg to bind the stuffing, or leave out the egg altogether and substitute a small eating apple, peeled and grated. If you are concerned that the meat may be dry, add a little stock to the cooking pan. (Calories lost: up to 1000.)

Food processor: ✓ for the stuffing.

TENDERLOIN OF PORK

The fillet – or tenderloin – of pork is a lean, economical cut of meat. A tenderloin weighs about 12–16 oz (350–450 g) and should be stuffed, marinated or larded to prevent the meat drying out.

PREPARATION TIME: *30 min*
COOKING TIME: *1½ hours*
INGREDIENTS *(for 6)*:
1½–2 lb (700–900 g) pork tenderloin
2 oz (50 g) unsalted butter
1 clove garlic
STUFFING:
4 oz (100 g) fine breadcrumbs
2 oz (50 g) mixed dried fruits
1 level tablespoon finely chopped parsley
1 heaped tablespoon finely chopped onion
1 clove garlic (optional)
½ level tablespoon chopped tarragon
2 oz (50 g) melted butter
1 orange
1 egg
Salt★ and black pepper
SAUCE:
1 lb (450 g) fresh apricots
1 tablespoon water
1 level tablespoon soft brown sugar
Juice of a lemon
½ level teaspoon curry powder
1 tablespoon Kümmel

Prepare the stuffing first: mix the breadcrumbs, the cut-up fruits, parsley, onion, crushed garlic and tarragon in a bowl. Stir in the melted butter. Add the grated rind of the orange, remove pith and membrane from the flesh, cut this up and mix into the stuffing. Beat the egg lightly and use to bind the mixture. Season with salt and freshly ground pepper.

Trim all the fat off each tenderloin and remove the transparent skin. Slit the meat lengthways through half its thickness, open it out and flatten with the fist or the edge of a cleaver.

Spread the stuffing over the tenderloins, roll them up tightly from the bottom and tie with string. Melt the butter in a flame-proof dish on the stove. Peel and slice the garlic and fry until brown, then remove. Fry the pork for a few minutes in the butter until evenly browned. Cover the pan with the lid and roast for 1 hour 20 minutes or 40 minutes to the lb (450 g) on the centre shelf of an oven pre-heated to 325°F (170°C, mark 3). Remove the lid for the last 10 minutes for the meat to brown.

To make the sauce, halve and stone the apricots, tie up the stones in a piece of cheesecloth and put them with the apricots in a saucepan. Add the water and stew until the apricots are tender, stirring constantly. Mix in the sugar, lemon juice and curry powder and cook for 5 minutes or until thick. Remove the stones; beat the apricots to a paste or liquidise in a blender before stirring in the Kümmel.

Before serving, remove the string and carve the meat into slices. Arrange on a serving dish and spoon over a little of the sauce. Offer the remaining sauce separately with, for example, sauté potatoes and broccoli.

KIDNEYS IN CREOLE SAUCE

Creole sauce, the classic sauce of the West Indies, is composed mainly of sweet peppers, tomatoes and fiery Tabasco sauce – which is hotter than sweet chili sauce. It is often served as a garnish with noodles or rice.

PREPARATION TIME: *15 min*
COOKING TIME: *15–20 min*
INGREDIENTS *(for 4–6)*:
1¼ lb (550 g) calf or pig kidneys
1 small onion
14 or 16 oz (400 or 450 g) tinned tomatoes
1 clove garlic
1 small green pepper
2 teaspoons capers
2 oz (50 g) unsalted butter or 2 tablespoons olive oil
1 level teaspoon soft brown sugar
1 level tablespoon tomato chutney
Salt★
Tabasco or chili sauce
Lemon juice
6–8 black olives

Skin the kidneys and cut them into thin slices. Snip out the white cores with scissors. Peel and thinly slice the onion. Peel the garlic. Wash the pepper, remove the stalk and the seeds and chop the flesh. Chop the capers.

Heat the butter, or oil, in a heavy-based pan and cook the onion over moderate heat until soft and transparent. Turn up the heat, add the sliced kidneys and fry them for 3–4 minutes or until browned, stirring frequently.

Crush the garlic into the pan and add the chopped tomatoes with their juices, the pepper and capers. Stir in the sugar and tomato chutney, and season to taste with salt, Tabasco or chili sauce and lemon juice.

Cover the pan with a lid or foil and simmer over low heat for 10–15 minutes. Meanwhile, halve and stone the olives and add them to the kidneys.

Spoon the kidneys and the sauce over ribbon noodles tossed in butter. A crisp green salad could be served as a side dish.

BRAISED OXTAIL

Oxtail is an inexpensive, nourishing but fatty meat. This stew is best cooked the day before so that the fat can settle and be lifted from the top before the stew is re-heated.

PREPARATION TIME: *40min*
COOKING TIME: *4¾ hours*
INGREDIENTS *(for 6)*:
2 oxtails
Seasoned flour (page 100)
1½ oz (40 g) beef dripping
2 onions
1 bottle red wine or 1½ pints (900 ml) beef stock
Bouquet garni (page 99)
Salt★ and black pepper
2 bay leaves
1 level tablespoon red currant jelly
Peel of half lemon and half orange
¾ lb (350 g) carrots
2 small turnips
1 tablespoon lemon juice
1 level tablespoon tomato paste
6 oz (175 g) mushrooms
GARNISH:
3 level tablespoons chopped parsley
2 level teaspoons grated lemon rind

Chop the oxtails into 2 in (5 cm) lengths and coat lightly with the seasoned flour. Peel and slice the onions.

Melt the dripping in a large sauté pan and fry the oxtails in the hot fat for 5 minutes until they glisten, then transfer to a large fireproof cooking pot. Fry the onions in the residue of the fat, and as soon as they begin to take colour add them to the oxtail. Pour the wine or beef stock over the oxtail and onions, put the pot over the heat and bring the wine to the boil. Add the bouquet garni, salt, pepper, bay leaves, jelly and peel, and simmer on top of the stove for 2 hours. Strain off the liquid into a wide bowl and leave to cool.

Peel and slice the carrots and turnips and add to the oxtail. Spoon as much fat as possible from the cooled liquid (if it is thoroughly cold, the fat will have settled in a layer on top and can easily be lifted off). Pour the liquid over the oxtail. Add the lemon juice and tomato paste, bring to the boil and immediately place on the lowest shelf of the oven, heated to 275°F (140°C, mark 1); cook for 2½ hours. Add the trimmed and sliced mushrooms to the dish for the last 10 minutes.

Serve sprinkled with parsley mixed with the lemon peel; rice with leeks would also be suitable.

KIDNEYS IN CREOLE SAUCE

GLUTEN-FREE★   WHOLEFOOD★
TOTAL CALORIES: ABOUT 1470

To reduce the **salt** level use fewer kidneys and olives, and add more onions. For a low-salt dish, replace the olives with grapes. Check the tomatoes are canned without added salt. The kidneys, although fairly low in **fat**, are quite high in **cholesterol**. However, the remaining cholesterol from the butter can be avoided by cooking the kidneys in oil; this gives an overall moderate level of cholesterol. The fat content can be reduced to low at the same time by using only 1 tablespoon of oil. (Calories lost: up to 300.)
Use **gluten-free** chutney.

Freezing: ☑ up to 2 months.
Microwave: ☑

BRAISED OXTAIL

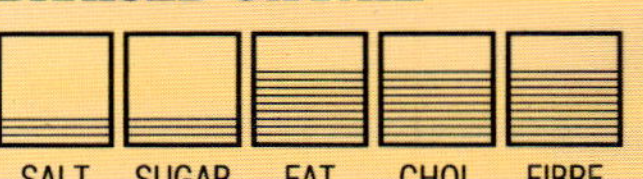

GLUTEN-FREE★   WHOLEFOOD★
TOTAL CALORIES: ABOUT 2500

For a low **fat** and **cholesterol** level trim the meat carefully, and let the dish chill so that fat settling on the top can be removed; brown the oxtails in a heavy pan brushed lightly with oil. (Calories lost: up to 350.)

Pressure cooker: ☑
Slow cooker: ☑
Freezing: ☑ up to 2 months.

ROGNONS TURBIGO

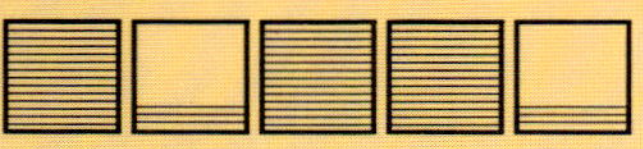

GLUTEN-FREE*
TOTAL CALORIES: ABOUT 1950

The raised **salt** level comes from the sausages and kidneys; using only 1 sausage will reduce it to medium.

To reduce the amount of **fat**, again use only 1 sausage (or omit the sausages completely and treble the amount of onion), as it is the sausages, with a typical fat level of at least 25%, which make this dish high in both fat and cholesterol.

The **cholesterol** level of this dish can be reduced by cooking the kidneys in 1 tablespoon of oil, omitting the butter, but will remain high, as organ meats have a much greater amount than other meats. However, this recipe does not use a large amount of kidney. Without the butter, with fewer sausages and if the sauce is made as suggested below, both fat and cholesterol will be medium. To make the sauce, substitute cornflour for the plain flour, slake with water to make a smooth paste, and work in the liquid when cold. Then heat gently together, stirring steadily, until boiling. Simmer for a few minutes before stirring in the tomato purée and sherry. (Calories lost: up to 850.)

Gluten-free sausages can often be produced on request by small butchers, and a cornflour sauce will be gluten-free. The dish is not really **wholefood**, as sausages generally contain additives.

Freezing: ✓ up to 2 months.
Microwave: ✓

ROGNONS TURBIGO

This French family meal consists of halved fried kidneys, supplemented with button onions and small sausages.

PREPARATION TIME: *25 min*
COOKING TIME: *20–25 min*
INGREDIENTS *(for 4):*
6 lamb kidneys
4 chipolata sausages
2 oz (50 g) unsalted butter
8 button onions
1 level tablespoon plain flour
½ pint (300 ml) chicken or beef stock
¼ pint (150 ml) dry white wine
1 rounded teaspoon tomato purée
2 tablespoons dry sherry
Salt★ and black pepper
1 bay leaf
GARNISH:
Chopped parsley and bread croûtons (page 96)

Skin the kidneys, cut them in half and snip out the white core with scissors. Separate the sausages and twist each in opposite directions so that they can be snipped in half.

Melt the butter in a large heavy-based pan. Gently fry the kidneys and sausages until brown, then remove from the pan and keep them hot.

Meanwhile, peel the onions, leaving them whole; put them in a saucepan and cover with cold water. Bring to the boil, simmer for 3–5 minutes, then drain.

Stir the flour into the hot fat remaining in the sauté pan, until well blended; cook gently for a few minutes. Gradually add the stock and wine, stirring well until the sauce is smooth. Bring to the boil, stir in the tomato purée and sherry; season to taste with salt

and freshly ground pepper.

Put the kidneys, sausages and onions back into the pan; add the bay leaf, cover tightly with a lid and simmer gently for 20–25 minutes.

Transfer the sausages, kidneys and onions to a hot serving dish. Remove the bay leaf, check seasoning and strain the sauce over the meat. Garnish with crisp bread croûtons and sprinkle with chopped parsley.

Spiced rice or creamed potatoes and broccoli go well with this dish.

LIVER WITH DUBONNET AND ORANGE

Lamb – or the more expensive calf – liver is most suitable for this recipe. The fruity, sweet-wine sauce blends surprisingly well with juicy, slightly undercooked liver.

PREPARATION TIME: *15 min*
COOKING TIME: *10–15 min*
INGREDIENTS (*for 6*):
1 lb (450 g) lamb liver
2 small onions
1 clove garlic
1 tablespoon olive oil
1½ oz (40 g) butter
Seasoned flour (page 100)
SAUCE:
1 tablespoon orange juice
8 tablespoons red Dubonnet
2 rounded tablespoons fresh
  chopped parsley
Rind of an orange, coarsely grated
1 teaspoon finely grated lemon
  rind

Wash the liver, trim off any tough and discoloured parts and dry it thoroughly. Cut the liver into slices, ½ in (1 cm) thick, and coat them with seasoned flour.

Peel and finely chop the onions and garlic. Heat the oil and butter in a large, heavy-based pan over moderate heat and cook the onion and garlic, covered, until soft and beginning to colour.

Add the liver slices to the onions, in a single layer, and cook over low heat. As soon as the blood begins to run, turn the liver over and cook the other side for a slightly shorter time.

When cooked, arrange the liver on a warm serving dish. Cover with the onion, lifted from the pan with a perforated spoon. Keep the dish hot.

To make the sauce, stir the orange juice and Dubonnet into the pan juices. Boil rapidly until the liquid has reduced by half. Take the pan off the heat and stir in most of the chopped parsley, grated orange and lemon rind, reserving a little for garnish.

Pour the sauce over the liver, sprinkle with the parsley and orange and lemon rind. Serve at once, with creamed potatoes and a green vegetable.

FRIED LIVER WITH ONION GRAVY

Liver, whether from lamb, calf or pig, is one of the most nourishing and digestible meats. The flavour is best preserved by steeping the liver in milk before frying.

PREPARATION TIME: *20 min*
COOKING TIME: *25 min*
INGREDIENTS (*for 4*):
1 lb (450 g) lamb liver
Seasoned flour (page 100)
1 lb (450 g) onions
5 oz (150 g) unsalted butter
1 level tablespoon plain flour
¼ pint (150 ml) beef stock
1 teaspoon vinegar
Salt and black pepper*

Cut away any skin and gristle from the liver and cut it into ¼ in (½ cm) slices. Soak the liver slices in milk for 1 hour. Drain the liver well, pat it dry on absorbent kitchen paper, then coat each slice with seasoned flour, making sure both sides are evenly coated.

Prepare the gravy before frying the liver: peel and thinly slice the onions. Melt 2 oz (50 g) of the butter in a large frying pan, add the onions and fry over low heat for about 20 minutes or until soft and golden brown. Turn frequently to prevent the onion sticking to the bottom of the pan.

LIVER WITH DUBONNET AND ORANGE

GLUTEN-FREE*   WHOLEFOOD*
TOTAL CALORIES: ABOUT 1815

Liver is high in **cholesterol** although fairly low in **fat**. For low fat, cook the onion and liver in a heavy-based pan brushed lightly with oil. (Calories lost: up to 350.)

FRIED LIVER WITH ONION GRAVY

GLUTEN-FREE*   WHOLEFOOD*
TOTAL CALORIES: ABOUT 2120

For a low **fat** (but still high **cholesterol**) dish, cook the onions in only 2 teaspoons of fat (butter, oil or vegetable margarine), adding a few tablespoons of the stock to prevent sticking, and cooking tightly covered so that the juices do not evaporate. To make the onions into gravy, thicken with cornflour, made into a smooth paste with a little cold stock or water, then mixed into the remaining stock. Heat gently, stirring, and simmer for 1–2 minutes. Do not add extra butter.
The liver itself can be grilled on a baking sheet lightly brushed with oil, for about 4 minutes each side. (Calories lost: up to 1000.)

DANISH LIVER PÂTÉ

SALT   SUGAR   FAT   CHOL   FIBRE

GLUTEN-FREE*   WHOLEFOOD*
TOTAL CALORIES: ABOUT 3680

To reduce the **salt** and **fat** to low and **cholesterol** to medium, line the pâté dish with a double layer of spinach leaves which have been softened by dipping in simmering water for about 40 seconds, and omit the streaky bacon and anchovies; replace the bacon in the pâté with 8 oz (225 g) chopped mushrooms; use skim milk and make the binding sauce by mixing a little of this with the flour, then working in the warm infused milk, and continuing with the recipe. Omit the butter. (Calories lost: up to 2600.)

Food processor: ☑
Freezing: ☑ up to 2 months.

BRAINS IN BLACK BUTTER

SALT   SUGAR   FAT   CHOL   FIBRE

GLUTEN-FREE   WHOLEFOOD
TOTAL CALORIES: ABOUT 2000

Although brains are high in **cholesterol**, the total fat content of the dish can be kept low if the brains are served with a non-buttery sauce. This can be a Chinese-style sweet-sour sauce, made by mixing 1 tablespoon each of soya sauce, brown sugar, wine vinegar, dry sherry and tomato purée with about 2 teaspoons cornflour worked to a paste with water. Heat gently until it thickens. (Calories lost: up to 1000.)

A pinch of sugar may help the onions to brown more quickly.

Blend 1 oz (25 g) of butter with the flour and add in knobs to the hot onions. Stir until melted and blended, then gradually stir in the hot stock. Bring the gravy to the boil, simmer for a moment, then stir in the vinegar and season to taste with salt and freshly ground pepper.

Melt the remaining butter in a heavy-based pan, add the liver slices and fry them quickly for about 5 minutes, turning once. Lift them out on to a hot serving dish and pour over the onion gravy. Creamed or boiled potatoes go well with the liver.

DANISH LIVER PÂTÉ

The inexpensive pig liver is not much used for grilling or frying, but is ideal for a pâté. This pâté should be left to cool under a heavy weight before being served. It will keep for up to a week in the refrigerator.

PREPARATION TIME: *35 min*
COOKING TIME: *2 hours*
INGREDIENTS *(for 6–8):*
1 lb (450 g) pig liver
½ pint (300 ml) milk
1 onion
1 bay leaf
6 oz (175 g) fat green back bacon rashers
6 anchovy fillets
Salt★ and black pepper
¼ level teaspoon each of ground nutmeg, cloves and allspice
1 oz (25 g) unsalted butter
1 oz (25 g) plain flour
1 egg
½ lb (225 g) streaky bacon rashers

Measure the milk into a saucepan. Peel the onion and cut in half; add it, with the bay leaf, to the milk and bring to the boil over gentle heat. Remove the saucepan from the heat and allow the milk to infuse for 15 minutes. Strain through a sieve and set the milk aside.

Trim the rind from the fat bacon rashers and remove any skin and gristle from the liver. Mince the bacon, the liver and anchovy fillets twice through the fine plate. Blend the mixture thoroughly and season to taste with salt, freshly ground pepper and the spices.

Melt the butter in a saucepan, add the flour and cook over low heat for 1 minute; gradually stir in the milk, beating continuously. Bring the mixture to the boil and cook for 2–3 minutes. Draw off the heat and blend in the liver mixture. Bind with the lightly beaten egg.

Line a 1 lb (450 g) loaf tin with the streaky bacon rashers, leaving the rashers to hang over the edges. Alternatively, bake the pâté in two smaller loaf tins and store one in the freezer. Spoon the pâté mixture into the tin and fold the bacon rashers over the top.

Cover the tin with a piece of buttered greaseproof paper and place in a large roasting pan holding 1 in (2½ cm) of cold water. Place in the centre of a pre-heated oven and bake for 2 hours at 325°F (170°C, mark 3). The pâté is baked when a stainless steel skewer comes away clean.

Remove the pâté from the heat, cover with freshly buttered greaseproof paper and place a heavy weight on top. Leave the pâté until quite cold, preferably overnight, before turning it out. Serve the pâté, cut into thick slices, with hot toast and butter.

BRAINS IN BLACK BUTTER

Calf brains are traditionally used in this classic French recipe. But they are often difficult to obtain, and lamb brains are also good.

PREPARATION TIME: *30 min*
COOKING TIME: *35 min*
INGREDIENTS *(for 4):*
2 sets lamb or calf brains
1 bay leaf
Salt★ and black pepper
6 oz (175 g) unsalted butter
½ tablespoon caper vinegar
1 tablespoon capers

Soak the brains in a bowl of cold, lightly salted water for at least 30 minutes to remove all blood. Drain the brains, remove any bone fragments and peel off the outer transparent skin. Rinse the brains again in cold water and divide each set into two (if using the larger calf brains, each set should be cut into thick slices).

Put the brains in a saucepan and cover with cold, lightly salted water. Bring to the boil over moderate heat, and carefully remove any scum. Lower the heat, add the bay leaf, and cover the pan with a lid; cook the brains gently for 20 minutes. Drain well and transfer the brains to a warm serving dish. Sprinkle with salt and freshly ground pepper.

Melt the butter in a small pan over moderate heat and let the butter brown without burning it. Stir in the vinegar and capers, and pour this sauce over the brains immediately.

Serve the brains with crusty bread to mop up the butter.

BRAINS IN CURRY SAUCE

Brains, like any other offal, require careful cleaning, and soaking for at least 1 hour. But they are so tasty, nourishing and inexpensive that they are worth a little trouble.

PREPARATION TIME: *15 min*
COOKING TIME: *30–35 min*
INGREDIENTS *(for 4–6):*
2 lb (900 g) calf brains
1 pint (570 ml) milk
1 onion
1 clove garlic
2 oz (50 g) butter
1 heaped tablespoon plain flour
1 rounded teaspoon curry powder
½ pint (300 ml) chicken stock
½–¾ lb (225–350 g) white or black
*   grapes*
¼ pint (150 ml) double cream
*   (optional)*
Salt and black pepper*

Cover the brains with cold water, add 2 level tablespoons of salt and leave to soak for 1 hour. Rinse them thoroughly under cold running water and remove the fine skin that covers the brains. Cut away any fibres and discoloured parts and remove any bone splinters. Put the brains in a pan with enough milk to cover. Bring to the boil and simmer for 10 minutes or until the brains are firm. Drain and set the milk aside. Cut the brains in ½ in (1 cm) thick slices. Arrange them on a dish, cover with foil and keep warm.

Peel and finely chop the onion and garlic. Melt the butter in a saucepan and cook the onion and garlic over gentle heat for 5 minutes. Stir in the flour and curry powder, mixing well. Gradually add the chicken stock and ¼ pint (150 ml) of the milk in which the brains were cooked; blend thoroughly. Simmer this sauce until it has reduced to the consistency of thick cream.

While the sauce is cooking peel the grapes and remove the pips (page 96). Add the grapes to the sauce and simmer for a further 5 minutes. Stir in the cream and season to taste with salt and freshly ground pepper.

Pour the sauce over the brains and serve with plain boiled rice and with triangles of toast.

SWEETBREADS WITH BEURRE NOISETTE

Ideally, this lunch or supper dish should be made with calf sweetbreads. These are often difficult to come by, and lamb sweetbreads make a good and inexpensive alternative. Both types of sweetbreads should be soaked for several hours before cooking.

PREPARATION TIME: *30 min*
COOKING TIME: *40 min*
INGREDIENTS *(for 4–6):*
1¼ lb (550 g) calf or lamb
*   sweetbreads*
4 tablespoons white wine vinegar
1 carrot
1 stick celery
¾ pint (425 ml) chicken or veal
*   stock*
½ bay leaf
1 sprig thyme
6 peppercorns
6 oz (175 g) clarified butter (page
*   95)*
Salt and black pepper*
Seasoned flour (page 100)
1½ oz (40 g) unsalted butter
1 tablespoon olive oil
GARNISH:
Chopped fresh parsley
Lemon wedges

Soak the sweetbreads for at least 3 hours in several changes of cold water to remove all traces of blood. For the last 1½ hours, soak the sweetbreads in fresh cold water with 1 tablespoon of vinegar. Put them in a pan with fresh cold water and bring slowly to the boil. Take the pan off the heat, drain the sweetbreads and cool under running water. Remove the black veins and pull off as much as possible of the thin skin around them, without tearing the sweetbreads. Wrap them in a

BRAINS IN CURRY SAUCE

GLUTEN-FREE*   WHOLEFOOD*
TOTAL CALORIES: ABOUT 3080

For notes on the **fat** and **cholesterol** content of brains, see the preceding recipe.
To give this dish a low overall fat content, use skim milk for cooking; cook the onion in a pan lightly brushed with oil, not in butter; do not add extra fat before stirring in flour and curry powder to make the sauce, but stir over lowest heat; replace the cream, if wished, with the same amount of smetana, quark or thick low-fat yogurt into which you have stirred a teaspoon of cornflour. (Calories lost: up to 1000.) This will be **gluten-free** if cornflour or potato flour is used for the sauce and there is no gluten in the curry powder – check the label.

Microwave: ☑

SWEETBREADS WITH BEURRE NOISETTE

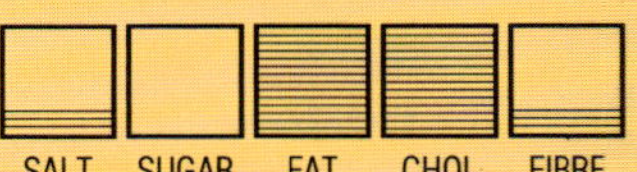

GLUTEN-FREE*   WHOLEFOOD*
TOTAL CALORIES: ABOUT 2780

Like liver and kidneys, sweetbreads are high in **cholesterol**, on a par with eggs, though much lower than brains. The cholesterol content of these cannot be reduced (except by using smaller portions), but although the remaining **fat** content is fairly low, reductions are possible here. If the meat is cooked in oil or vegetable fat rather than butter, the cholesterol level will be medium to high. To reduce the fat content to low, either sauté in a heavy pan brushed lightly with oil or grill on a baking sheet brushed with oil. The butter sauce can be replaced by a Chinese-style sauce (see the notes on Brains in Black Butter on the previous page), or by a purée of boiled beetroot, flavoured with a little lemon juice or vinegar. (Calories lost: up to 1550.)

COEUR CORIANDRE

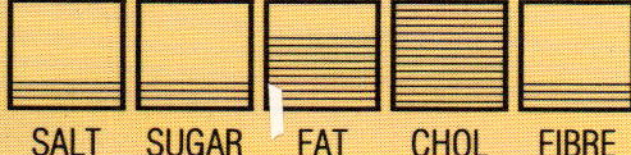

SALT   SUGAR   FAT   CHOL   FIBRE

GLUTEN-FREE *   WHOLEFOOD *
TOTAL CALORIES: ABOUT 1650

Like kidney and liver, heart is higher in **cholesterol** than it is in **fat**; it has less than the two other organ meats, but more than most meats. As this cannot be reduced, avoid the remaining fat in this dish (from the butter) by browning the meat in a non-stick or heavy pan brushed lightly with oil, rather than in butter. After adding the onion, add a few tablespoons of stock and cover tightly to avoid drying out. This gives a low-fat dish, although the cholesterol remains medium to high. (Calories lost: up to 300.)

Pressure cooker: ☑
Slow cooker: ☑
Freezing: ☑ up to 2 months.

clean cloth and let them cool between two weighted plates or wooden boards to flatten them. Meanwhile, scrape, wash and slice the carrot and celery.

Put the sweetbreads in a pan, cover with the stock by about 1 in (2½ cm) and add the carrot, celery, bay leaf, thyme and peppercorns. Put the pan over low heat and bring slowly to simmering point; cook for 10 minutes, uncovered. Remove the sweetbreads, strain the stock through a fine sieve and leave the sweetbreads in the stock until they are cool enough to handle.

Remove the sweetbreads from the stock and dry them on a clean cloth. Heat the remaining vinegar in a small pan and boil until it has reduced by two-thirds. In a separate pan, heat the clarified butter gently and, when light brown, stir in the vinegar. Season to taste with salt and freshly ground pepper.

Cut the sweetbreads into thick slices and coat lightly with seasoned flour. Melt the unsalted butter and oil together over moderate heat and cook the sweetbreads in it for about 3 minutes on each side, or until lightly browned. Remove the sweetbread slices to a heated serving dish and pour the brown butter over them.

Sprinkle with chopped parsley and serve at once garnished with wedges of lemon. They go well with boiled rice and cucumber au gratin.

COEUR CORIANDRE

Hearts are usually stuffed and braised slowly for several hours as they tend to be dry. In this French farmhouse recipe they are marinated in lemon juice before being braised in an apple and cider sauce, with an unusual spicing of coriander.

PREPARATION TIME: *20 min*
COOKING TIME: *1–1½ hours*
INGREDIENTS *(for 4)*:
4 lamb or 2 calf hearts
Juice of a lemon
½ lb (225 g) onions
2 medium cooking apples
2–3 tablespoons plain flour
1½ oz (40 g) butter
Salt * *and black pepper*
2 bay leaves
¼ pint (150 ml) cider
1 level teaspoon crushed coriander seeds
1 level teaspoon caster sugar
2 thin slices unpeeled lemon

Cut the hearts in slices, about ½ in (1 cm) thick, and remove all fat, gristle and blood vessels. Put the slices in a basin with the lemon juice and leave to marinate for 30 minutes. Meanwhile, peel and slice the onions and the cored apples.

Dry the heart slices and coat them with flour, then fry them in the butter in a flameproof casserole over high heat. Add the onion and continue frying until pale golden. Season well with salt and freshly ground pepper. Add the bay leaves and the cider. Cover the heart slices with the apple and sprinkle them with coriander seed and sugar. Lay the lemon slices on top of the apples.

Put the lid on the casserole and cook over low heat on top of the stove or in a pre-heated oven, at 300°F (160°C, mark 2), for about 1 hour or until tender. When cooked, remove the lemon slices and bay leaves and stir the apple slices into the sauce.

Serve the casseroled hearts with creamed potatoes.

Offal

TRIPE PROVENÇALE

Tripe, which is associated with onions and the near-extinct tripe parlours of the Midlands and the North of England, has a long history. The Normans introduced it as a food to Britain; the following recipe comes from southern France.

PREPARATION TIME: *20 min*
COOKING TIME: *2½ hours*
INGREDIENTS *(for 6)*:
2 lb (900 g) thick tripe
1 pint (570 ml) chicken stock
Salt★ and black pepper
1 onion
1 clove garlic
1 oz (25 g) unsalted butter
1 lb (450 g) tomatoes
Dried thyme
4 tablespoons dry white wine
1 level tablespoon chopped parsley

Wash the tripe thoroughly. Put it in a saucepan and cover with cold water. Bring to the boil. Remove from the heat, drain the tripe and rinse under cold running water. Cut into 2 in (5 cm) cubes and return them to the saucepan. Pour over the boiling stock and add a pinch of salt. As soon as the stock is boiling again, reduce the heat. Cover the pan with a lid and simmer the tripe for 2 hours.

Meanwhile, peel and roughly chop the onion, and skin and crush the garlic. Melt the butter in a frying pan and gently fry the onion and garlic for about 5 minutes until transparent. Skin the tomatoes (page 97) and chop them roughly; add them, with a pinch of dried thyme, the wine and parsley, to the frying pan. Bring this mixture to the boil over gentle heat, cover with a lid and simmer for 30 minutes. Season to taste with salt and freshly ground pepper. If the sauce is still thin, remove the lid and boil the sauce over high heat for 5 minutes until it has reduced and thickened.

When the tripe has finished cooking, drain it and stir it into the tomato mixture. Cook over low heat for a further 10 minutes. Arrange the tripe on a hot serving dish and surround it with plain boiled rice.

TRIPE WITH ONIONS

Fresh, ready-to-cook tripe usually needs only about 2 hours' cooking time, but it is best to check with the butcher.

PREPARATION TIME: *10 min*
COOKING TIME: *approx. 2¼ hours*
INGREDIENTS *(for 4)*:
1 lb (450 g) tripe
3 large onions
1 pint (570 ml) milk
1 oz (25 g) butter
1 oz (25 g) plain flour
Salt★ and black pepper
1 rounded tablespoon finely
*   chopped parsley*

Cut the tripe into ¾ in (2 cm) pieces, and peel and roughly chop the onions. Place these ingredients in a heavy-based pan, pour over the milk to cover (if necessary, top up with water). Cover the pan and cook over gentle heat for about 2 hours or until the tripe is tender. Strain through a coarse sieve and set aside about 1 pint (570 ml) of the liquid.

Make a roux (page 82) from the butter and flour and gradually blend in the liquid. Bring to the boil and season to taste with salt and ground pepper. Re-heat the tripe and onions in the sauce, add the parsley and serve.

BRAWN WITH SPICED PRUNES

Brawn is a traditional English dish made from pork trimmings and pig's head. It dates from the 15th century and is always served cold, usually as a first course. However, it also makes an attractive main course for lunch or supper. Preparations should begin at least 2 days in advance.

PREPARATION TIME: *1¾ hours*
COOKING TIME: *4 hours*
INGREDIENTS *(for 8)*:
½ pig's head
8 oz (225 g) rock or sea salt
2 onions
4 shallots
2 carrots
2 turnips
12 whole allspice
Bouquet garni (page 99)
4 cloves
2 blades mace
6 peppercorns
Juice of a lemon
Oil
Salt★ and black pepper
SPICED PRUNES:
1 lb (450 g) prunes
1 pint (570 ml) cold tea
¾ pint (425 ml) white wine
*   vinegar*
½ lb (225 g) brown sugar
1 level teaspoon pickling spice
GARNISH:
Cucumber and tomato slices

Make the spiced prunes first, as they have to steep in pickling liquid for 24 hours. Soak the prunes in the cold tea for 8 hours or overnight. Cook the prunes, with the cold tea, over low heat for 20 minutes or until tender.

Meanwhile, put the vinegar into a separate pan and stir in the sugar. Add the pickling spice,

TRIPE PROVENÇALE

GLUTEN-FREE   WHOLEFOOD
TOTAL CALORIES: ABOUT 1400

Tripe is lower in both **salt** and **fat** than most kinds of meat. If you wish to reduce the **cholesterol** and fat level of this recipe further, substitute vegetable fat or oil for the butter, and use only half as much of it. (Calories lost: up to 100.)

Pressure cooker: ✓
Freezing: ✓ up to 1 month.

TRIPE WITH ONIONS

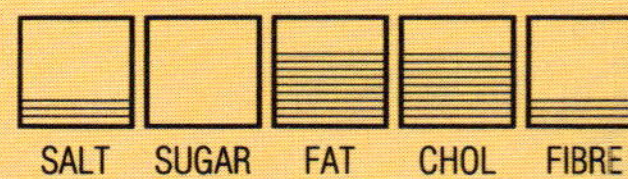

GLUTEN-FREE★   WHOLEFOOD★
TOTAL CALORIES: ABOUT 1280

As tripe is naturally lower in **salt** and in **fat** than most meats, the fat and **cholesterol** content of this dish can both be low if skim milk is used, and the sauce made either with vegetable margarine (lowering cholesterol only), or with half the amount of fat (lowering fat). (Calories lost: up to 300.)

Pressure cooker: ✓
Freezing: ✓ up to 1 month.

BRAWN WITH SPICED PRUNES

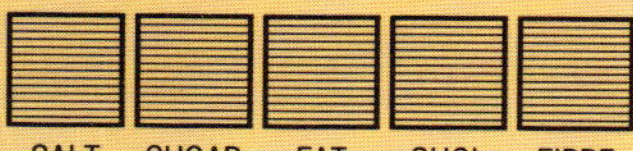

| SALT | SUGAR | FAT | CHOL | FIBRE |

GLUTEN-FREE   WHOLEFOOD
TOTAL CALORIES: ABOUT 4725

The **salt** content is difficult to judge, as it depends how much salt the meat picks up from the brine. If wished, omit this step, giving a low salt level.

The high **sugar** content can simply be reduced (to medium-low) by not adding more than a few tablespoons of sugar to the vinegar. Prunes are quite sweet by themselves.

The dish will be fairly fatty. Even if the fat that solidifies on top of the meat is carefully removed, the **fat** level is still likely to be medium.)

The **cholesterol** level will also be high, because brains are extraordinarily high in this sterol. However, only those on strict low-cholesterol regimes need avoid occasional use of this recipe.

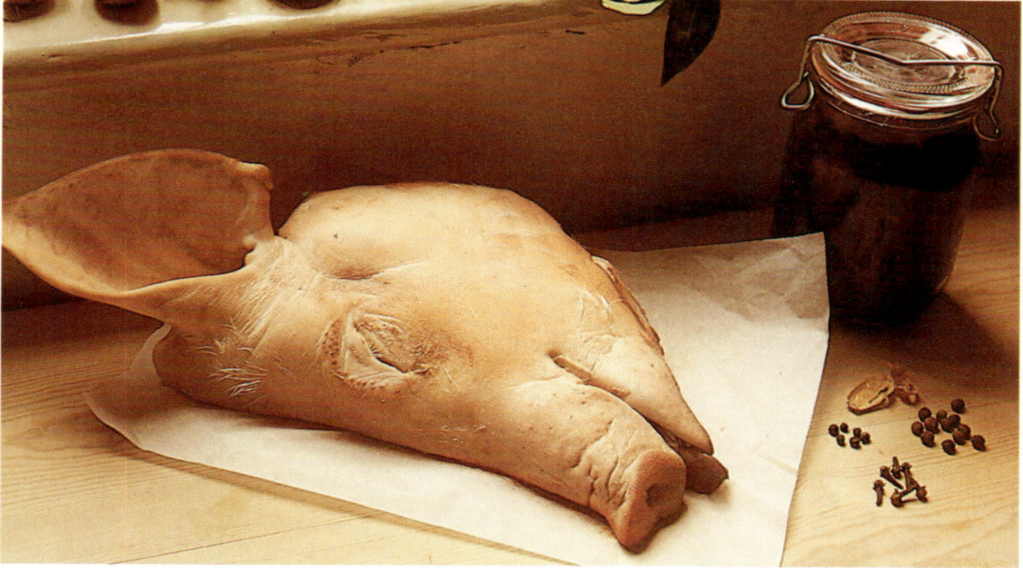

wrapped in muslin. Bring to the boil and simmer briskly for 5 minutes. Remove the pan from the heat and stir in half the cooking liquid from the prunes. Drain the prunes and pack them into a preserving jar, pour over the spiced vinegar and seal immediately. The prunes are ready for use 24 hours later.

Ask the butcher to cut the half pig's head in two and to remove the eye. Scrub the portions under cold running water until thoroughly clean. Leave them to soak for 12 hours in a bowl of cold water to which the salt has been added.

Remove the pig's head, rinse it thoroughly in fresh water and put it in a large saucepan. Cover with fresh cold water. Bring to the boil, and cook the pig's head at near-boiling point for 2 hours or until the flesh leaves the bones easily. Remove the meat from the pan. Strip all the flesh, including the ear, tongue and brain, from the bones – it should yield approximately 2 lb (900 g) of meat. Return the bones to the pan with the cooking liquid and bring back to the boil.

Meanwhile, peel and roughly slice the onions, shallots, carrots and turnips. Add the vegetables to the boiling liquid, together with the allspice, bouquet garni, cloves, mace, peppercorns and lemon juice. Continue boiling this stock, uncovered, for about 1 hour until the liquid has reduced to just over $\frac{1}{2}$ pint (300 ml). Remove from the heat, strain and set the liquid aside until cold.

Skin the tongue and dice that and all the meat finely. Put the meat in a large bowl and work it through the fingers until thoroughly mixed, discarding any pieces of gristle. Remove the solidified fat from the surface of the cold stock, and strain the liquid through two thicknesses of cheesecloth into a clean pan. Season with salt and freshly ground pepper and bring to the boil. Remove the pan from the heat immediately and stir in the chopped meat.

Clean and thinly slice the cucumber and the tomato. Brush a 2 pint (1·2 litre) tin mould with oil and decorate the bottom with thin slices of cucumber and tomato, and a few cut-up prunes. Spoon the brawn carefully into the mould, without disturbing the decorative pattern. Firm the top of the brawn and set it aside for 1 hour.

Cover the brawn with a wooden board, with a heavy weight on top, and chill in the refrigerator for at least 24 hours.

To serve, turn the brawn out of the mould. Arrange the spiced prunes around the brawn, garnished with a few tomato slices for added colour.

Beef

Beef comes from castrated bullocks and young heifers which have never calved. The male produces a better proportion of lean meat to fat, but the heifer carries less bone. The best beef comes from young animals, but even so it must, after slaughtering, be matured or 'hung', at low temperatures, to tenderise the meat with the minimum loss of weight and to improve its keeping qualities. Until a few years ago, a hanging period of 12–14 days at a temperature of 36–40°F (2–4°C) was considered ideal, but with the tendency to slaughter younger animals, the hanging period is now a good deal less.

On properly hung beef, the lean meat should be plum-red in colour and slightly moist. Very bright red meat denotes that the beef has not been hung sufficiently and is therefore not tender. Dark red, lean and sinewy beef indicates cuts from an animal not of prime quality and likely to be tough. Such cuts are suitable for slow cooking, provided they are well flecked with fat, which will give tenderness, heighten flavour and prevent the meat becoming too dry.

Quality beef should have a good outside covering of fat, creamy to pale yellow and of firm texture. The bones should be shiny and pinkish with a blue tinge. There should be little or no gristle; on steaks, for example, a thick and fibrous strip of gristle running between the fat and lean layers indicates an old and tough piece of meat.

Prime quality meat is the most expensive. It is juicy, fine-textured, well marbled (streaked with fat), full of flavour, and very tender. In choice meat, the lean is usually plum red but slightly less marbled than prime lean. The covering of fat is firm, thick, and white or creamy white.

Cheap cuts are as nutritious as expensive ones, the only difference being the time spent on preparing and cooking them. Another point to bear in mind is that price is controlled by supply and demand: because only a given number can be cut from one animal, grilling steaks are always expensive. In summer, stewing and braising beef are not popular, and so are relatively inexpensive. They are ideal for using in dishes that can be stored in the home freezer.

Cuts of beef – and the names by which they are known – vary considerably. Avoid unrecognisable cuts, especially nondescript rolled joints which invariably disintegrate during cooking.

The cuts and joints illustrated here may not always be available from supermarkets which specialise in pre-packed meats, but a good butcher will supply a cut of meat at a few days' notice.

As well as home-grown beef, imported beef is also available. This beef is vacuum-packed and either chilled or blast frozen. The fat on imported beef is nearer white and the meat is pale pink. By law, all butchers must label beef with the country of origin.

Some meat carries a purple inspection mark, indicating that certain standards of hygiene and health have been met. The purple dye is harmless; however, for the sake of appearance it can be cut away.

Blade bone Sold as braising steak and often included with chuck which is similar (in Scotland, the blade and chuck together is known as a shoulder). Many butchers dice blade of beef and mix it with chopped kidney; it is marketed as fillings for pies and puddings. Being fairly lean, blade is also excellent for slow-cooked casseroles and stews.

Brisket on the bone A whole brisket weighs 16–18 lb (7·2–8·2 kg); it is usually cut up into joints, ideally of 4½–5 lb (2–2·3 kg) because of the amount of bone to meat. Choose a joint with a fair proportion of meat to fat and bone. Best pot-roasted or braised, but may also be boiled if ordered salted.

Brisket, rolled Boned and rolled joints are suitable for slow pot-roasting and braising. It is also sold salted, ready for boiling. It is then pressed between weights and served cold, cut into thin slices. Brisket is an excellent economical buy, especially when catering for large numbers. Order at least one week in advance and ask the butcher to trim the joint of excess fat.

Chuck The best type of stewing steak, known in the North of England as a chine. It is best braised, stewed or used for pie and pudding fillings. As it is gristly and coarse, do not attempt to fry or grill.

Clod or sticking Also known as neck. This muscular cut is useful for gravy beef, stewing or casseroles. It is usually fairly inexpensive, but has a high proportion of gristle which must be cut from the meat.

Fillet This lean and boneless piece, which lies below the ribs of the sirloin, is the most expensive. It is usually sliced into steaks of about 6–8 oz (175–225 g) each. Tiny flecks of fat running through the lean are good signs that the steaks will grill well. It is also sold, on order, whole or in large portions for such dishes as boeuf en croûte. As the fillet is lean, it must be larded with thin strips of bacon fat.

Flank An inexpensive, rather fatty joint. It is excellent for pot-roasting, braising or boiling.

Leg This always refers to one of the hind legs, which contain a large proportion of tissue and gristle. Although the meat is lean and has a good flavour it needs long and slow cooking. It is best used for stews, casseroles, puddings and pies, and it is also used for consommé and beef tea.

Rib (fore) One of the larger roasting joints, which can be cooked either on the bone or boned and rolled.

Rib (top and back) Usually known as middle rib, this cut comes from the ribs between fore ribs and the shoulder. The joint is divided into two: top and back ribs which are partially boned and rolled for easier carving. These joints have less bone than fore rib and are good slow-roasted.

Rib (wing or prime) This large joint, from between the fore ribs and sirloin, is one of the most expensive cuts. It is an excellent joint for roasting, ranging from 4 lb (1·8 kg) to 12 lb (5·4 kg). It should have a good eye muscle of meat and a good outer layer of firm and creamy yellow fat.

Rump, top A large joint from the hind leg, also known as thick flank. It is usually cut into two joints and tied with fat. It may be slow-roasted at low temperature, but is better pot-roasted. It can also be sliced for braising or cut into cubes and used for casseroles and stews.

Shin This comes from the foreleg and is usually fairly gristly. It is normally sold for stews, casseroles, puddings or pies and, because of its high gelatine content, for brawns. It is relatively inexpensive, but also wasteful.

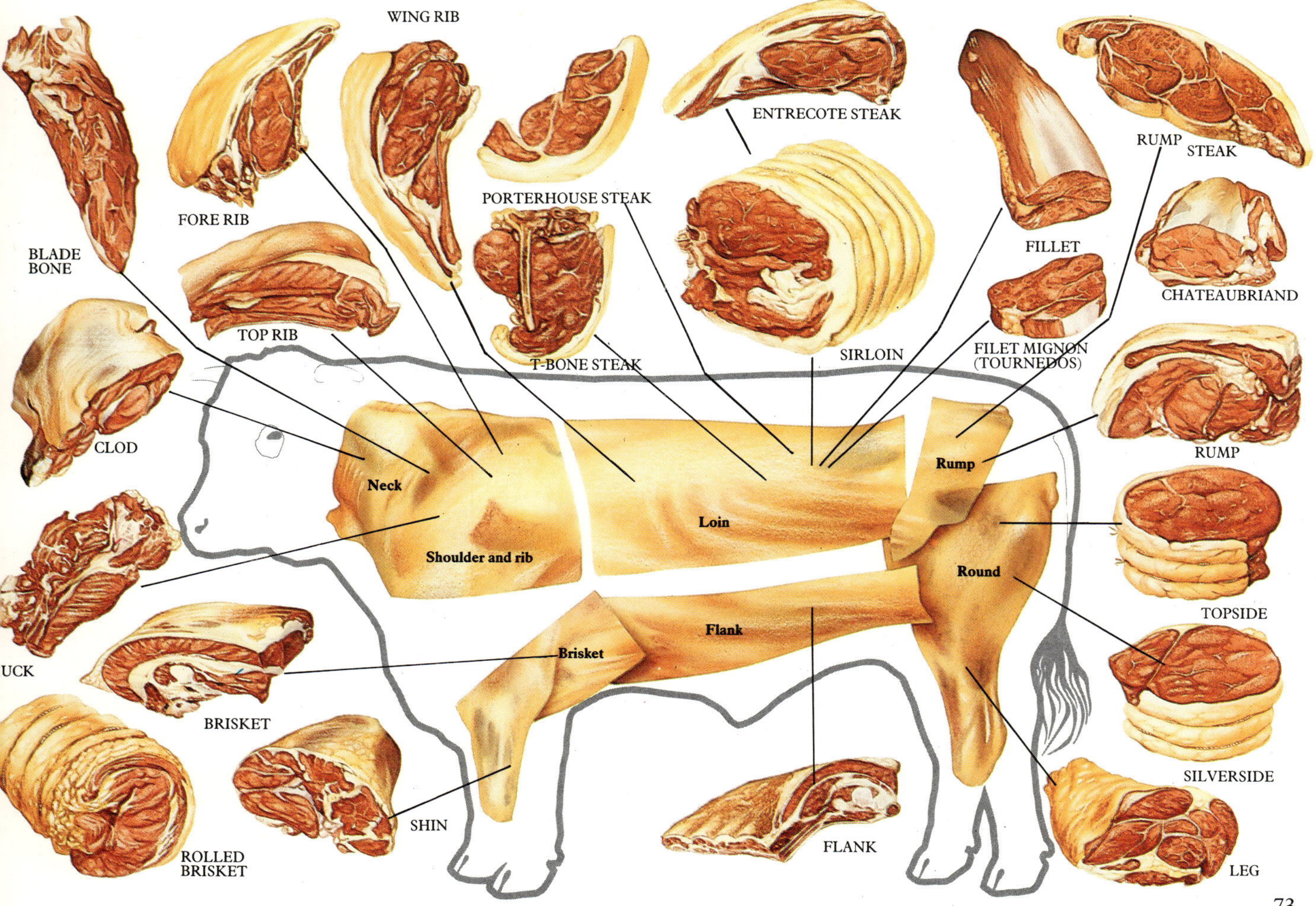

Silverside A boned joint most commonly used for spiced or salted beef for slow-boiling to serve hot or, after pressing, cold. Unsalted, the joint may be pot-roasted or larded and used for boeuf à la mode.

Sirloin This is the national joint and traditional roast beef of old England. It is said to have been knighted by a king of England after he had feasted well on a roast loin of beef. It is the ideal roast for flavour and tenderness, but also the most expensive. Can be bought on the bone or boned and rolled. It is sold with the fillet attached; if bought on the bone, the fillet can be removed and cooked separately.

Skirt There are several skirts, the best being rump skirt. This is usually thick and heavy with membranes and gristle. These must be trimmed off and the meat cut into cubes and minced or used for stews and casseroles.

Steak, chateaubriand A tender, expensive steak, ideally about $1\frac{1}{4}$ in (3 cm) thick and cut from the centre of the fillet. Grill or fry. It is generally large enough to serve two people.

Steak, entrecôte The lean, tender eye muscle from a boneless sirloin. Usually $1–1\frac{1}{2}$ in ($2\frac{1}{2}$–4 cm) thick, and one of the most popular steaks as it can be cut to uniform weight and size.

Steak, mignon Also known as filet mignon or tournedos. It is a small cut from the centre of the fillet, but it is not as thick as chateaubriand steak. Filet mignon is best grilled or sautéed. Tournedos are usually larded, tied and skewered to keep their shape during cooking.

Steak, porterhouse A thick steak cut from the chump end of the sirloin, containing part of the fillet. Usually $\frac{3}{4}$–1 in (2–$2\frac{1}{2}$ cm) thick; excellent for grilling, especially over charcoal. Make sure the butcher trims off all excess fat.

Steak, rump This is considered the best-flavoured steak, excellent for grilling, or frying with onions. This steak should have about $\frac{1}{4}$ in ($\frac{1}{2}$ cm) fat on the outside edge and no gristle.

Steak, T-bone This thick steak is cut on the bone, from between the chump end and wing rib. It is usually cut to serve two portions, but may also be cut out as individual steaks. Grill or fry.

Topside A very lean, boneless joint with a fine grain to the meat. It is best slow-roasted or pot-roasted, but it may also be braised. If topside is used for roasting, ask the butcher to tie a piece of good larding fat round the joint to keep it moist during cooking.

Veal

Veal is often in short supply, except in large towns. As it is very dry with little fat, veal requires careful cooking. On its own, veal tends to be bland, and sauces, stuffings and seasonings are often used to provide additional flavour to the tender succulent meat.

When buying veal, look for soft, finely grained and moist flesh, varying in colour from off-white to palest pink. Avoid flabby and wet veal, and also meat which is dry and brown or has a blue tinge or mottling. The lean should have a fine texture with a thin outside layer of firm, creamy-white fat. Bones should be soft and almost translucent. Do not be put off by what may seem excessive gelatinous tissue around the meat: this is a natural characteristic of the young animal, and the tissues normally shrink and soften during cooking.

Most of the best veal comes from milk-fed calves which are slaughtered at the age of three months. They have been reared on milk and fatty foods which help to produce white flesh. These calves give high-quality veal, but as it is extremely expensive it is sold almost exclusively to the hotel and restaurant trade, although it can be purchased from specialist butchers. Older calves, from 14 weeks to 1 year old, provide most veal for the home market. It is less expensive than milk-fed veal, but apart from the leg, this type of veal is more suitable for roasts, pie fillings and stews and casseroles.

Imported veal is usually paler in colour than home-killed veal, but it compares well for both flavour and quality.

Best end neck A medium-priced cut sold on the bone for roasting. It can also be boned, stuffed and rolled for roasting whole, but is more often sold as neck cutlets.

Best end neck cutlets These cutlets should have the tip of the chine bone removed before being cut about 1 in ($2\frac{1}{2}$ cm) thick. Each cutlet should have a good round eye of meat; grill or fry.

Breast One of the most economical cuts of veal. It may be roasted on the bone or be boned, stuffed and rolled first. Cut into 1 in ($2\frac{1}{2}$ cm) thick strips, it is excellent for braising or stewing.

Escalopes From the prime muscle of the leg, such as the topside. They are cut, with the grain, no more than $\frac{1}{4}$ in ($\frac{1}{2}$ cm) thick and beaten into thin slices.

Fillet This lies at the top of the hind leg and is the most expensive of veal cuts, usually weighing 8–12 oz (225–350 g). There is, however, no wastage, and it is both tender and delicately flavoured. It is normally cut into fillet steaks, but may also be larded and roasted whole.

Knuckle or shin One of the cheaper cuts, this comes from the lower part of the hind or fore leg. The hind knuckle is the more tender of the two; it can be slow-roasted on the bone or cut into $1\frac{1}{2}$–2 in (4–5 cm) pieces and used for osso buco. The fore leg knuckle is only suitable for boiling, or it may be boned and cut up and used for stews and casseroles.

Leg This is one of the largest and most expensive joints with plenty of meat to bone. The whole leg, after the hind knuckle has been removed, may be roasted on the bone, but usually the topside, known as cushion of veal, is cut off for escalopes, and the remainder boned and rolled for smaller roasting joints.

Loin A prime cut, taken from between the best end and the leg. It is sold as a whole joint on the bone, or already boned and stuffed, suitable for roasting.

Loin chops Single bone portions, suitable for grilling and frying. They sometimes include the kidney.

Middle neck An economical cut, but with a high proportion of bone, usually sold in cutlets for stewing or boned as pie veal.

Scrag Mainly sold in one piece for boiling or stewing. It is inexpensive, but there is a high percentage of bone to meat. Most butchers chop scrag and offer it for casseroles.

Shoulder This is also known as the oyster of veal after the fore knuckle has been removed. It is the cheapest veal roasting joint, sold on the bone, but better boned, stuffed and rolled.

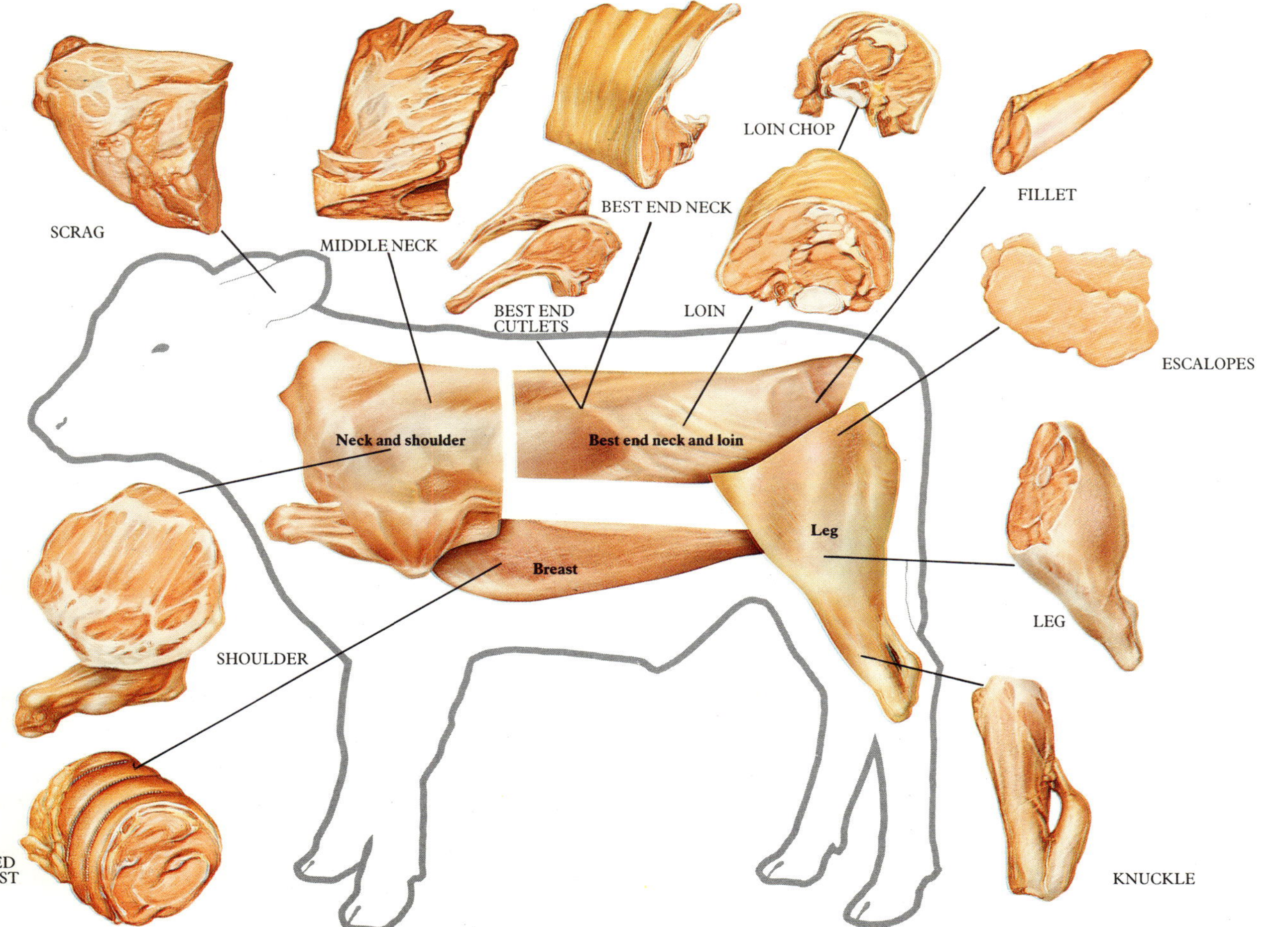

Lamb

Most lambs are slaughtered when they are less than a year old. The spring lamb, however, is ready for the market at 5–7 months, and the baby lamb in 6–8 weeks. The term 'mutton' is usually applied to the flesh of sheep at least eighteen months to two years old. Lamb is delicately flavoured, and a rich source of iron and other important minerals; it is rich in vitamins, especially those of the B complex, essential for the release of energy from all foods and for the general health of skin and nerve tissues.

Lamb varies in colour according to the age and breed of the animal. Meat from a young lamb is usually pale pink; red meat comes from an older animal. But some breeds, hill lambs for example, have a deep colour even when young. The fat should be creamy-white, not oily or yellow – a yellowish tinge shows excessive age.

Frozen lamb has a less delicate flavour than fresh and it looks different; the lean is paler and does not have the bloom of fresh meat, while the fat is whiter and crumbles more easily. If the fat looks very brittle it is a sign that the lamb has been frozen for a long time; it will generally shrink during cooking and have a bland taste.

A joint of lamb should have a good depth of lean meat covered by a moderate layer of fat. The skin should be pliable to the touch, not hard or wrinkled. Legs and shoulder joints should have a plump, not flat appearance. A blue tinge in the knuckle and rib bones indicates that the animal is young.

Although the choicest cuts of lamb for roasting, grilling and frying comes from the loin, legs and shoulders, do not ignore the cheaper cuts. Best end of neck, scrag, middle end and breast may take more time to prepare but they can be as delicious and are as nourishing as the prime, expensive cuts.

Best end of neck A tasty and versatile cut from between the middle neck and the loin. It may be braised and is excellent as a small roast on the bone. For a whole roast, the butcher will saw through the vertebrae – the bone known as the chine bone – without removing it from the joint. He will also strip off the outer thin skin.

Two best ends of neck are used to shape a crown, from which the skin and excess fat have been removed. The top of the rib bones are trimmed of meat. Most butchers will prepared a crown roast on request. Fill the hollow of the crown with a stuffing.

Guard of honour is another popular roast, shaped from two best ends and joined in such a way that the trimmed rib bones criss-cross on top. Give the butcher a few days' notice to prepare either of these joints.

Breast A very economical cut, which is usually sold boned, stuffed and rolled, for roasting or braising. As it is a fatty joint, it is not much in demand.

Chops These individual cuts of lamb come either from the loin or the leg of the animal. They are suitable for grilling, frying or braising.

Chump chops These chops, ¾–1 in (2–2½ cm) thick, are cut from between the leg and the loin. They are oval with a small central bone, and are more expensive than loin chops because each leg of the animal gives only two chops.

Loin chops Cut from the loin, about 1 in (2½ cm) thick, they have a small T-shaped bone. They should be fairly lean with a thin layer of fat on the outside edge.

Cutlets These are taken from the best end neck, as individual cuts. They have a characteristic long bone, a thin layer of fat and a small round eye of sweet lean meat. Suitable for grilling and frying; allow two cutlets per person. French lamb cutlets are also from the best end, the only difference being in the method of preparation. On French cutlets, the chine bone is removed and the rib bone is trimmed of meat and fat for about 2 in (5 cm). To serve cutlets traditionally, put paper frills on the bare rib ends after cooking.

Middle neck cutlets These are fattier and more gristly than best end cutlets and are best stewed or braised.

Fillet The upper part of the leg, frequently sold as a separate joint. It has lean meat, little bone and no gristle. It is suitable for roasting whole on the bone.

Knuckle The lower part of the hind leg, usually sold as a separate, fairly expensive joint for roasting on the bone. It may also be boned, stuffed and rolled.

Leg The most popular large roasting joint, weighing 4–5½ lb (1·8–2·5 kg). It is sold on the bone or can be ordered boned and rolled. The leg, being so large, is often divided into two joints: knuckle and fillet. Whole leg of lamb is good for roasting, braising and boiling. Lamb steaks are cut from boned leg.

Loin This prime joint is usually sold on the bone for roasting whole. A complete loin weighs about 4 lb (1·8 kg), but it is also sold in smaller portions. It has a thin even layer of fat just below the skin. Ask the butcher to saw through the chine bone for easier carving. The loin can also be ordered boned, then stuffed with the chopped kidneys and rolled to make a good roast for a small number of people.

Middle neck Comes from between the best end of neck and the scrag; it is sometimes sold in one piece including the scrag. It has a large proportion of bone and fat to meat and is best used for stews; boned, it may also be sliced and fried.

Noisettes These are small round and thick slices cut from the loin or best end. They are boned, trimmed of fat and shaped and tied into round fillets, each weighing about 6 oz (175 g). The butcher requires notice to pre-pare noisettes, or they can easily be shaped at home. They are suitable for grilling or frying.

Rib The complete rib section is seldom sold whole, but cut into three portions: best end of neck, middle neck and scrag.

Saddle A large prime joint com-prising both loins and cut from the best end to the legs; the tail is left on. The butcher requires a few days' notice to dress a saddle. The meat is skinned and the cleaned kidneys are skewered and tied to the end of the loins, with the slit tail wrapped round them. A saddle weighs about 8 lb ($3\frac{1}{2}$ kg) and makes an ideal, if expensive, large roast.

Scrag end of neck This cut nearest the head contains much bone and gristle. It is sold already chopped and is used for stews and soups and broths.

Shoulder A roasting joint from the fore-quarter; usually weighs $3\frac{1}{2}$–4 lb (1·6–1·8 kg). It is the least expensive of the roasting joints, fattier than the leg, but with a sweeter flavour. The shoulder is more difficult to carve than the leg and is therefore often boned and rolled.

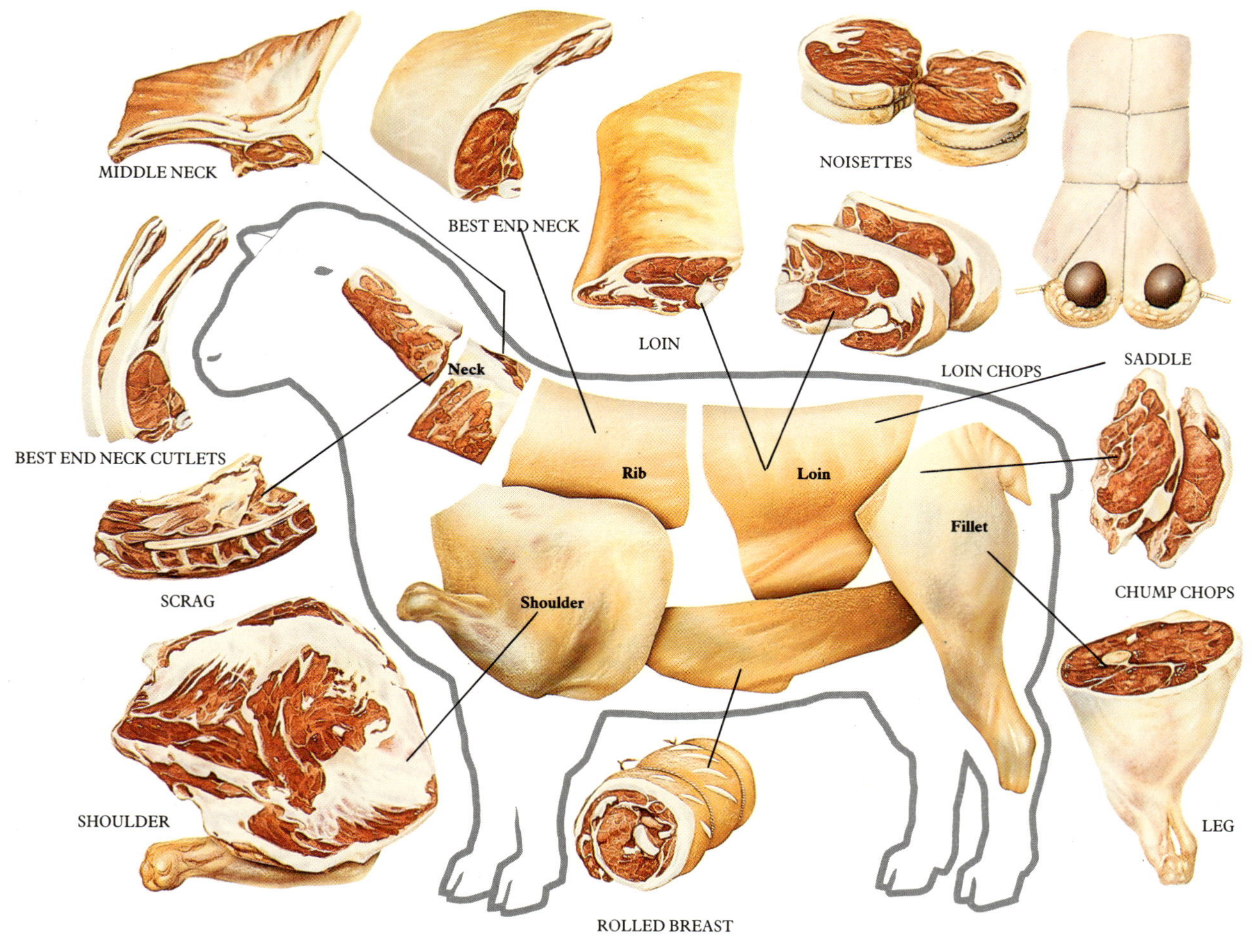

Pork

Most pigs are slaughtered young, mainly because of the growing demand for lean pork. Prime pork should be well developed, with small bones and without excessive fat – about $\frac{1}{2}$ in (1 cm) fat over the lean meat of a loin, for example, is considered ideal.

Fresh pork does not keep as well as lamb or beef, and needs more care in buying, preparation and cooking. Pork is highly nutritious, and contains more B_1 vitamins, which prevent fatigue and stimulate the appetite, than any other meat.

The fat should be firm and a clear milky-white colour. Avoid cuts with soft, grey and oily fat which leads to excessive weight loss in cooking and difficulties in carving. The lean should be pale pink, firm and smooth to the touch and with very little gristle. Freshly cut surfaces should look slightly moist and the bones should be pinkish-blue. A good butcher will present pork with clean-cut edges.

For crackling, make sure that the butcher scores the rind carefully so that the cuts are close together and penetrate the rind.

All pork joints can be roasted and, with the exception of the loin, salted and boiled. It is often more economical to buy whole joints, such as hand and spring, rather than small portions. The joint can then be separated, by the butcher or at home, into cuts for roasting, boiling or salting, and chops for grilling or frying. Pork has more flavour if cooked on the bone, but many joints are often sold boned and rolled.

Cured pork comes from pigs especially reared to produce certain proportions of lean meat to fat. Bacon, from the body of the pig, and gammon, from the hind legs, are cured in brine and may or may not undergo smoking, which increases their keeping quality. Ham, from the hind legs, is salted and then cured. Both shoulder and collar can be cured in the same way as ham and can be used instead of it.

Belly, belly pork This is sometimes known as streaky, draft or flank pork. It is fairly fatty, and the best cut is the thicker part of the belly which has a good proportion of lean meat. It is a cheap cut which is sold fresh or salted. Fresh belly pork is good for roasting and can be boned, stuffed and rolled. It can also be chopped up for stews or sliced for grilling. Salted belly pork should be soaked before boiling.

Blade A small, reasonably priced joint cut from the shoulder. It weighs about 2 lb (900 g) and may be roasted on the bone, or boned, stuffed and rolled for roasting.

Chops These large, fairly expensive slices, generally 1 in ($2\frac{1}{2}$ cm) thick, come from the loin or the spare rib joints. They are all suitable for grilling, frying or baking.

Chump chops Cut from the chump end which lies between the loin and the leg. They have a round central bone. A boned chump is cut into $\frac{3}{4}$ in (2 cm) thick pork steaks or even thinner and beaten flat into pork escalopes.

Loin chops Cuts from either the end of the fore loin or from the hind loin. They all have a T-bone, and chops from the hind loin usually come with the kidney left in. If the chops are bought with rind on, snip through it with scissors to prevent the chop curling during cooking. However, most loin chops are cut from 'hogmeats', a term for loins that have had the rind and excessive fat trimmed off.

Spare rib chops Cuts from the spare rib joint which have a smaller eye of meat than chump and loin chops. They contain little bone, however, and have a sweeter taste. Grill or fry. Do not confuse them with spare ribs, which come from the belly.

Fillet or tenderloin This is the lean and tender muscle which lies underneath the backbone in the hind loin. It is obtained from bacon pigs when the carcasses are cut up for curing. This choice cut for roasting, braising, grilling and frying is covered in a near-transparent thin skin which must be peeled off. For roasting whole, the fillet is best cut through half its thickness, spread with a stuffing and rolled up.

Fillet half leg The top end of the hind leg. It is roasted whole on the bone or cut into steaks.

Hand The lower part of the shoulder, usually more expensive than the complete hand and spring. It has a large area of rind for crisp crackling and is also ideal, boned, stuffed and rolled, for roasting.

Hand and spring Sometimes known as the shoulder. It is the lower shoulder (the hand), with the jowl, knuckle and trotter as well as the first three or four bones of the belly. Sold fresh or salted. When buying this joint, look for one which is compact and well fleshed with fat. It is particularly economical when bought whole. The knuckle end can be cut off and salted for boiling; two or three steaks can be cut from the thin end and used for grilling or frying, while the centre portion can be roasted whole.

Knuckle This large joint is also known as hough. It is cut from the lower part of the leg. Knuckle is fairly expensive and can be roasted whole or boned and stuffed. It is also excellent for boiling and stewing. On a prime joint, the knuckle bone should have a tinge of blue.

Leg A prime, expensive roasting joint sometimes known as gigot. A whole leg weighs 10–15 lb ($4 \cdot 5$–$6 \cdot 8$ kg) and is usually sold cut into two joints: the fillet half leg and the knuckle half. Both are excellent roasted on the bone. Whole legs are sometimes partly boned and tied by the butcher so that smaller roasting joints from $2\frac{1}{2}$ lb ($1 \cdot 1$ kg) upwards can be cut.

Loin Considered by many to be the choicest cut of pork, the loin is also the most expensive. The whole loin weighs 9–10 lb (4–$4\frac{1}{2}$ kg). It may be roasted whole, but is more often cut into smaller joints. The choicest part of the loin (hind loin), which has the kidney and the fillet attached, is usually dearer than the rib end (fore loin). The rib end is similar in appearance to best end of lamb, although much larger. It can be prepared by the butcher for a large crown roast to serve at least ten people, at a few days' notice.

When buying loin of pork look for a good proportion of pale pink meat to fat.

Neck end A fairly inexpensive joint which is the upper part of the shoulder and consists of the blade and spare rib, sometimes known as a chine. In Scotland it is called shoulder and is cut larger, weighing up to 20 lb (9 kg). Look for a compact joint, with an even distribution of fat and a large amount of lean meat. It can be boned and rolled and cut into joints of varying sizes, or sold separately as blade and spare rib.

Spare rib The cut left on the upper part of the shoulder after the blade has been removed from the neck end. Suitable for roasting, braising or stewing.

Spare ribs In spite of the name, these do not come from the spare rib, but are cut from the rib part of the belly. Rind and all excess fat are removed and the ribs are cut into single bone strips. Much used in Chinese cooking, for roasting and for barbecues.

Sucking (suckling) pig A young pig from three weeks to two months old when slaughtered. It is usually spit-roasted.

CURED PORK PRODUCTS

These include bacon, gammon and ham. Unsmoked (green) gammon and ham are less expensive than smoked, but do not keep as well. Ham is cured in various ways. Many hams are lightly cured or smoked and intended for cooking, while others, such as the air-dried Parma ham, are eaten raw.

Bacon Whether green or smoked, bacon should have firm, moist flesh and the fat should be white or cream with no yellow or green tinges. The best joints come from the back, while the collar (neck) and forehock (foreleg) give more economical joints. Rashers come from the back and belly. Top back rashers are always lean; they have a distinctive flavour, sweeter than other rashers. Long and short back rashers are good quality but expensive. Streaky bacon rashers, from the belly, have alternate layers of fat and lean meat and always contain some gristle which must be cut out.

Gammon A whole gammon, 12–14 lb (5·4–6·4 kg), is the hind leg of a bacon pig and is cut square at the top, unlike ham. Gammon is more expensive than other bacon joints; it may be par-boiled and baked whole, but is usually cut into smaller joints.

Ham This is the hind leg of the pig and corresponds to the gammon except for its characteristic round top. It is removed from the carcass before salting. A whole ham weighs between 10 and 16 lb (4·5 and 7·2 kg).

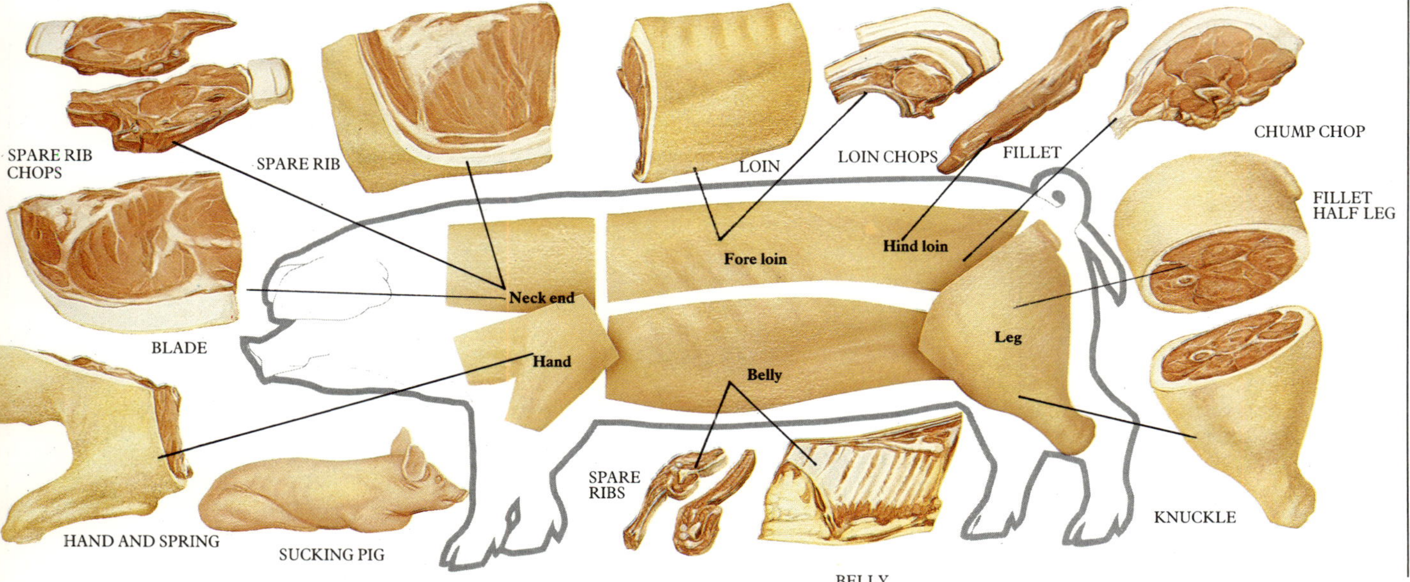

Offal

Many types of offal – liver for example – are excellent sources of the minerals and vitamins necessary for good health. Much offal – brains, sweetbreads and tripe, to mention a few – is also easily digestible and therefore suitable for a building-up diet.

Ironically, certain types of offal, such as brains, calf's liver and sweetbreads, are considered such gourmet's delicacies that they are often priced out of the market for the average housewife. But generally, offal compares favourably with meat in price. It seldom requires lengthy preparation and cooking, and as it contains no bones and little fat or gristle, wastage is cut to the minimum.

Offal does not store well; it should be used on the day of purchase and stored in the refrigerator until prepared for cooking.

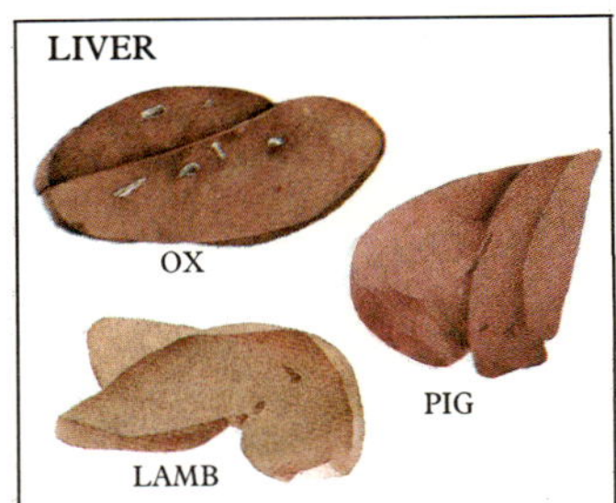

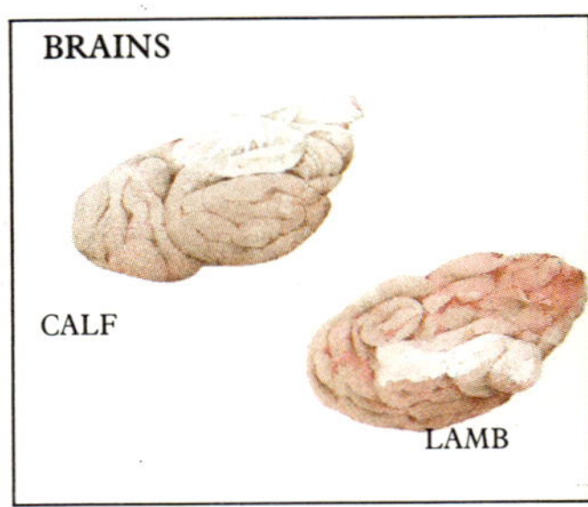

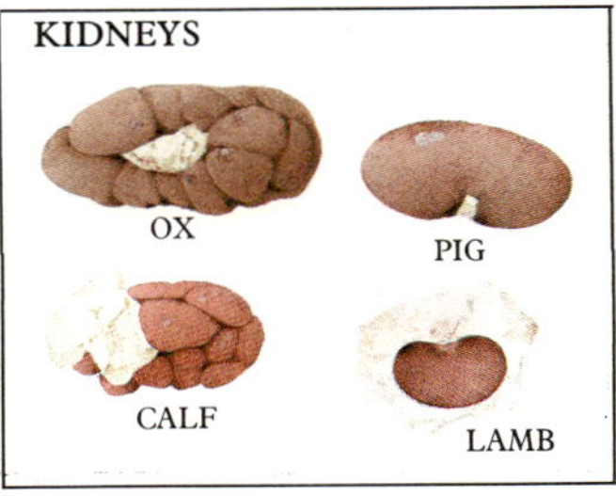

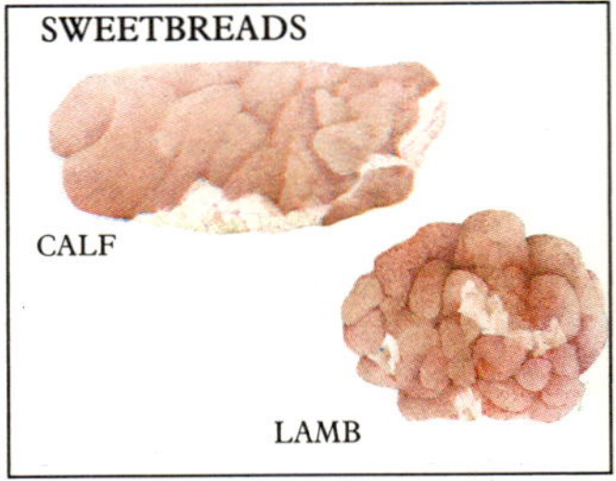

Liver Calf's liver is the best and most expensive, ox liver the cheapest and coarsest, with the strongest flavour. Calf's liver should be pale milky brown in colour and soft to the touch. Make sure the butcher removes the inedible main pipes. Lamb's liver should be light brown in colour; avoid any that is dark brown and therefore from an older animal. Pig's liver is stronger in flavour and softer in texture than either calf's or lamb's liver.

Kidneys Ox kidney is the largest and coarsest, followed by the similar but smaller and more tender calf's kidney, which is light brown with creamy-white suet. Lamb's kidney has a different shape, and is usually surrounded by a thick, white deposit of suet. Choose firm, light brown kidneys, avoiding any that are dark or strong-smelling. Pig's kidney is similar to lamb's in colour and texture, but is more elongated and flatter with no suet.

Tongues Ox and lamb's tongues are the most readily available. Calf's tongue is rare, and pig's tongue is usually sold with the head. Ox tongue is often sold ready cooked, but can also be bought fresh or salted. Lamb's tongues are usually sold fresh and should be soaked in lightly salted water before cooking.

Brains Calf's brains have the most delicate flavour, but lamb's brains are sometimes more easily available and may be used in any recipe for calf's brains.

Heads Pig's, sheep's and sometimes calf's heads are sold whole or in halves. Calf's and pig's heads make good brawn. Sheep's or lamb's head can be boiled or stewed after thorough scrubbing and used as a base for broths or for pie fillings. The cheeks of a pig's head are sometimes cured and boiled, to be sold as Bath chaps.

Hearts All hearts make good nutritious eating, but require long slow cooking. Lamb's heart is the smallest and most tender. Choose bright red, firm hearts; avoid any that are grey. Pig's heart is larger and less tender than lamb's heart.

Sweetbreads This is the name given to the two portions of the thymus gland, one in the throat and one in the chest cavity. Calf's sweetbreads are considered the finest but are in short supply. Lamb's sweetbreads are more readily available, but smaller. Ox sweetbreads are large and tough, with a strong flavour; pig's sweetbreads are not sold.

Feet Excellent for making jellied stock, pig's trotters are the ones most frequently seen, either fresh or brined. Calf's foot is rare but can sometimes be had if it is ordered well in advance; it may be bought in concentrated form in jars.

Tripe This comes from the ox and is the lining of the stomach. Tripe from the first stomach is the smoothest and is known as blanket. Honeycomb tripe comes from the second stomach. Both types of tripe should be thick, firm and white; avoid any that is slimy and grey or has a flabby appearance.

Oxtail This is sold ready skinned and jointed; the fat should be a creamy-white and the lean meat deep red. Excellent braised and as a basis for soups.

Sausages These are made by blending lean and fat meat with cereal, seasonings and additives. **Beef sausages** are available as chipolatas or small sausages. They should contain at least 50 per cent meat, of which at least half should be lean. **Pork sausages and chipolatas** should contain at least 65 per cent meat, and at least 50 per cent should be lean.

Black pudding This is a mixture of pig's blood and pork fat stuffed into pig's intestines and boiled. Cut black pudding in half lengthways or into thick slices and fry in butter or grill.

Stocks and Soups

The basis for all soups is good fresh stock usually made from the bones and flesh of fish, meat and poultry, with added vegetables, herbs and spices. Fresh bones and meat are essential ingredients for brown and white stocks. Use marrow bone and shin of beef for brown stock and knuckle of veal for a white stock. Ask the butcher to chop the bones into manageable pieces. The chopped bones release gelatine while cooking, which gives body to the stock.

Vegetables give additional flavour, but avoid potatoes, which make the stock cloudy. Strong-flavoured vegetables, such as turnips, swedes and parsnips, should be used sparingly.

STOCKS

Brown Stock
PREPARATION TIME: *15 min*
COOKING TIME: *5 hours*
INGREDIENTS *(for 6 pints,*
    3¼ litres):
1 lb (450 g) marrow bones
2–3 lb (1–1½ kg) shin of beef
1½ oz (40 g) butter or dripping
1–2 leeks
1 large onion
1–2 celery sticks
½ lb (225 g) carrots
2 bouquets garnis (page 99)
Salt★ and black peppercorns

Blanch the bones for 10 minutes in boiling water, then put them, with the chopped meat and butter or dripping, in a roasting tin. Brown the bones in the centre of the oven for 30–40 minutes, at a temperature of 425°F (220°C, mark 7). Turn them over oc-casionally to brown them evenly. Put the roasted bones in a large pan, add the cleaned and sliced vegetables, the bouquets garnis and peppercorns. Cover with cold water, to which ½ teaspoon of salt has been added.

Bring the contents slowly to boiling point, remove any scum from the surface and cover the pan with a tight-fitting lid. Simmer the stock over lowest possible heat for about 4 hours to extract all flavour from the bones. Top up with hot water if the level of the liquid should fall below the other ingredients.

Strain the stock through a fine sieve or muslin, into a large bowl. Leave the stock to settle for a few minutes, then remove the fat from the surface by drawing absorbent paper over it. If the stock is not required immedi-ately, leave the fat to settle in a surface layer which can then be easily lifted off.

Once the fat has been removed from the stock, correct seasoning if necessary.

White Stock
This is made like brown stock, but the blanched veal bones are not browned. Place all the in-gredients in a large pan of water and proceed as for brown stock.

Cooking stock in a pressure cooker
Place the stock ingredients, with lightly salted water, in the pres-sure cooker – it must not be more than two-thirds full. Bring to the boil and remove the scum from the surface before fixing the lid. Lower the heat and bring to 15 pounds (6·8 kg) pressure. Re-duce the heat quickly and cook steadily for 1 hour. Strain the stock and remove the fat.

Storing stock
After the fat has been removed, pour the cooled stock into a container and cover with a lid. It will keep for three or four days in the refrigerator, but to ensure absolute freshness, boil up the stock every two days.

Freezing stocks
Stocks can be satisfactorily stored in a home freezer, where they will keep for up to two months. Boil the prepared stock over high heat to reduce it by half. Pour it into ice cube trays, freeze quickly and transfer the stock cubes to poly-thene bags. Or, pour the stock into freezing containers, leaving a 1 in (2½ cm) space at the top.

To use frozen stock, leave it to thaw at room temperature, or simply turn it into a saucepan and heat over low heat, stirring occa-sionally. Add 2 tablespoons water to every cube of concen-trated stock.

Ready-made stocks
Many ready-made stock prep-arations are available, usually in the form of bouillon cubes, meat extracts, and meat-and-vege-table extracts. In an emergency, these preparations are acceptable replacements for home-made stocks, but they have a sameness of flavour and lack body and jellying qualities. As they are highly seasoned, be careful about extra flavourings until the soup has been tasted.

SKIMMING STOCK

Lifting scum from boiling stock

Removing surface fat

SOUPS

Beef Consommé

A consommé is a clear soup made from meat, poultry, fish or vegetables and clarified stock. Consommés are particularly suitable for party menus and may be served piping hot or chilled as a jellied soup.

PREPARATION TIME: *15 min*
COOKING TIME: *2 hours*
INGREDIENTS (*for 6*):
½ lb (225 g) lean beef
1 small carrot
1 small onion or leek
3 pints (1¾ litres) brown stock
Bouquet garni (page 99)
1 egg white

Shred the meat finely, and peel and chop the vegetables. Put all the ingredients in a large pan, adding the egg white last. Heat gently, whisking continuously with a wire whisk, until a thick froth forms on the surface. Cease whisking, reduce the heat immediately and simmer the consommé very slowly for 1½–2 hours. Do not let the liquid reach boiling point, as the foam layer will break up and cloud the consommé.

Strain the consommé into a bowl through a double layer of muslin, or a scalded jelly bag. Strain the consommé again through the egg foam in the muslin – it should now be perfectly clear and sparkling.

Reheat the consommé, correct the seasoning if necessary, and serve hot or cold.

Broths

These semi-clear soups are easy to make and consist of uncleared brown or white stock with added meat, vegetables, rice or barley. The recipe given below is a good example.

Scotch Broth

This is a nourishing, easily prepared soup which is a complete meal in itself.

PREPARATION TIME: *30 min*
COOKING TIME: *2–3 hours*
INGREDIENTS (*for 8*):
1 lb (450 g) flank of mutton or
*   scrag end or middle neck of*
*   lamb*
2 oz (50 g) barley
2 onions
½ lb (225 g) carrots
½ lb (225 g) turnips
3 leeks
Salt★ and black pepper
Finely chopped parsley

Ask the butcher to chop the meat into small pieces. Put the meat with 6 pints (3½ litres) of water in a large pot. Bring to the boil and remove any scum from the surface. Reduce the heat, add the barley and simmer for 20–30 minutes.

Meanwhile, peel and finely chop the onions, carrots and turnips. Trim and thoroughly wash the leeks, then cut them into thin rounds. Add all the vegetables to the pot, with 1 teaspoon salt and several twists of pepper. Cover the pot and simmer for 2 hours. Lift out the bones, strip off as much meat as possible and stir this back into the broth. Adjust seasoning to taste and serve the broth sprinkled with finely chopped parsley.

Sauces & Dressings

Sauces first came into widespread use in the Middle Ages, to disguise the flavour of long-stored meat that had been inadequately cured. Today, they are used to add flavour to bland food, colour to simple meals and moisture to otherwise dry foods.

BASIC WHITE SAUCE

This is prepared by either the roux or the blending method:

Roux method

A roux is usually composed of equal amounts of butter and flour which are then combined with liquid (usually milk) to the required consistency. Melt the butter in a heavy-based pan, blend in the flour, and cook over low heat for 2–3 minutes, stirring constantly with a wooden spoon.

Gradually add the warm or cold liquid to the roux, which will at first thicken to a near solid mass. Beat vigorously until the mixture leaves the sides of the pan clean, then add a little more milk. Allow the mixture to thicken and boil between each addition of milk. Continuous beating is essential to obtain a smooth sauce. When all the milk has been added, bring the sauce to the boil; let it simmer for about 5 minutes and add the seasoning.

A basic white sauce can also be made by the one-stage method. Put the basic ingredients (fat, flour and liquid) into a pan. Cook over low heat, beating until the sauce has thickened. Boil for 3 minutes and season.

Blending method

For this method the thickening agent is mixed to a paste with a little cold milk. Mix 1 oz (25 g) plain flour with a few tablespoons taken from ½ pint (300 ml) of cold milk. Blend to a smooth paste in a bowl, and bring the remaining milk to the boil.

Pour the hot milk over the paste and return the mixture to the pan. Bring to the boil over low heat, stirring continuously with a wooden spoon. Simmer the sauce for 2–3 minutes, until thick. Add a knob of butter and seasoning and cook for 5 minutes.

A basic white sauce can be made into other savoury sauces, such as béchamel and velouté.

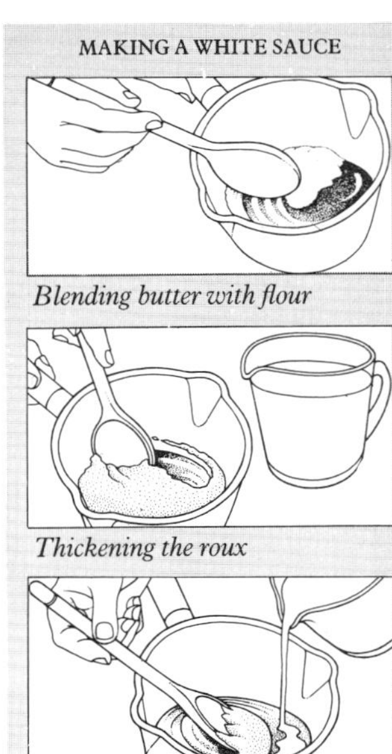

Blending butter with flour

Thickening the roux

Adding the remaining milk

Béchamel Sauce

PREPARATION TIME: *20 min*
COOKING TIME: *5–10 min*
INGREDIENTS (*½ pint, 300 ml*):
½ pint (300 ml) milk
½ small bay leaf
Sprig of thyme
½ small onion
¼ level teaspoon grated nutmeg
1 oz (25 g) butter
1 oz (25 g) plain flour
Salt⋆ and black pepper

Put the milk with the bay leaf, thyme, onion and nutmeg in a pan, and bring slowly to the boil. Remove from the heat, cover with a lid and leave the milk to infuse for 15 minutes. In a clean heavy-based pan, melt the butter, stir in the flour and cook the roux for 3 minutes.

Strain the milk through a fine sieve and gradually blend it into the roux. Bring to the boil, stirring, then simmer for 2–3 minutes. Adjust the seasoning.

Velouté Sauce

PREPARATION TIME: *5–10 min*
COOKING TIME: *1 hour*
INGREDIENTS (*½ pint, 300 ml*):
1 oz (25 g) butter
1 oz (25 g) plain flour
1 pint (570 ml) white stock
Salt⋆ and black pepper

Make the roux with the butter and flour. Gradually stir in the hot stock until the sauce is quite smooth. Bring to boiling point, lower the heat, and let the sauce simmer for about 1 hour until reduced by half. Stir the sauce occasionally. Strain through a sieve and season to taste.

BROWN SAUCES

A basic brown sauce is made by the roux method, using the same proportions of flour, fat and liquid (brown stock) as for a basic white sauce.

Melt the fat in a pan and stir in the flour. Cook the roux over low heat, stirring continuously with a wooden spoon, until the roux is light brown in colour. Gradually stir in the brown stock and proceed as for a white sauce.

Espagnole Sauce

PREPARATION TIME: *10 min*
COOKING TIME: *1¼ hours*
INGREDIENTS (*approx. ½ pint, 300 ml*):
1 carrot
1 onion
2 oz (50 g) green streaky bacon
1 oz (25 g) butter
1 oz (25 g) plain flour
¾ pint (425 ml) brown stock
Bouquet garni (page 99)
2 level tablespoons tomato paste
Salt⋆ and black pepper

Peel and dice the carrot and onion. Remove rind and gristle from the bacon and chop the rashers. Melt the butter in a heavy-based pan, and cook the vegetables and bacon over low heat for 10 minutes or until light brown.

Blend in the flour, stirring the roux until brown. Gradually blend in ½ pint (300 ml) stock, stirring constantly until the mixture has cooked through and has thickened. Add the bouquet garni, cover with a lid and set the pan on an asbestos sheet. Simmer

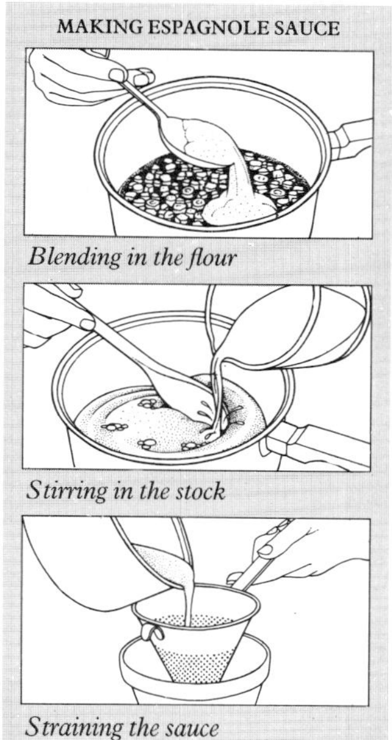

for 30 minutes. Add the remaining stock and the tomato paste. Cover the pan again, and continue cooking for 30 minutes, stirring frequently. Strain, skim off fat and adjust seasoning.

Gravies

The most frequently used brown sauce is gravy, made from the pan residues of a roast joint.

Thick gravy

Pour off most of the fat from the roasting tin, leaving about 2 tablespoons of the sediment. Stir in 1 level tablespoon plain flour and blend thoroughly with the fat. Stir constantly with a wooden spoon, cooking until the gravy thickens and browns. Gradually blend in ½ pint (300 ml) hot brown stock or vegetable liquid. Bring to boiling point, and cook for 2–3 minutes. Season to taste, strain and serve hot with a roast.

Thin gravy

Pour all the fat from the pan, leaving only the pan residues. Add ½ pint (300 ml) hot vegetable liquid or brown stock. Stir well and boil for 2–3 minutes to reduce slightly.

Thickening agents for sauces

Basic white and brown sauces can be thickened or enriched with various other liaisons: cornflour or arrowroot with water; beurre manié (kneaded butter and flour); egg yolks and cream.

Cornflour and arrowroot

To thicken ½ pint (300 ml) of liquid to a sauce of coating consistency, stir 1 level tablespoon cornflour with 2 tablespoons cold water, and mix into a smooth paste. Blend a little of the hot liquid into the liaison, then return this to the sauce. Bring the sauce to the boil, stirring constantly for 2–3 minutes to allow the starch to cook through.

Arrowroot is best used to thicken clear sauces that are to be served at once. To thicken ½ pint (300 ml) sauce use 2¼ level teaspoons arrowroot mixed to a paste with water. The sauce cannot be reheated and quickly loses its thickening qualities.

Beurre manié

This liaison is ideal for thickening sauces, casseroles and stews at the end of cooking. Knead an equal amount of butter and flour, about 1 oz (25 g) each, into a paste with a fork or the fingers. Add small pieces of the beurre manié to the hot liquid. Stir or whisk continuously to dissolve the butter and disperse the flour. Simmer the sauce until it is thick and smooth and has lost the starchy taste of raw flour. Do not let it boil or the beurre manié will separate out.

EGG-BASED SAUCES

These rich sauces require care and practice to prevent them curdling. They are made from egg yolks and a high proportion of butter. Through continuous whisking, these two main ingredients are emulsified to a thick and creamy consistency.

Hollandaise Sauce
PREPARATION AND COOKING
    TIME: *20 min*
INGREDIENTS (*½ pint, 300 ml*):
3 tablespoons white wine vinegar
1 tablespoon water
6 black peppercorns
1 bay leaf
3 egg yolks
6 oz (175 g) soft butter
Salt★ and black pepper

Boil the vinegar and water with the peppercorns and the bay leaf in a small pan, until reduced to 1 tablespoon. Leave to cool. Cream the egg yolks with ½ oz (10 g) butter and a pinch of salt. Strain the vinegar into the eggs, and set the bowl over a pan of boiling water. Turn off the heat. Whisk in the remaining butter, ¼ oz (5–10 g) at a time, until the sauce is shiny and has the consistency of thick cream. Season with salt and pepper.
    Until the technique of egg-

Whisking in pieces of butter to thicken Hollandaise sauce

based sauces has been mastered, a Hollandaise sauce may sometimes curdle during preparation. This is usually because the heat is too sudden or too high, or because the butter has been added too quickly. If the finished sauce separates, it can often be saved by removing from the heat and beating in 1 tablespoon of cold water.

Béarnaise Sauce
This sauce is similar to Hollandaise sauce, but has a sharper flavour. It is served with grilled meat and fish.

PREPARATION AND COOKING
    TIME: *20 min*
INGREDIENTS (*½ pint, 300 ml*):
2 tablespoons tarragon vinegar
2 tablespoons white wine vinegar
½ small onion
2 egg yolks
3–4 oz (75–100 g) butter
Salt★ and black pepper

Put the vinegars and finely chopped onion in a small saucepan; boil steadily until reduced to 1 tablespoon. Strain and set aside to cool. Follow the method used for making Hollandaise sauce.

Mayonnaise
Mayonnaise and its variations are the most widely used of savoury cold sauces. They are served with hors d'oeuvre, salads, cold meat, poultry and vegetable dishes. Mayonnaise, like Hollandaise and Béarnaise sauce, is based on eggs and fat, but oil is used instead of butter.
    It is essential that all the ingredients and equipment are at room temperature.

PREPARATION TIME: *20 min*
INGREDIENTS (*¼ pint, 150 ml*):
1 egg yolk
¼ level teaspoon salt
½ level teaspoon dry mustard
Pinch caster sugar
Black pepper
¼ pint (150 ml) olive oil
1 tablespoon white wine vinegar
    or lemon juice

Beat the egg yolk in a bowl until thick. Beat in the salt, mustard, sugar and a few twists of freshly ground pepper. Add the oil, drop by drop, whisking vigorously between each addition of oil so that it is absorbed completely before the next drop. As the mayonnaise thickens and becomes shiny, the oil may be added in a thin stream. Finally, blend in the vinegar.
    A mayonnaise may curdle if the oil was cold or was added too quickly, or if the egg yolk was stale. To save a curdled mayonnaise, whisk a fresh yolk in a clean bowl, and gradually whisk in the curdled mayonnaise. Alternatively, whisk in a teaspoon of tepid water until the mayonnaise is thick and shiny.
    To make **tartare sauce**, combine ¼ pint (150 ml) mayonnaise with 2 teaspoons capers, 3 finely-chopped cocktail gherkins, 1 teaspoon finely-chopped chives and 1 tablespoon double cream.

MISCELLANEOUS SAUCES

Horseradish Sauce
PREPARATION TIME: *10 min*
INGREDIENTS (*about ⅓ pint, 200 ml*):
3 rounded tablespoons fresh grated horseradish
¼ pint (150 ml) soured cream
Salt★ and black pepper
Pinch dry mustard

Fold the horseradish into the soured cream and season to taste. Serve with roast beef.

Mint Sauce
PREPARATION TIME: *10 min*
RESTING TIME: *30 min*
INGREDIENTS (*for 4–6*):
Small handful mint leaves
1–2 level teaspoons caster sugar
2 tablespoons vinegar

Wash and dry the mint leaves. Put them on a board, sprinkle with the sugar, and chop them finely. Put the chopped mint in a jug and stir in 2 tablespoons boiling water. Add the vinegar and leave the sauce to stand for 30 minutes. Serve with roast lamb.

Apple Sauce
PREPARATION TIME: *10 min*
INGREDIENTS (*½ pint, 300 ml*):
1 lb (450 g) cooking apples
1 oz (25 g) unsalted butter
Caster sugar (optional)

Peel, core and slice the apples. Put them in a pan with 2–3 tablespoons of water and cook over low heat for about 10 minutes. Rub the cooked apples through a coarse sieve or purée them in the liquidiser. Stir in butter and season with sugar. Serve with roast pork and goose.

A good dressing is essential to a salad, but it must be varied to accord with the salad ingredients. A sharp vinaigrette sauce is probably best for a green salad, but egg, fish, meat and vegetable salads would nearly always need additional flavours.

Sauce Vinaigrette
PREPARATION TIME: *3 min*
INGREDIENTS (*¼ pint, 150 ml*):
6 tablespoons oil
2 tablespoons vinegar
2 teaspoons finely chopped herbs
Salt★ and black pepper

Put the oil and vinegar in a bowl or in a screw-top jar. Whisk with a fork or shake vigorously before seasoning to taste with herbs, salt and freshly ground pepper.

French Dressing
PREPARATION TIME: *3 min*
INGREDIENTS (*⅓ pint, 200 ml*):
8 tablespoons oil
4 tablespoons vinegar
2 level teaspoons French mustard
½ level teaspoon each salt★ and
*   black pepper*
Caster sugar (optional)

Whisk or shake all the dressing ingredients together, seasoning with sugar (optional). Any of the following ingredients can be added to a basic French dressing: 1–2 crushed garlic cloves; 2 tablespoons chopped tarragon or chives; 1 tablespoon tomato paste and a pinch of paprika; 2 tablespoons each finely chopped parsley and onion; 1 teaspoon anchovy essence (for cold fish).

Meat

Fresh, good-quality home produce is more highly prized, and consequently more expensive, than imported chilled and frozen meat.

Frozen meat is usually sold thawed, but if it is still chilled or frozen when purchased, it should be allowed to thaw at room temperature before cooking. Fresh meat will keep for two to three days in the refrigerator. Remove the wrapping paper as soon as possible after purchase and wipe the meat with a damp cloth to remove any blood or sawdust. Put the meat on a clean dish, wrap it loosely in plastic film and store in the refrigerator.

Minced meat and offal do not keep well and should preferably be used on the day of purchase. Once meat has been cooked, it should be cooled as quickly as possible before storing.

COOKING METHODS

There are no set rules for cooking meat, as each cut lends itself to preparation, cooking and presentation in several different ways. In general, however, the tender cuts are roasted or grilled, while the tougher cuts are more suitable for pot-roasting, boiling, braising, frying and stewing.

Roasting
This is the traditional method for cooking large joints of meat. It can be done in several ways, oven roasting being the most common, and again there are two methods. With quick-roasting, the meat is cooked at a high temperature which quickly seals in the juices, thus preserving the full flavour. At the same time, however, the joint shrinks.

Slow-roasting is done at low temperature over a long period. This method reduces shrinkage of the meat and produces a joint that is usually more tender.

Whichever roasting method is used, the joint must first be weighed and the cooking time calculated. Put the meat, fat side up, on a wire rack in a shallow roasting tin. Rub a lean joint with dripping or lard first.

Place the tin in the centre of the oven. During roasting the melting fat naturally bastes the joint; otherwise spoon the pan juices over it from time to time.

Roasting times and temperatures
The size and shape of a joint, and the way in which it has been prepared, influence cooking times. Large joints require less roasting time for their weight than small ones, and joints on the bone cook more quickly than boned joints because bones are a conductor of heat. A joint on the bone is considered to have a better flavour. Joints on the bone, especially from the loin and breast portions, usually have the chine bone removed by the butcher.

Rolled joints with a wide diameter take less cooking time than roasts with a narrow diameter although they may weigh the same. Joints which weigh less than 3 lb (1½ kg) should always be slow-roasted for at least 1½ hours. Smaller joints are unsatisfactory for roasting as they shrink and dry out.

Meat thermometer
A meat thermometer, which registers the internal temperature of meat, is useful for assessing roasting times. Before cooking, insert the thermometer into the thickest part of the meat, but make sure that it does not touch bone or fat. When the thermometer registers the required internal temperature, the joint will be cooked.

This type of thermometer is particularly useful for cooking beef, where there are wider margins of 'doneness' dictated by personal preference.

Spit-roasting
This traditional roasting method has been revived by the invention of the rôtisserie. This device is attached to a cooker and consists of a horizontal revolving shaft or spit driven by electricity or by clockwork. The spit can hold large joints of meat, whole game (such as hare or partridge) or poultry and kebabs.

Spit-roasting can be applied to prime joints, but for even roasting the joint must have a uniform shape. Rolled and stuffed joints must be tied firmly or skewered so as to keep their shape.

Thread the meat on the spit so that the weight is evenly distributed; place it on the rôtisserie and operate it according to the manufacturer's instructions. While the joint revolves, it is basted with its own juices and cooks evenly.

Foil roasting

Roasting in foil is becoming more and more popular, mainly because it saves the oven from being spattered with the roasting juices. Wrap the joint loosely in foil, sealing the edges firmly; basting is unnecessary, but remove the foil for the last 20–30 minutes of cooking to brown the joint. Foil wrapping is particularly recommended for slightly tough joints as the moist heat tenderises the meat. At the same time, foil deflects heat, and the oven temperature should consequently be raised.

Clear plastic roasting bags are now available—which completely eliminate splashing of the oven, and the joint bastes and browns during roasting. Do not remove the bag until the joint is finished.

Pot-roasting

This is particularly suitable for smaller and slightly tougher joints, such as brisket and topside of beef. Melt enough fat to cover the base of a deep, heavy-based pan, put in the meat and brown it over high heat. Lift out the meat, put a wire rack or a bed of root vegetables in the bottom of the pan, and replace the joint.

Cover the pan with a tight-fitting lid and cook over low heat until the meat is tender; allow 45 minutes per pound (450 g). Turn the meat frequently.

Alternatively, put the browned meat in a deep baking dish, cover it tightly and cook in the centre of a pre-heated oven, at 325°F (170°C, mark 3); allow 45 minutes per pound (450 g). Lift out the cooked meat, drain the fat from the juices and use them for gravy or sauce.

Braising

A cooking method used for smaller cuts of meat, such as less tender chops and steaks, and for large offal such as hearts. Coat the meat with seasoned flour (page 100) and brown it evenly in hot fat. Set the meat on a bed of diced, lightly fried root vegetables in a casserole or heavy-based saucepan. Pour over enough water or stock and tomato purée to cover the vegetables; add herbs and seasonings.

Cover the casserole with a tight-fitting lid and cook in the centre of a pre-heated oven, at 325°F (170°C, mark 3), or on the stove until tender for 2–3 hours. Add more liquid if needed.

Stewing

This long, slow-cooking method is suitable for the tougher cuts of meat. Cut the meat into 1 in (2½ cm) cubes, coat them in seasoned flour (page 100) and brown them quickly, in a pan of very hot fat.

Lift the meat on to a plate and fry a few sliced carrots, onions and turnips in the fat until golden brown. Sprinkle in 1–2 tablespoons of flour, or enough to absorb all the fat; fry until the mixture is pale brown. Stir in sufficient warm stock or water to give a pouring consistency, season with salt, freshly ground black pepper and herbs and bring the sauce to the boil.

Put the meat in a flameproof casserole, pour over the sauce and vegetables and cover with a tight-

COOKING TIMES

Cooking methods	Quick-roasting at 425°F (220°C, mark 7)	Slow-roasting at 350°F (180°C, mark 4)	Stuffed joints	Meat thermometer: recommended internal temperatures	Boiling	Grilling and frying
Beef	*On the bone* 15 mins per lb (450 g) + 15 mins extra *Off the bone* 20 mins per lb (450 g) + 20 mins extra	*On the bone* 20 mins per lb (450 g) + 20 mins extra *Off the bone* 30 mins per lb (450 g) + 30 mins extra	+ 5–10 mins per lb (450 g)	Rare: (flesh and juice bloody) 140°F (60°C) Medium: (juices bloody) 160°F (70°C) Well done: (flesh brown) 170°F (75°C)	20 mins per lb (450 g) + 20 mins extra Salt beef: 25 mins per lb (450 g) + 25 mins extra	Steaks Rare: 7 mins Medium: 10 mins Well done: 15 mins
Veal	*On the bone* 25 mins per lb (450 g) + 25 mins extra *Off the bone* 30 mins per lb (450 g) + 30 mins extra	*On the bone* 35 mins per lb (450 g) + 35 mins extra *Off the bone* 40 mins per lb (450 g) + 40 mins extra	+ 5–10 mins per lb (450 g)	180°F (80°C)	20 mins per lb (450 g) + 20 mins extra	Chops: 12–15 mins Escalopes (beaten and crumbed): 2 mins each side
Lamb	*On the bone* 20 mins per lb (450 g) + 20 mins extra *Off the bone* 25 mins per lb (450 g) + 25 mins extra	*On the bone* 25 mins per lb (450 g) + 25 mins extra *Off the bone* 35 mins per lb (450 g) + 35 mins extra	+ 5–10 mins per lb (450 g)	180°F (80°C)	Mutton: 20 mins. per lb (450 g) + 20 mins extra	Cutlets: 7–10 mins Chops: 12–15 mins Kidneys: 5–10 mins Liver: 4–6 mins
Pork	*On the bone* 25 mins per lb (450 g) + 25 mins extra	*Off the bone* at 375°F (190°C, mark 5) 35 mins per lb (450 g) + 35 mins extra	+ 5–10 mins per lb (450 g)	190°F (85°C)	20 mins per lb (450 g) + 20 mins extra	Chops: 15–20 mins Sausages: 10–15 mins
Bacon and Gammon				160°F (70°C)	Cured bacon and ham 25 mins per lb (450 g) + 25 mins extra. Weigh after soaking	Bacon rashers: 5–10 mins Gammon steaks: 10–15 mins Bacon chops: 10–15 mins

fitting lid. Simmer the stew on top of the stove or in an oven, at 325°F (170°C, mark 3), until tender, after 1½–3 hours.

Boiling
Suitable for whole joints, tongues and salted joints. Bring a pan of water, in which the joint will fit snugly, to the boil. Add 2 level teaspoons of salt to each 1 lb (450 g) of meat, a bouquet garni (page 99), a large onion studded with cloves, and the meat. Bring the contents of the pan to the boil, remove any scum from the surface, then cover the pan with a tight-fitting lid and lower the heat.

Simmer the meat over very low heat until tender. Add a selection of chopped root vegetables to the pan for the last 45 minutes of cooking, if the joint is to be served hot. For a cold, boiled joint, leave the meat to cool in the cooking liquid. Drain the meat thoroughly before serving.

Salted joints should be placed in cold water and brought quickly to the boil. Drain the meat and proceed as already described. A very salty joint should be soaked in water overnight or for several hours before being boiled. If possible, change the water at least once.

Grilling
This quick-cooking method is suitable for small tender cuts, such as prime steaks, chops and cutlets, and for sausages, liver, kidney, bacon and gammon rashers.

Brush the meat with oil or melted butter, and sprinkle with a little salt and pepper (omit salt on beef steaks as this draws out the juices, and on bacon and gammon rashers). On pork chops, use sharp scissors to snip the outer layer of fat or rind at 1 in (2½ cm) intervals to prevent curling and shrinkage during grilling.

Grease the grill bars of the pan with oil or butter to prevent the meat from sticking to them. Put the meat on the pan and set it under a pre-heated grill. Turn the meat once only during grilling and baste with the pan juices if the meat begins to dry out.

Frying
Another quick-cooking method for the same types of meat as suggested for grilling. Frying times are the same (see chart on opposite page).

Melt just enough butter or oil to cover the base of a frying pan (dripping may be used for beef and lard for pork), and heat it quickly. Put the meat in the pan and cook it on a high heat, turning once only. For thick cuts, lower the heat after the meat has browned and continue frying until tender.

Lift out and drain the fried meat and keep it warm while making the gravy. Pour the fat from the pan, and stir a little stock or wine into the pan juices. Bring to the boil, correct seasoning and pour the gravy into a warm sauce boat.

Bacon rashers need little or no extra fat for frying. Place the rashers so that the lean parts overlap the fat in a cool pan, then fry over moderate heat, turning over, until the rashers are cooked.

Sausages are often pricked with a fork before they are fried, to prevent the skins bursting. This is unnecessary if they are fried over low heat for about 20 minutes.

BEEF

Allow 8–12 oz (225–350 g) per person from a joint on the bone, and 6–8 oz (175–225 g) per person from boned joints. For average portions, allow a 5–6 oz (150–175 g) steak per person.

Roasting
The best beef joints for roasting include sirloin, the rib joints, thick flank and whole fillet. Topside and rump, too, may be slow-roasted, but are more suitable for pot-roasting.

Sirloin and rib joints are sold on the bone or as rolled joints. Boning and rolling may also be done at home without a lot of trouble.

Boning and rolling (of sirloin)
Lay the joint, bones down, on a steady board. Using a sharp, broad knife, cut the joint across the grain at the thick bone at the top of the joint (chine bone). Insert the knife at the top where the meat has been loosened and move it downwards, following the bones carefully, in sawing movements until the meat comes away from the bones in one piece. Use the bones for stock or a soup.

Lay the boned joint on the board, skin side up, and roll it tightly from the thickest end. Tie it securely with a piece of string to hold its shape. Cut 2 in (5 cm) strips of pork fat and tie them, slightly overlapping, round the joint. A wider strip of fat may be tied over the top of the rolled joint to provide extra fat during roasting. Remove this piece of fat before carving.

Larding (fillet)
A whole piece of fillet is an excellent, if expensive, joint for roasting. As it has no fat this must be added in some form to prevent the meat drying out during roasting. First trim any skin or sinews from the fillet, then cut fat pork or green bacon rashers into strips narrow enough to be threaded through the eye of a larding needle. Thread short lengths of the fat at intervals through the fillet, about ½ in (1 cm) deep and on all four sides. A fillet encased in pastry does not need larding.

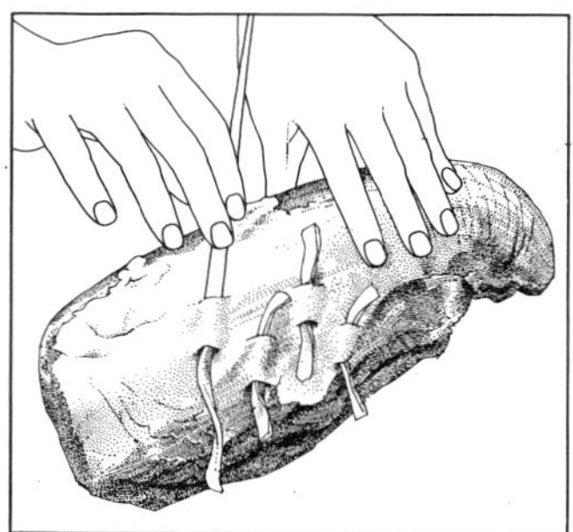

Lard beef fillet by threading short lengths of fat through the meat

Alternatively, wrap thin fat bacon rashers, slightly overlapping, round the fillet and secure with thin string. Fillet should be quick-roasted, at 12–15 minutes per pound (450 g), or roasted on a spit, when 15–20 minutes per pound (450 g) should be allowed.

Pot-roasting and braising
Flank, brisket, topside, rump and silverside are the best joints for pot-roasting or braising; for cooking these joints, follow the directions given under Meat.

Boiling
Silverside and brisket are ideal for slow boiling with vegetables. These joints can often be bought

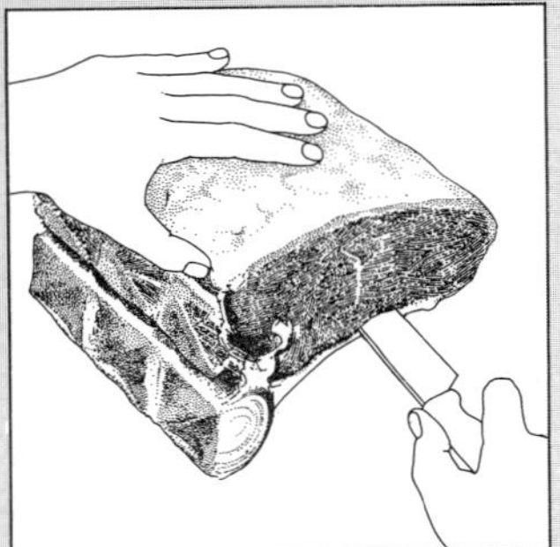

1. Severing the meat from the bone

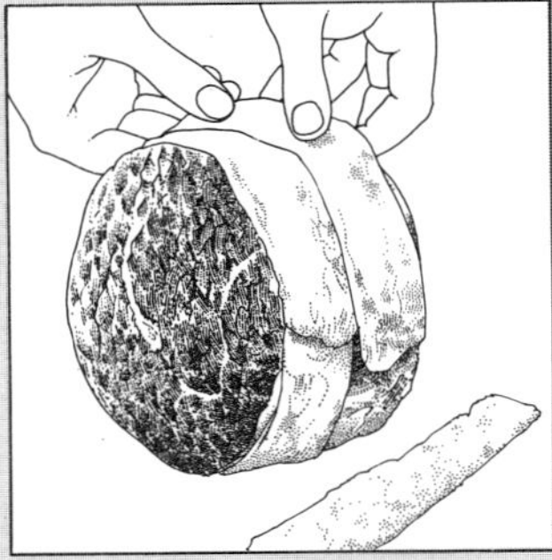

3. Laying pork fat round the joint

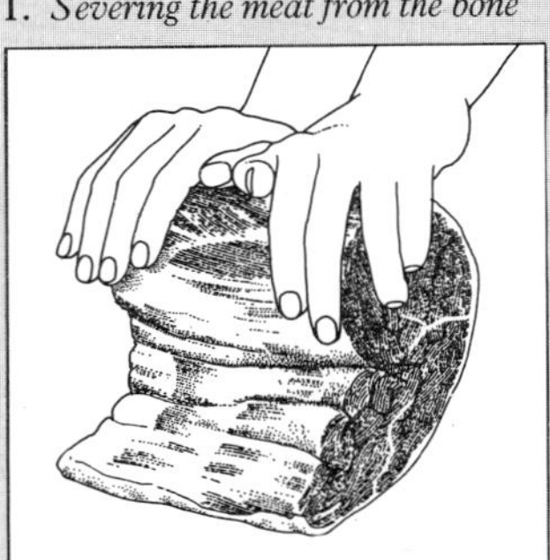

2. Rolling up the boned meat

4. Rolled joint with fat tied on top

salted or pickled, or the pickling may be done at home. See recipe for Spiced Brisket of Beef on page 24.

Salting or pickling
(silverside, brisket)
Put 1 gallon cold water with 1½ lb (700 g) salt, 1 oz (25 g) saltpetre and 6 oz (175 g) brown sugar in a large pan. Bring to the boil and boil for 20 minutes. Strain the liquid through muslin into a large earthenware bowl and leave to cool. Put the meat in the liquid, and keep it submerged by covering it with a weighted plate. Leave the meat in the salting liquid for 5–10 days, depending on thickness. Soak in cold water for about 1 hour before boiling.

Grilling and frying
These cooking methods are suit-able for all steaks – fillet, sirloin, rump, porterhouse and T-bone. Follow the general directions, but never sprinkle beef with salt as this draws out the juices.

Stewing
This slow-cooking method is ideal for all the tougher cuts of beef, such as flank, chuck, clod and shin. Stews store well in a home freezer. Many people consider them best if cooked a day in advance, but pre-cooked stew must be heated through thoroughly before being served.

The Hungarian stews, known as goulashes, are internationally famous and differ from a British stew in their piquant, sweet and spicy flavour. They are ideally made from chuck steak, but lean boned shoulder of lamb or pork may also be used.

VEAL

The flavour of veal is delicate, and the flesh tends to be dry unless carefully cooked. It does not keep well and should be used on the day of purchase. Allow 8 oz (225 g) per person from veal on the bone, and about 6 oz (175 g) per person of boneless veal.

Roasting
This method is suitable for large joints such as shoulder and loin, both of which may be roasted on the bone or boned and stuffed. As the meat is fairly dry, it must be basted frequently. Boned breast is the most economical veal joint. It is ideal for stuffing – allow 1 lb (450 g) stuffing to a 6 lb (2·7 kg) breast. Use the slow-roasting method rather than the quick-roasting one.

Pot-roasting and braising
Boned and stuffed shoulder and middle neck can be pot-roasted or braised. Stuffed breast is also recommended for braising, allowing about 3 hours for a 6 lb (2·7 kg) stuffed joint.

Boiling and stewing
Veal sold for stews and pies usually comes from the neck and knuckle. Both of these contain a large amount of bone, and if bought on the bone, allow 1 lb (450 g) per serving.

Grilling and frying
Thick cutlets cut from best end of neck are suitable for grilling, frying and braising.

For frying, the most popular veal cuts are escalopes. These are cut from the tender fillet, or frequently from the top of the leg. The latter are less tender than fillet slices, and as both are often sold ready prepared it is often difficult to see the difference.

For escalopes, buy ideally ¼ in (½ cm) thick slices from the butcher. Put them between sheets of waxed paper and beat them flat with a meat hammer or rolling pin. They should be as thin as possible, and are then dipped in beaten egg and coated with fresh white breadcrumbs. Fry in hot butter for 5 minutes, turning once.

LAMB AND MUTTON

Lamb is a rather fatty meat, and mutton even more so, and the fat which rises to the surface from stewed, boiled or braised lamb should be skimmed off. Dust the basted skin of roast lamb with seasoned flour (page 100) to absorb excess fat and to crisp the top.

Allow ¾ lb (350 g) lamb on the bone per person, and 6–8 oz (175–225 g) of boned lamb per serving.

Roasting
The double or single loin, with the kidneys attached, can be roasted whole.

Whole leg and shoulder of lamb are among the most popular cuts. They are usually sold on the bone, but may also be purchased boned for stuffing and rolling.

Best end of neck is probably the most versatile joint of all meats. It is relatively inexpensive and can be used in a number of ways. It is the basis of classic stews – Lancashire hot pot, navarin of lamb, Scotch broth, to name but a few – but the joint is also excellent for roasting when prepared in classic joints, such as crown roast and guard of honour.

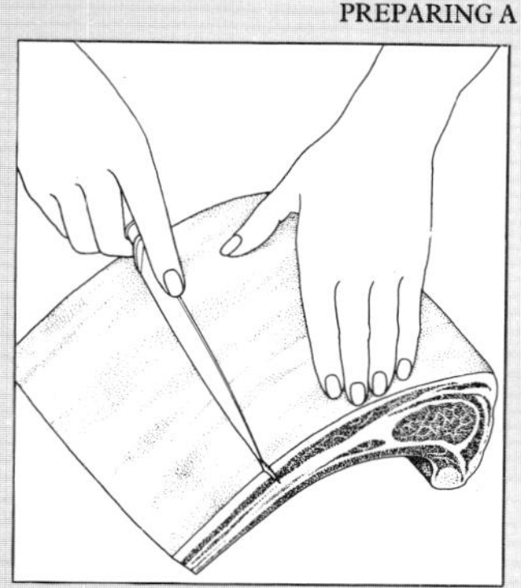

1. *Trimming meat from bones*

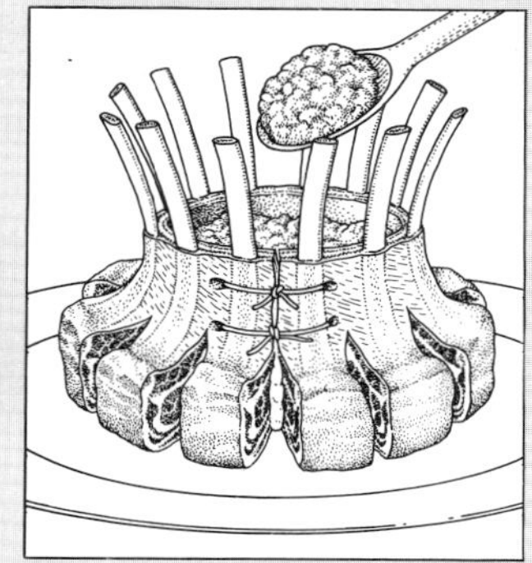

2. *Scraping bone ends clean*

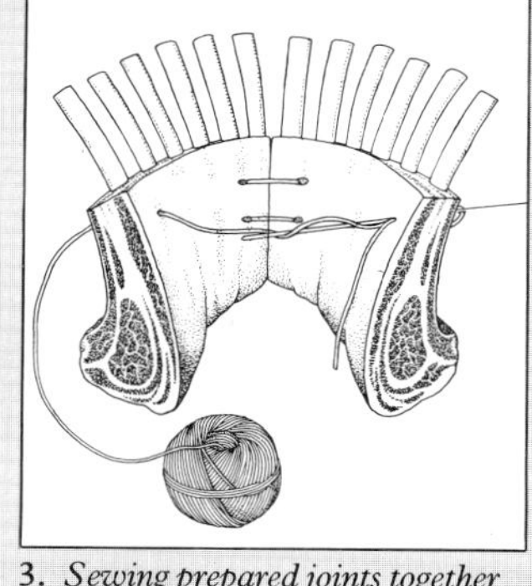

3. *Sewing prepared joints together*

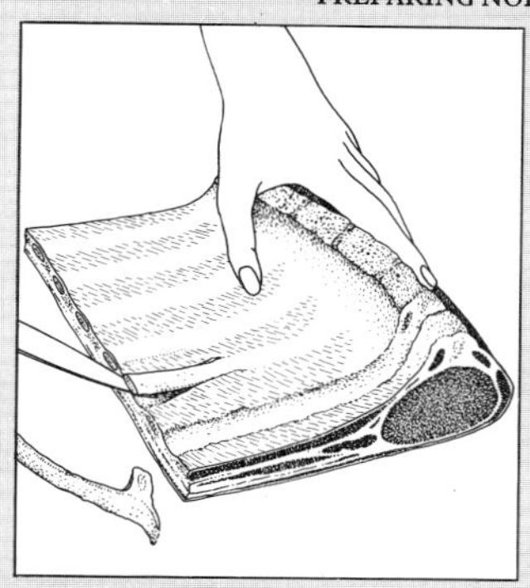

4. *Filling the crown with stuffing*

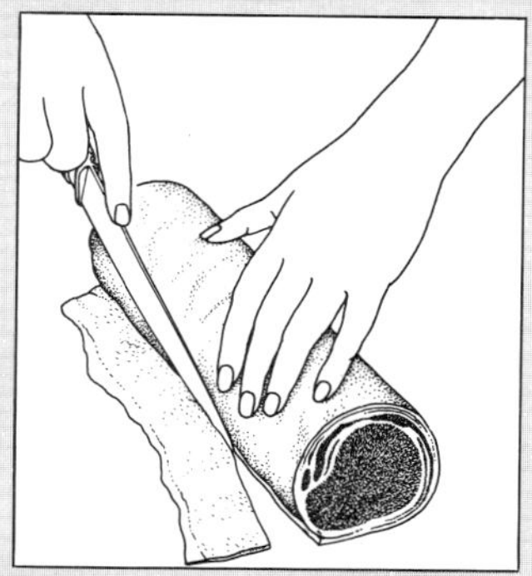

1. *Easing out rib bones*

2. *Rolling up the boned joint*

3. *Trimming the rolled joint*

4. *Cutting joint into noisettes*

Crown roast

Many butchers will prepare a crown roast if given a few days' notice, but if this is not possible, buy two matching pieces of best end, each containing seven to eight rib portions or cutlets.

Trim the fat from the thick part of each best end, and with a sharp knife cut the top 1½–2 in (4–5 cm) layer of meat from the thin end of the bones. Scrape off all gristle and meat to leave the bone ends clean. When the two pieces of meat have been prepared, sew them together, with a trussing needle and fine string, having the thick ends of the meat as the base of the crown.

Slit the lower half of the formed crown between each bone, about two-thirds up from the base and, if necessary, tie a piece of string round the middle. Fill the cavity of the crown with stuffing and slow-roast the joint.

Butchers who sell prepared crowns often put the trimmings of the joint into the hollow crown. Remove them before stuffing and roasting. The circle of fat covering the trimmings may be replaced on top of the stuffing as it bastes the joint during roasting, but it should be removed for the last 30 minutes.

Pot-roasting and braising

Boned breast of lamb is the best joint for pot-roasting and braising. It is usually bought already boned, stuffed and rolled, but make sure most of the fat has been trimmed off.

Guard of honour

This is also prepared from two best ends, but the bones are trimmed clean to about 2½–3 in (6½–7½ cm). The two pieces of meat are then joined and sewn together, skin side up, along the bottom meaty part of the joints. Fold the meat together, skin outside, so that the cleaned bones meet and criss-cross on top. Protect these with foil. Fill the cavity with a savoury stuffing; tie the joint at intervals to keep its shape; roast at low temperature.

Stewing and boiling

Breast of lamb, middle and scrag are the best and most economical cuts for stews and casseroles. Trim off as much fat as possible before cooking.

Grilling and frying

Cutlets, from best end of lamb and with a high proportion of bone, may be grilled or fried. Chops from the loin are thicker and less bony than cutlets, and chump chops have even less bone. Both types of chops are excellent for grilling and frying.

Noisettes

These are trimmed, round slices from a best end of lamb. Cut off the thick chine bone at the thick end of the best end and trim away all excess fat from the meat. Cut along either side of each rib bone and ease it out. Roll up the boned joint, trim it and tie with string at ½ in (1 cm) intervals. Cut the rolled joint into 2 in (5 cm) thick slices and fry or grill.

PORK

Pork must be thoroughly cooked to be digestible, and underdone pork can be dangerous. A pork joint should have a moderate amount of fat – lean pork is generally lacking in flavour, and fatty pork is wasteful. Allow ½–¾ lb (225–350 g) of pork on the bone per person, 6 oz (175 g) of boned meat.

Roasting
All pork joints are suitable for roasting, on or off the bone. The leg and the loin, both large and expensive joints, together with the more reasonably priced blade joint, have the largest area of skin, which gives good crackling.

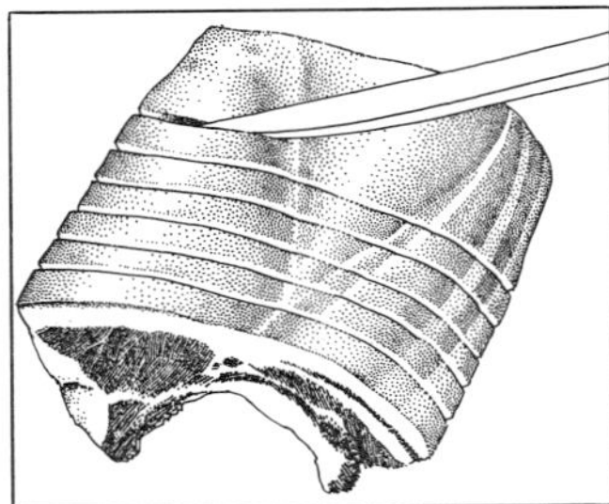

Scoring a loin of pork, making deep, even cuts through the rind

To obtain the characteristic crackling, the skin on these joints must be evenly and deeply scored. The butcher will usually do this, but before roasting make sure that all the score marks penetrate the depth of the skin and that they follow the grain of the meat. Rub the skin with olive oil or vegetable oil and with coarse salt to ensure crisp crackling. This can be removed to make carving easier.

Leg and the fore-end of loin are often boned, stuffed and rolled before roasting; hand of pork, which is an awkward joint to carve, should also be boned and rolled.

Boiling
The most suitable joints for this cooking method are fresh or salted hand, salted leg (or the knuckle end) and salted belly pork. These cuts are sold already salted, having been immersed in brine for 7–10 days.

Boiled joints of pork may be served hot with vegetables, but are more often served cold with salads.

Grilling and frying
All types of chops are suitable for these methods. Large loin chops often have a thick strip of fat around the outer edge. This fat tends to curl during cooking, and to prevent this snip the fat with scissors at 1 in (2½ cm) intervals.

Lean spare rib cutlets are usually grilled or braised, as are Chinese spare ribs which are cut from the lower rib section of the belly. Belly pork may be cut into ½ in (1 cm) thick slices and grilled or coated with beaten egg and breadcrumbs and then fried. Slices of lean fillet may be cooked in the same way, but pork fillet is usually stuffed and roasted or braised.

BACON, GAMMON AND HAM

These cured meats are sold as whole joints or as rashers and steaks. They are suitable for boiling and for grilling and frying.

Cooking methods
Whole joints of bacon and gammon should be soaked in cold water for at least 2–3 hours, or preferably overnight, to remove excess salt. They are then boiled or parboiled before being roasted or baked. Joints suitable for boiling and roasting include the fore hock, collar, back and ribs, and the gammon cuts.

Put the joint in a large pan, cover with cold water and bring slowly to boiling point. Cover the pan with a lid and reduce the heat so that the meat is cooked at a slow simmer. Fast boiling hardens the tissue and causes shrinkage of the meat. For a boiled joint, follow the times given in the chart on page 86.

Lift out the boiled joint, allow it to cool and set slightly, then peel off the skin and serve the bacon hot. Alternatively, leave the bacon to cool in the cooking liquid, peel off the skin and cover the joint with toasted breadcrumbs. Serve cold.

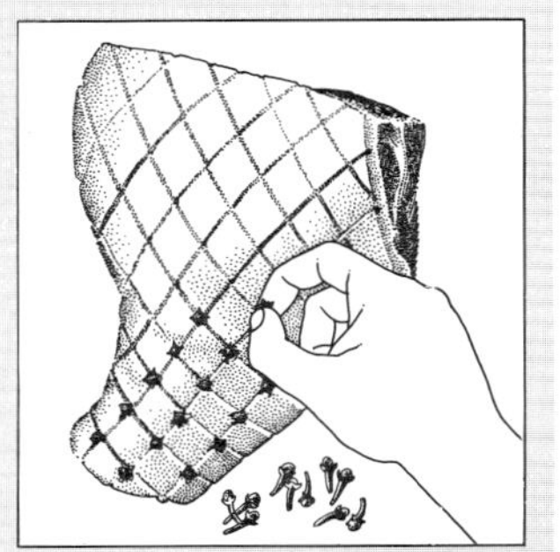

Skimming a gammon joint

Studding the joint with cloves

To roast or bake a bacon joint, first simmer it for half the cooking time. Then wrap the joint in foil and cook in the centre of a pre-heated oven at 350°F (180°C, mark 4) for the remaining cooking time. Half an hour before cooking is completed, remove the foil and peel off the skin.

To finish the joint, score a diamond pattern in the exposed fat, insert whole cloves in the intersections and pat brown sugar over the top of the joint to glaze it. Return the joint to the oven and roast at 425°F (220°C, mark 7) for the last 30 minutes. Honey, golden syrup or marmalade may be used for glazing instead of brown sugar. Large gammon joints may be studded with tinned half pineapple rings or apricot halves and basted with the syrups from these fruits.

Cured hams are sold with cooking instructions which vary according to the curing methods. Follow the manufacturers' instructions carefully when cooking these hams.

Grilling and frying
All bacon rashers (streaky, long and short back, best back) and corner gammon rashers, usually cut ¼ in (½ cm) thick, are suitable for both grilling and frying. Thicker rashers, such as bacon chops, ½–¾ in (1–2 cm) thick and cut from best back, and gammon steaks, are also ideal for grilling. To prevent the fatty edges curling during cooking, snip them as for pork chops.

Before cooking bacon rashers, the rind and any gristle or small bones must be cut off. The rind is most easily removed with sharp kitchen scissors: cut out the gristle with a knife.

Bacon rolls

Streaky bacon rashers are used for barding and are also rolled up, grilled or baked, and used as a garnish with poultry. Before rolling or tying streaky bacon rashers, they must be stretched. Lay the rashers on a board and run the blade of a knife over each rasher. For bacon rolls, rind and gristle must be removed, but this is not necessary for barding.

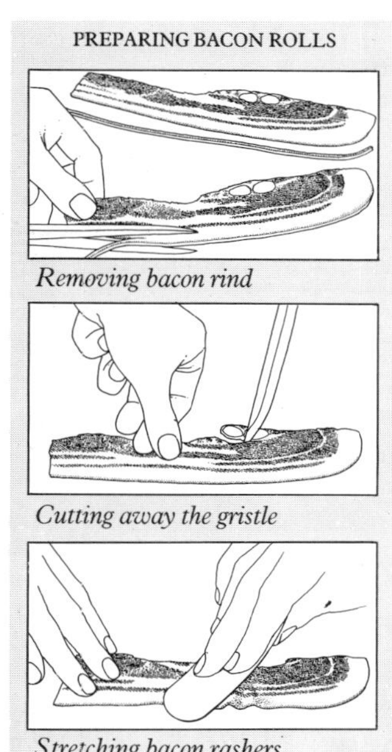

Removing bacon rind

Cutting away the gristle

Stretching bacon rashers

Bacon rashers should also be stretched when they are used for Devils on Horseback (prunes wrapped in bacon, fastened with a wooden toothpick and grilled).

OFFAL

Some of the internal organs, known as offal, of beef, veal, lamb and pork, are edible. These organs include the hearts, kidneys, livers, brains, tongues and sweetbreads. By extension, offal also includes beef and veal marrow bones, oxtail, and pigs' heads and trotters, as well as pork sausages, and black and white puddings. Offal is highly nutritious, easily digestible and generally cheap.

Brains

Calf, lamb and pork brains may all be prepared and cooked in the same manner. Soak the brains in lightly salted cold water to remove all traces of blood. Snip off any pieces of bone and all fibres. Put the brains in a pan of well-flavoured stock, bring to the boil and simmer over low heat for about 20 minutes. Drain thoroughly, then leave the brains to cool and press under a weight.

Cut the cold brains into $\frac{1}{2}$ in (1 cm) slices, coat them in beaten egg and breadcrumbs and fry in butter until golden brown. Alternatively, coat the slices in batter and deep fry them. Allow 2 sets of brains per person.

Hearts

Ox, calf and lamb hearts are used. They are usually stuffed and pot-roasted, braised or stewed. Ox heart, however, being very tough and muscular, is better chopped and used in casseroles. Calf and lamb hearts are more tender; allow one heart per person.

Rinse off all the blood under cold running water and snip out the stumps from the arteries and the tendons with scissors. Stuff the hearts with an onion or sage stuffing and sew up the opening. Pot-roast or braise the hearts for $1\frac{1}{2}$–2 hours or until tender.

Kidneys

Ox kidneys are strongly flavoured and are used, chopped, for braising, or in pies and puddings. Calf, lamb and pig kidneys are all suitable for grilling and frying, although pork kidneys are less tender than calf and lamb. Allow two or three kidneys per person.

Kidneys are sometimes sold in a thick layer of solid fat; this must be removed, and the thin transparent skin surrounding the kidneys must be peeled off. Cut the kidney in half lengthways and snip out the central core.

Brush the kidneys with melted butter, sprinkle with salt and pepper, and grill or fry them for not more than 6 minutes, turning them once only.

Fat from lamb kidneys can be rendered down for frying and roasting; fat from ox kidneys is used for suet crust and, after rendering down, is also suitable for deep-frying.

Liver

Ox liver, which is slightly coarse and tough, should be soaked for at least 1 hour in cold water to remove excess blood. It is best braised, although it can be sautéed like calf, lamb and pork liver.

Cut ox liver into $\frac{1}{4}$ in ($\frac{1}{2}$ cm) slices, coat with seasoned flour (page 100) and brown in butter together with thinly sliced onion and a few bacon rashers. Put the liver in a casserole dish, with the onion and bacon, cover with stock or tomato sauce. Put the lid on the dish and cook in the centre of a pre-heated oven, at 350°F (180°C, mark 4), for 45 minutes.

For grilling and frying, calf and lamb liver are preferable. Cut off any gristly portions and remove, with a knife or scissors, any central cores. Wash and dry the liver thoroughly, then cut into $\frac{1}{4}$ in ($\frac{1}{2}$ cm) thick slices. Brush with melted butter and sprinkle with salt and pepper before grilling the liver.

Alternatively, coat the slices in seasoned flour (page 100) and fry in butter over gentle heat. Avoid overcooking liver as this toughens it – as soon as blood begins to run, turn over the slices and cook the other side for a shorter time.

Pork liver may be prepared and cooked as calf and lamb liver, and is also used in pâtés, stews and casseroles.

Paunch

The stomach of a sheep is used for the traditional Scottish haggis. It is turned inside out and thoroughly cleaned and scrubbed before being stuffed. The stuffing consists of the cooked, minced heart, lungs and liver, seasoned with salt, pepper, cayenne, nutmeg and grated onion. This is mixed with 8 oz (225 g) oatmeal and 8 oz (225 g) shredded beef suet. The stuffing should only fill half the paunch as it swells during cooking. Add 2 tablespoons white stock and sew up the opening. Wrap the haggis in a clean cloth and boil over gentle heat for 3 hours.

Sweetbreads

Calf and lamb sweetbreads are prepared in the same way. One pair of sweetbreads will serve two people. Soak the sweetbreads in cold water for 1–2 hours to remove all blood. Drain and put in a pan with cold water.

Bring to the boil and drain off the liquid immediately; cover the sweetbreads with cold salted water and bring them to the boil again over low heat. As soon as boiling point is reached, lift out the sweetbreads and rinse under cold running water. Remove the black veins which run through the sweetbreads and as much as possible of the thin membranes which cover them.

Put the sweetbreads in a pan, barely cover with white stock and add a knob of butter and a squeeze of lemon juice. Bring to the boil, cover the pan with a lid and simmer gently for 15–20 minutes. Leave the sweetbreads to cool in the liquid, then drain. Coat with seasoned flour, beaten egg and breadcrumbs and fry in butter or bacon fat until golden brown. Serve with a creamy sauce and sautéed mushrooms. They can be used as a filling for vol-au-vents.

Tongues

Ox tongue is the largest, weighing 4–6 lb (1·8–2·7 kg). It can be purchased salted or fresh, and is cooked whole and usually served cold. Soak a salted tongue overnight in cold water, drain and put in a large pan. Cover with cold water, bring to the boil, then drain thoroughly. Return the tongue to the pan, cover with fresh cold water and add 6 peppercorns, 1 bouquet garni (page 99) and a sliced onion. Bring to the boil, cover with a lid and simmer for 2–3 hours or until tender (cook a fresh tongue for 5–6 hours).

Plunge the cooked tongue into cold water, then peel off the skin, starting from the tip end. Remove bones and gristle from the root end; trim it off neatly. Arch the tongue into a round shape and press it into a deep, round cake tin, about 7 in (18 cm) wide. Spoon over a little of the strained stock, cover the tongue with a weighted board and leave to set.

Lamb tongues are much smaller, weighing only about 8 oz (225 g) each. Soak them for 1–2 hours in lightly salted water. Boil the tongues, with 1 sliced onion, 1 bouquet garni (page 99), a few peppercorns and enough water to cover, for about 2 hours. Peel the tongues and serve them hot with parsley sauce made from the stock, or press the tongues in jellied stock as described for ox tongue and serve cold.

Tripe, ox

This is sold blanched and partly cooked, and additional cooking time varies according to the pre-cooking. Always check with the butcher how much longer the tripe should be cooked.

Marrow bones

The marrow contained in the large thigh and shoulder bones of the ox is considered a delicacy. Have the bones sawn into manageable lengths, scrape and wash them before sealing the ends with a flour and water paste. Tie each bone in a piece of pudding cloth, cover with water and simmer gently for 1½–2 hours. Drain, then extract the marrow with a teaspoon and spread on toast.

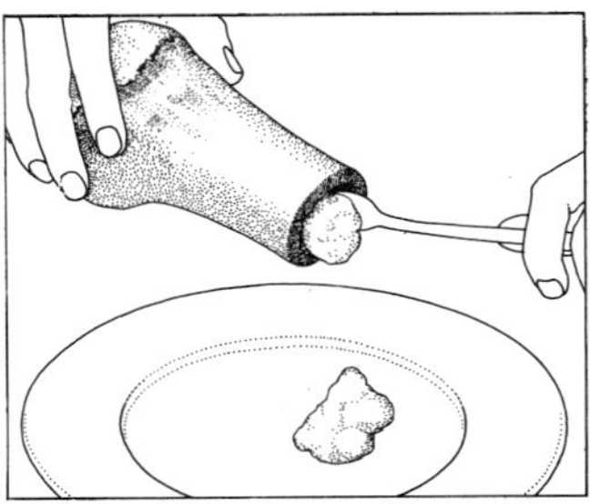

Scoop cooked marrow from the bone, using a small, pointed teaspoon

Veal bones

The bones of young calves contain a large quantity of gelatine which sets to jelly after boiling. Calf's head and feet are ideal for jellied stocks and brawns; they are, however, scarce and pigs' trotters, which also contain gelatine, may be used instead.

Oxtail

Although not strictly offal, this is often classed as such. It is sold skinned and jointed into pieces about 2 in (5 cm) long and is ideal for rich stews. As oxtail has a high proportion of fat and bone, allow one oxtail for 3–4 servings.

PREPARATION TIME: *25 min*
COOKING TIME: *3–3½ hours*
INGREDIENTS *(for 4)*:
1 oxtail
1 oz (25 g) seasoned flour (page 100)
2 oz (50 g) dripping or oil
2 onions
½ lb (225 g) carrots
2 sticks celery
½ pint (300 ml) brown stock (page 81)
Bouquet garni (page 99)

Trim as much fat as possible from the jointed oxtail and toss in seasoned flour. Heat the dripping in a heavy-based pan and brown the oxtail over high heat. Lift out the oxtail and put in a casserole. Fry the sliced onions, carrots and celery in the fat until lightly brown, sprinkle in the remaining seasoned flour and cook until it has absorbed all the fat. Stir in the stock gradually, then pour this sauce over the oxtail. Add the bouquet garni, cover the casserole and cook on a low oven shelf, at 300°F (160°C, mark 2), for about 3 hours. Add more stock during cooking if necessary.

Pig's head

This is often used for making brawn. It must be soaked for at least 24 hours in cold salted water before being boiled. Calf's head, too, makes an excellent brawn, but is now rarely obtainable.

Sausages

Pork – and beef – sausages are rarely home-produced today. Originally, they consisted of equal amounts of lean minced meat and fat, seasoned with salt, pepper and herbs. This mixture is stuffed into the blanched intestines with the aid of a sausage funnel attached to a mincer. Twist the filled intestines every 3–4 in (7½–10 cm). Many sausages contain up to one-third of their weight in breadcrumbs.

Black and white puddings

Black puddings are made from seasoned pig's blood and suet, and white puddings from white minced pork meat and fat. These mixtures are stuffed into blanched pig intestines and slowly poached before being marketed. Cut the puddings in half lengthways or into thick slices and fry in hot butter.

Trotters

Pig's feet or trotters contain a large amount of gelatine and are used, with pig's or calf's head, to produce brawn or jellied stock.

Carving Meat

Boned and rolled joints present no carving problems as the bones have already been removed. But for many people, carving meat with the bone in can be daunting. However, knowing about the position of the bones in the joints makes carving them less difficult. When carving, it is essential to use a sharp knife and a two-pronged fork with a thumb guard. With this equipment, the carver can produce neat slices which leave the joint looking respectable enough to serve cold. Meat may be carved across the grain, because this makes it more tender. Beef should be thinly sliced; pork and veal are sliced slightly thicker than beef; and lamb is sliced fairly thickly.

WING RIB OF BEEF

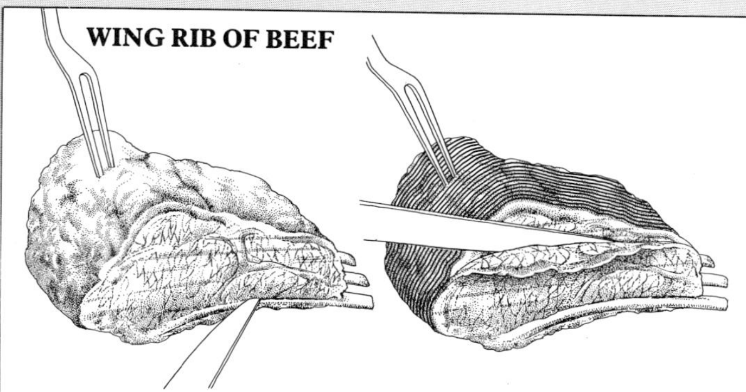

Remove the chine bone at the thick end of the joint and loosen the meat from the narrow ribs.

Carve the meat in thin downward slices; they should come away easily from the rib bones.

SIRLOIN OF BEEF

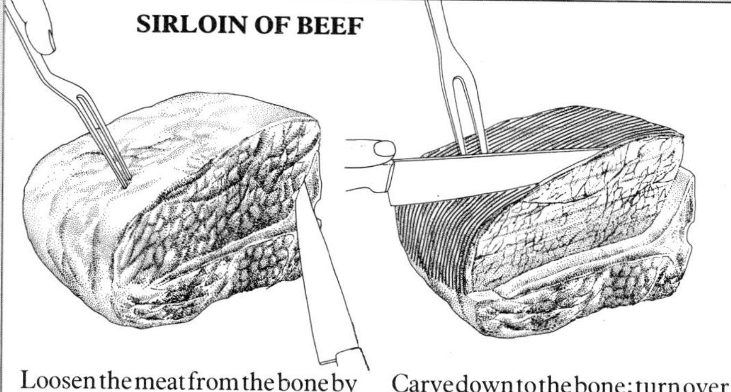

Loosen the meat from the bone by inserting a sharp knife between the meat and the bone.

Carve down to the bone; turn over the joint, remove the bone and carve the remaining meat.

WHOLE GAMMON

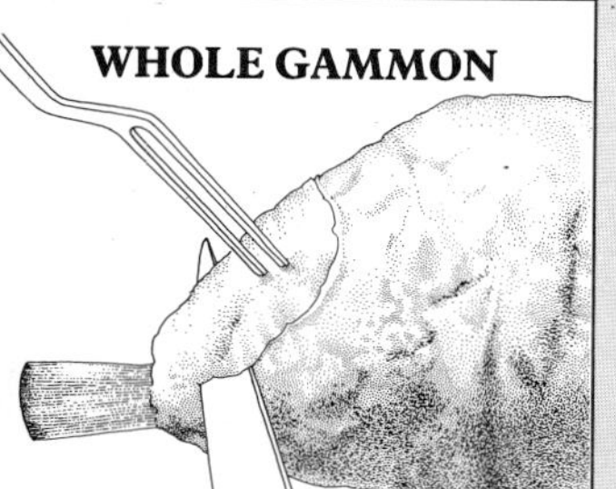

Remove a triangular section next to the knuckle end. Carve in a 'V' formation along the bone, taking a slice first from one side, then from the other.

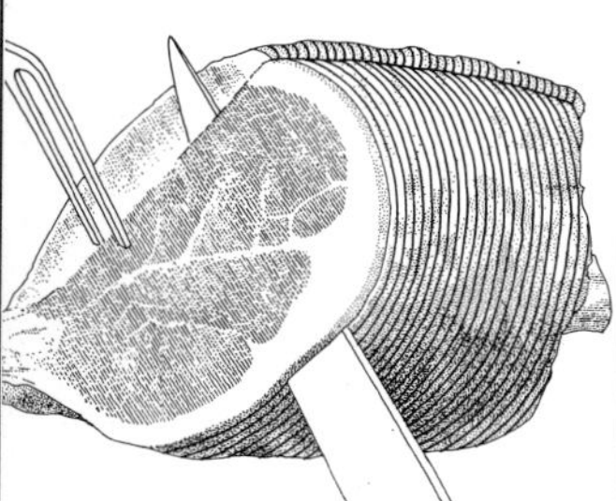

Continue carving, with the knife held at an oblique angle, and cutting long, thin slices from either side of the bone until the gammon is used up.

MIDDLE GAMMON

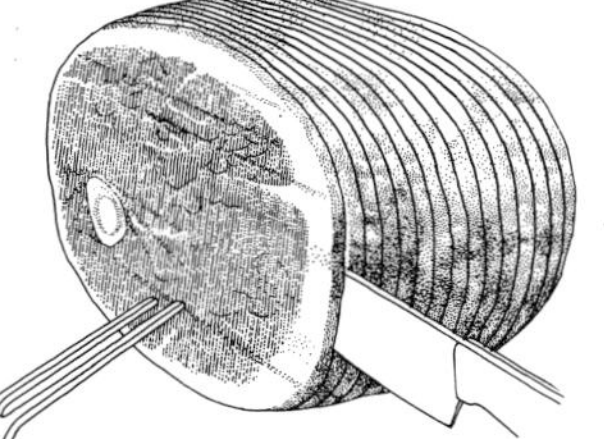

This is the prime cut of the whole gammon. It narrows towards the bone end, so the cuts made into the joint opposite the bone should be thicker at the outside, then taper towards the bone.

PORK LOIN

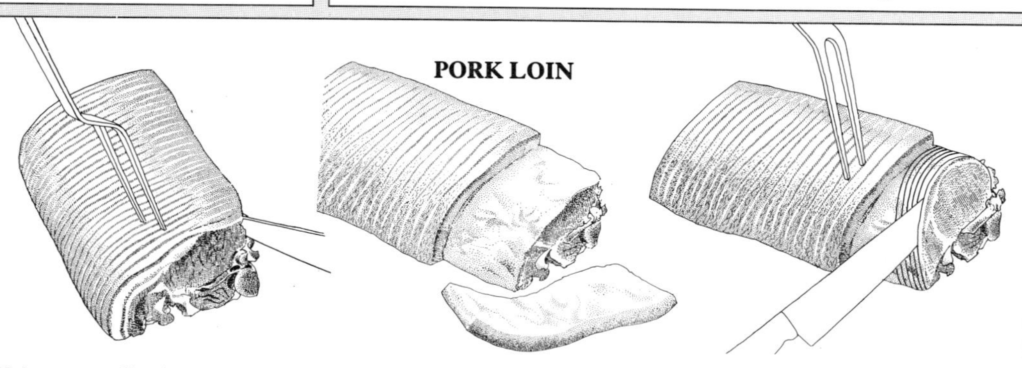

Using a small, sharp knife, remove the chine bone and free the meat. Leave crackling on.

Alternatively, remove the crackling in sections from the top of the joint to make carving easier.

Slice the loin at a slight angle so that the pieces are not too small. Carve pork thicker than beef.

LEG OF LAMB

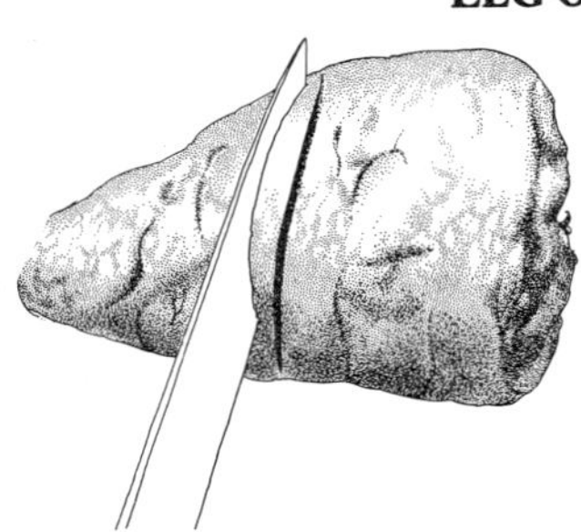 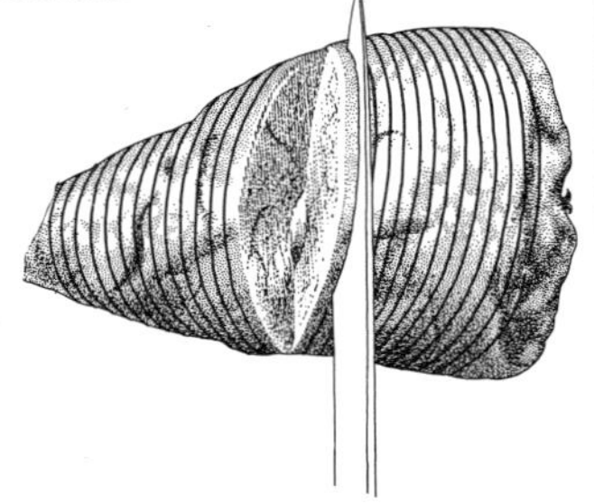

Use a cloth to hold the shank end of the joint and turn the meatiest side of the joint uppermost. Take out two slices, about $\frac{1}{4}$ in ($\frac{1}{2}$ cm) thick, from the centre of the leg, cutting to the bone.

Continue slicing from both sides of the first cut, and gradually angling the knife to obtain longer slices. Turn the joint over, remove any unwanted fat and carve horizontal slices along the leg.

LAMB LOIN

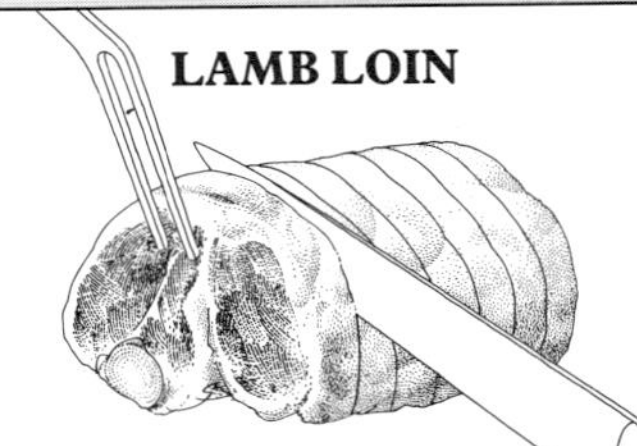

Remove the chine bone to loosen the meat from the bone. Carve the joint downward, in thick slices or chops, following the natural divisions of the bones. Boned, rolled and stuffed loin of lamb can be carved in thinner slices.

SADDLE OF LAMB

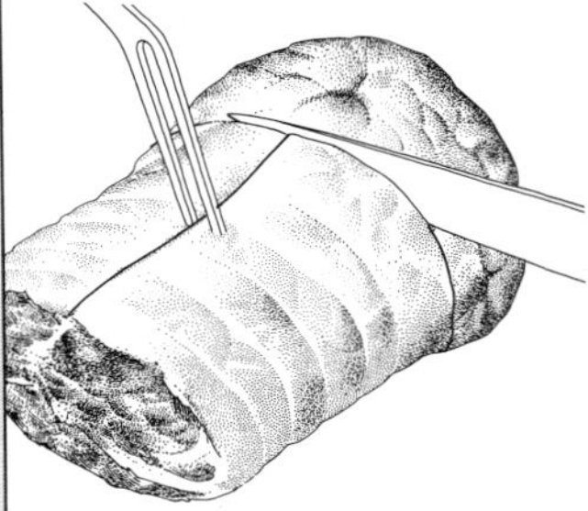

Cut across the base of the chump and at a right angle down the centre of the saddle, thus forming a 'T' shape.

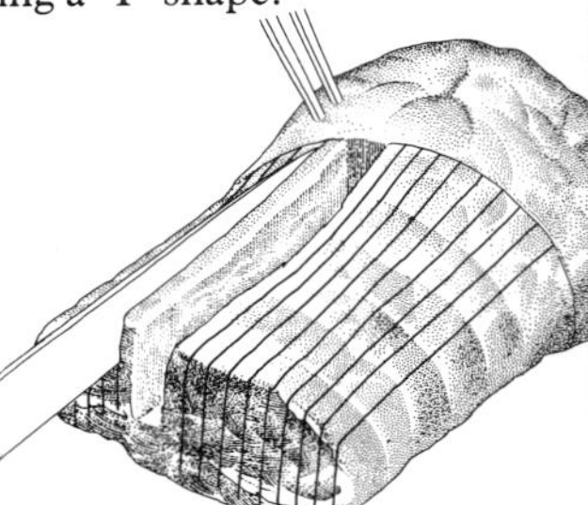

To carve the French way, cut fairly thick even slices down the length of the saddle.

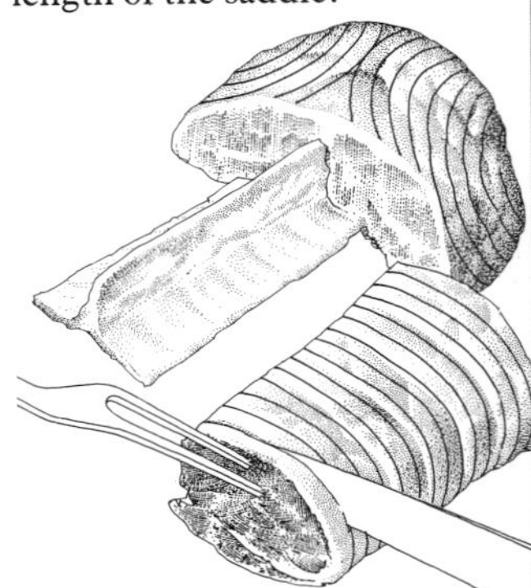

The English way is to remove the meat completely before it is carved. The chump end is carved from each side in turn, slanting the knife towards the middle. Turn the joint over and slice the fillet lengthways.

SHOULDER OF LAMB

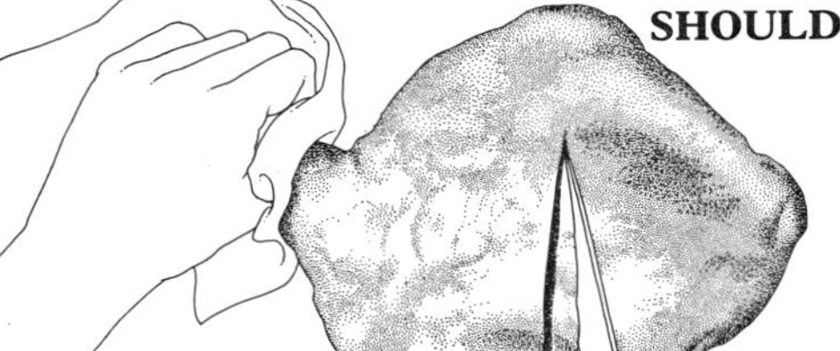

Use a cloth to hold the shank end of the joint. Turn the joint so that the thickest part – with the crisp skin – is uppermost. Cut a long slice, about $\frac{1}{4}$ in ($\frac{1}{2}$ cm) thick, from the centre of the joint down to the bone.

Carve thick slices from both sides of the first cut. Slices from the wedge of the blade bone will be smaller.

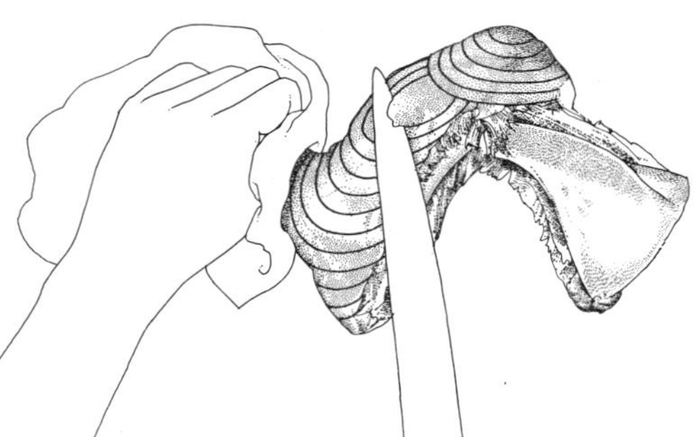

Cut horizontal slices from the shank bone until all the meat has been carved from the top of the joint.

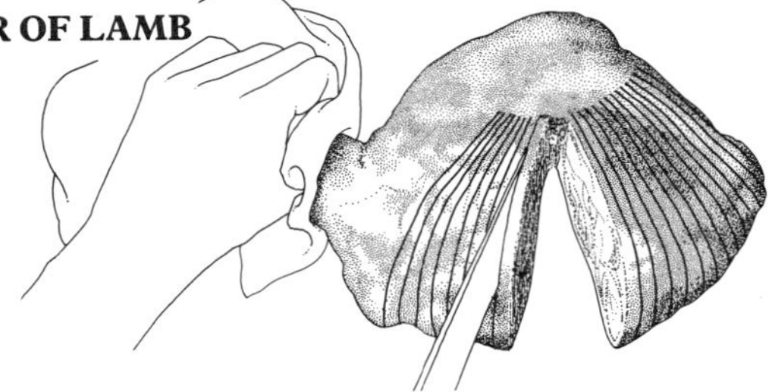 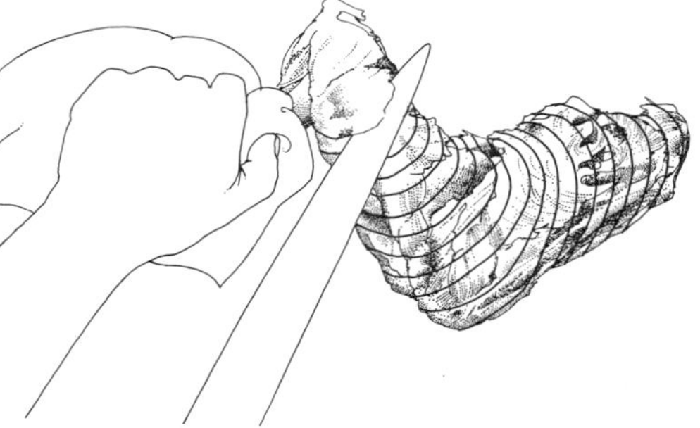

Turn the joint over, remove any unwanted pieces of fat from the underside of the shoulder, and carve thin horizontal slices from the remaining meat. The small succulent bits are the carver's pieces.

Fats and Oils

Fats and oils play an important part in cooking, as they contribute to or sometimes alter the flavour of food, especially when frying. The term "fat" can be taken generally to include all fatty substances, but it can also mean those which are solid at room temperature, those which are liquid being called "oils". Conveniently, this division more or less coincides with the division into saturated and unsaturated fats.

FATS

These are mainly derived from animal foods, such as meat and dairy products, but can also be produced from oily fish, nuts and vegetables.

Butter

Butter is made from the fatty substances skimmed from full cream milk. It is churned and then pressed to squeeze out water, and sometimes salt is added. It is used as the cooking medium for egg dishes and for sautéing and shallow frying over moderate heat. It is not suitable for frying at high temperatures as it burns easily, but a mixture of oil and butter will withstand quite a high heat without turning black.

Clarified butter, or ghee

This can be heated to a much higher temperature than ordinary butter without burning, and is therefore more suitable for frying and also for brushing food, for example fish, that is to be grilled. It is an expensive cooking medium, as 1 lb (450 g) of butter produces only about 10 oz (275 g) of clarified butter. To make it, melt the butter in a small pan over gentle heat and cook without stirring until the butter begins to foam. Continue to cook without letting it brown until the foaming stops. Remove the pan from the heat and let it stand until the milky deposits have sunk to the bottom, leaving a clear yellow liquid. Pour this carefully through muslin into a bowl. Clarified butter can be used in liquid or solid form and will keep well in the refrigerator.

Maître d'hôtel butter

A popular garnish for grilled meat or fish. Blend a tablespoon of finely chopped parsley with 4 oz (100 g) of softened butter and season to taste with salt, freshly ground pepper and a few drops of lemon juice. Other herbs, such as tarragon, chervil or chives, can also be used.

Dripping

This is the rendered fat from beef, mutton or poultry. A roast joint or bird will usually yield quite a lot, or it can be bought already rendered down. As it has a fairly high water content, it tends to splatter and is better used for roasting and shallow-frying than for deep-frying.

Lard

This is processed from pure pork fat and is excellent for frying. It is also used in baking some pastries and cakes.

Margarine

Made from vegetable oils blended with milk and vitamins, and sometimes with butter, margarine is interchangeable with butter for baking purposes and for sautéing. Most margarines are highly processed and therefore not acceptable to wholefood devotees. The fat content is the same as that of butter. From the point of view of low cholesterol content, soft margarines made from polyunsaturated vegetable oils are the best. Harder margarines are likely to have been processed in a way which in effect turns unsaturated fats into saturated ones.

Suet

Suet is the fat deposit from the loins and round the kidneys of beef or sheep. It is sold fresh for grating or already shredded and packed; it can be used in pastries, puddings and stuffings.

OILS

Edible oils are derived from fish, vegetables, cereals, fruit, nuts and seeds. They vary in colour and flavour, and choice is a matter of individual taste. Cold-pressed oil is the most natural (and most expensive) form, smelling and tasting strongly of its origin. Refined oil (often misleadingly called "pure") has had most of the vitamins and virtue bleached out or otherwise chemically removed, although some vitamins may be added back.

Corn oil

Fairly inexpensive and a good all-purpose oil with a mild taste.

Olive oil

Valued for its distinctive fruity taste and its affinity with certain foods. Suitable for frying and also for salad dressings: for these the best, but alas expensive, is the first pressing, also known as virgin oil.

Peanut oil

Also known as groundnut or arachide oil, this is a pleasant-tasting oil which will withstand quite high heat without burning.

Safflower oil

Expensive, but often recommended for a cholesterol-lowering diet as it is extremely high in polyunsaturated fats and in particular linoleic acid, the one essential fatty acid which cannot be manufactured by the body.

Sesame oil

Made from sesame seeds, this has a distinctive taste. It is much used in the Middle East for baking and also makes a good salad dressing.

Soya oil

A neutral-tasting oil, this is high in polyunsaturates and not too expensive.

Sunflower oil

An excellent all-round oil: can be used for frying and for salad dressings, high in polyunsaturates but cheaper than safflower oil.

Walnut oil

Very expensive; its strong nutty taste is much appreciated in salad dressings.

Garnishes

A well-chosen garnish adds texture, colour and flavour to a dish. It should be fresh and simple rather than cluttered, and if the dish is hidden by a sauce, the garnish should give a clue to what is in the sauce. For instance, a dish served *à la véronique* – that is, with a sauce containing white grapes – is always garnished with small bunches of grapes. Many garnishes are classic – lemon and parsley, for example, are traditional with fried fish.

Bread croûtons

Bread croûtons are a classic garnish with thick soups. Remove the crusts from $\frac{1}{2}$ in (1 cm) thick slices of bread; cut into cubes and toast or fry in a little butter until crisp and golden. Serve in a separate dish or sprinkled over the soup.

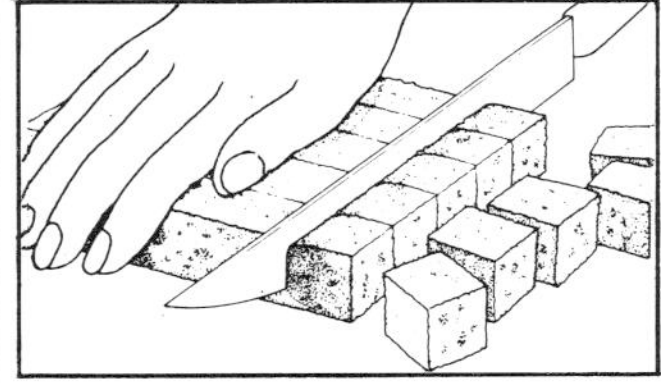

Cutting bread croûtons

Breadcrumbs

Fried crumbs are a traditional garnish for game and *au gratin* dishes. Melt 1 oz (25 g) butter or margarine in a frying pan, stir in 4 oz (100 g) fresh breadcrumbs and fry over moderate heat until the crumbs are evenly browned and golden. Turn frequently.

Celery tassels

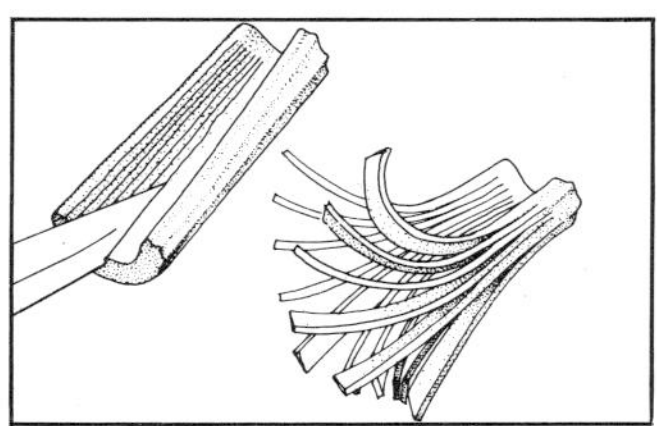

Edible garnish used with dips. Scrub the celery stalks, cut them in 2 in (5 cm) lengths, then cut down the lengths at narrow intervals almost to the base. Leave the stalks in a bowl of water to curl.

Cucumber

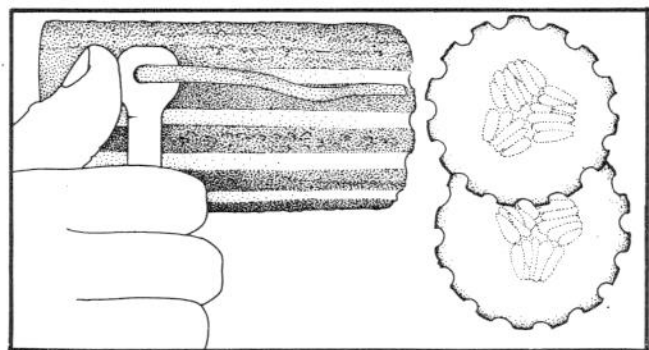

Sliced cucumber is a traditional garnish to a cold mousse or terrine. Deckled or ridged cucumber makes a more unusual decoration: wipe but do not peel a piece of cucumber; score it along the length with a fork or canelling knife, so that it has a serrated edge when cut into slices.

Gherkin fans

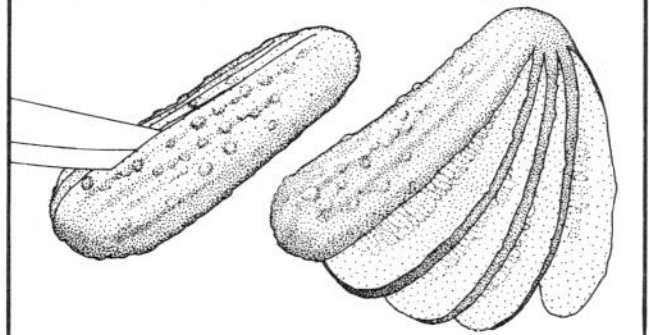

Drain cocktail gherkins thoroughly, then slice each three or four times lengthways almost to the stalk end. Ease the slices apart to open out like a fan.

Grapes

Most grapes are easily peeled, away from the stem end using the fingernails. If the skins are difficult to remove dip a few grapes at a time in boiling water for 30 seconds, then plunge them immediately into cold water.

Remove the pips from whole grapes by digging the rounded end of a clean new hair grip into the stem end of the grape; scoop out the pips. Alternatively, make a small cut down the length of the grape, being careful not to cut right through, and ease out the pips with the tip of the knife.

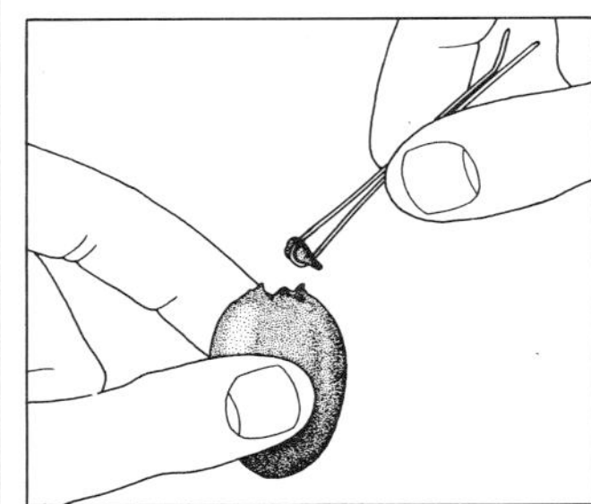

Mushrooms

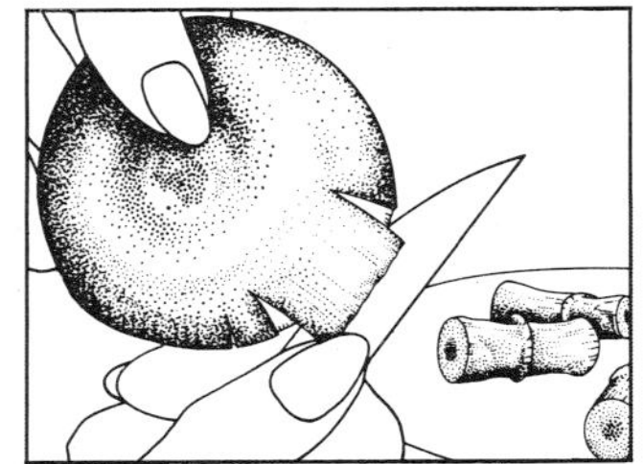

Trim by removing stalks, and peeling ragged skin

'Turned', these are a traditional garnish with grilled meat. Choose large button mushrooms, wipe with a damp cloth and trim the stem level with the cap. Peel off any ragged skin. With a sharp knife make a series of curving cuts, $\frac{1}{4}$ in ($\frac{1}{2}$ cm) apart, following the natural shape of the cap and from the top of the cap to the base. Take out a narrow strip along each indentation.

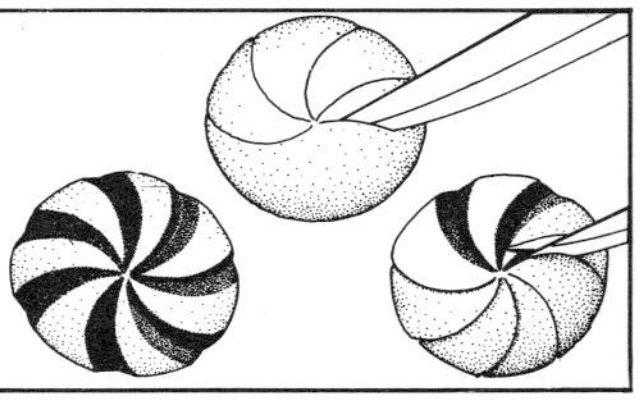

Nuts

Almonds are bought whole, halved or finely chopped (nibbed almonds), or flaked. Whole almonds, bought with or without their skins, can be used whole, split in two along their natural seam, cut into slivers or chopped. For slivered almonds blanch whole unskinned almonds in boiling water for 2–3 minutes; rub off the skins and, while still soft, cut the almonds into strips. For toasted almonds, spread the nuts in a shallow pan and brown under a grill.

Hazel nuts need to be toasted before the skins can be removed. Place the shelled nuts in a single layer on a shallow pan and toast under a medium grill until the skins are dry and the nuts begin to colour. Cool slightly, then rub the nuts against each other in a bag to loosen the skins.

Onions

Diced onions can be scattered over salads and other dishes. Peel off the skin and trim the root. Cut the onion in half through the root, then cut downwards in slices. To chop, turn the onion and slice across the first cuts. To dice, chop again across these cuts.

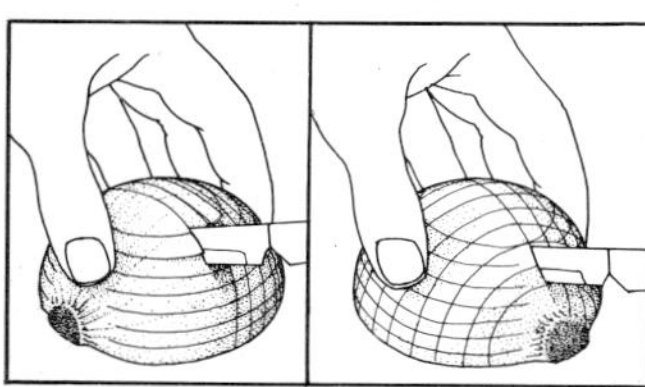

Parsley

Wash freshly picked parsley as soon as possible, shake well and remove long stems. Place in a jar of water reaching to the base of the leaves, or put in a polythene bag, tied at the neck. Parsley will then stay crisp and green for several days. Change the water in the container daily.

Scissors can be used for chopping parsley, but the result is coarser than when chopped with a knife. Gather the parsley into a tight bunch and with scissors snip off as much as is required straight on to the dish to be garnished.

To chop parsley, put the leaves on a chopping board. Hold the handle of a sharp straight-bladed knife firmly with one hand and the tip of the knife blade with the other; lift the handle in a see-saw action, gradually chopping the parsley finely or coarsely as required. Alternatively, bunch the parsley leaves in one hand on the chopping board and, using the knife, gradually shred the parsley, moving the fingers back to reveal more parsley.

Radish roses

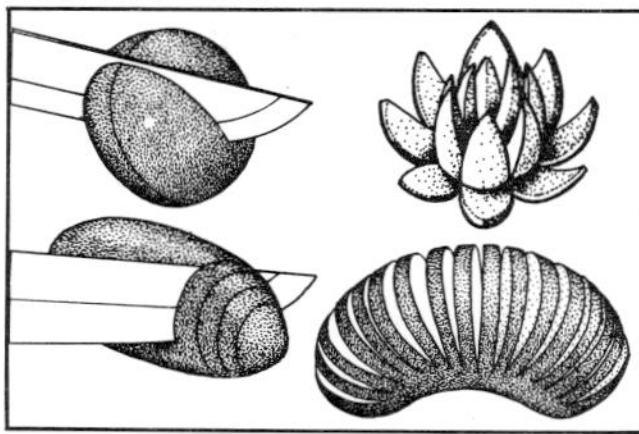

Used to garnish cold entrées, open sandwiches, hors d'oeuvre and salads. Make 6–8 cuts lengthways through a radish from the base towards the stalk; put the radishes in a bowl of iced water until they open like flowers. Long radishes look attractive when cut at intervals along the length to open out concertina-fashion.

Tomatoes

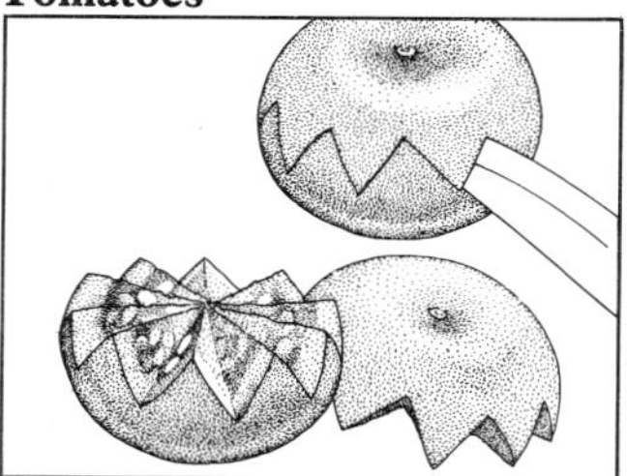

Serrated or vandyked tomatoes can be stuffed or used as tomato halves as a garnish for salads, flans, fried or grilled fish and meat. Choose firm tomatoes of even size. Using a small sharp knife, make a series of small V-shaped incisions around the circumference of the tomato. Carefully pull the two tomato halves apart. Oranges, grapefruit and melons may also be separated in this way.

Twists and butterflies

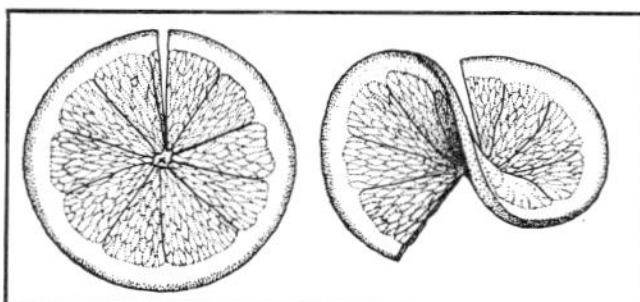

Tomatoes, cucumbers, beetroot, lemons and oranges make attractive garnishes to any number of dishes, both savoury and sweet. Slice the vegetable or fruit thinly, though not wafer-thin. For twists, cut each slice through to the centre, then twist the two halves in opposite directions and place in position. For butterflies, cut two deep V-shaped incisions to meet near the centre of each round lemon slice. Remove the two wedges in order to leave a butterfly shape.

Watercress

Another favourite garnish for meat, poultry and fish dishes. Trim off the stems, and wash the watercress leaves in plenty of salted water. Lift out, rinse and shake well. Discard any ragged and yellow leaves; arrange the watercress in small bunches to be added as garnish just before the dish is served. Washed watercress, with part of the stem left on, will keep for 1 day in the refrigerator if stored in a polythene bag.

TWO WAYS OF SKINNING FRESH TOMATOES

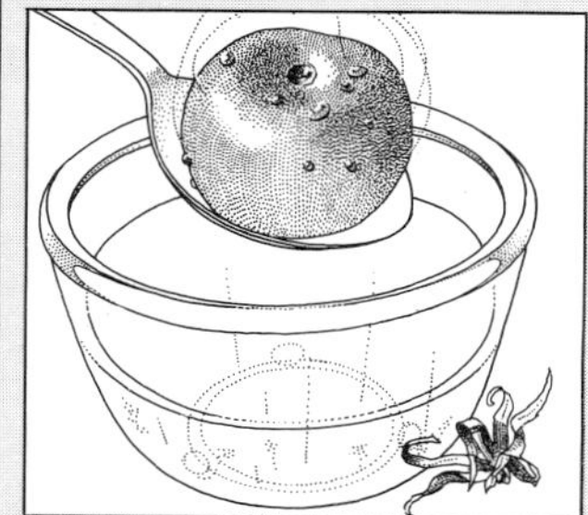

1. Put in hot water for 1 min

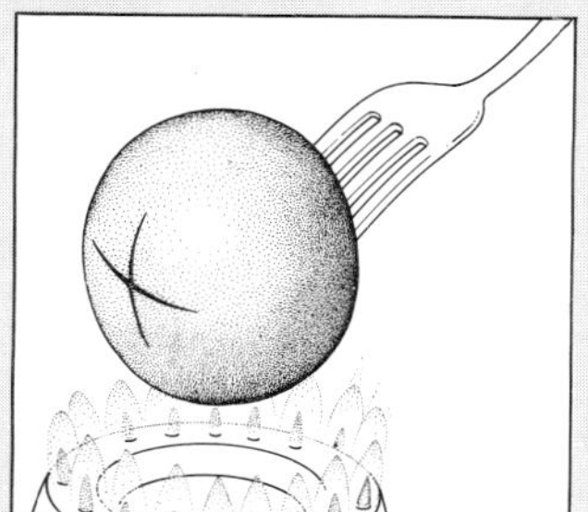

1. Hold tomato over open gas flame

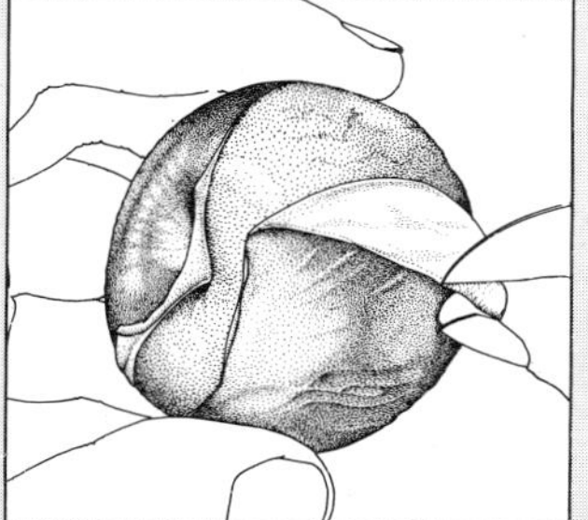

2. Peel soft skin from wet tomato

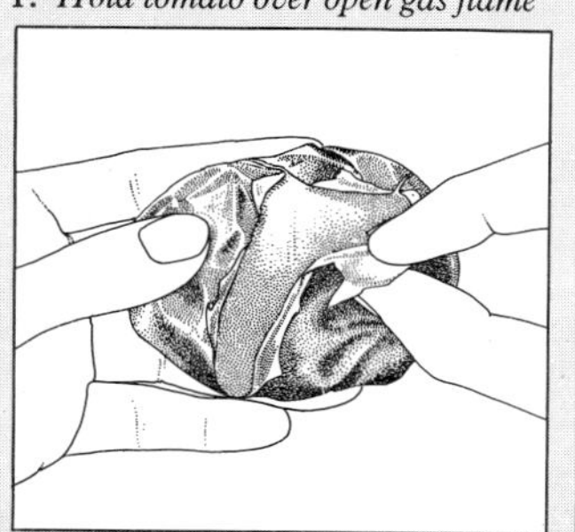

2. Peel away charred tomato skin

Home Freezing

The freezer is a time and money saver for anyone who cooks for a family. It enables a cook to plan well ahead, both in bulk-buying and in cooking. And, if the rules for the preparation, packaging and thawing of the raw materials are carefully followed, frozen food loses nothing in freshness and quality. Being able to freeze pre-cooked dishes for later use also has numerous advantages. Leftovers can be stored for later use. Time can be spent in the kitchen when it is convenient. Quantities of recipes can be doubled to save time, energy and cooking expense, with one dish eaten at once and the other frozen.

FREEZING PRE-COOKED FOOD

For successful freezing follow these pointers:

1. Working surroundings must be scrupulously clean, as freezing does not destroy germs in food.

2. Use top-quality ingredients and season lightly; more seasoning can always be added later.

3. Always slightly undercook dishes which are to be frozen, allowing for the time the food will be in the oven to heat up.

4. When recipes for soups, sauces and casseroles call for the addition of cream or egg yolks, omit these before freezing and add them when the dishes are being reheated. Do not freeze dishes with custard or mayonnaise.

5. Omit garlic before freezing (it can be added later) unless the food is going to remain in the freezer for only a short time.

6. Be generous with sauces, so that meat, chicken, fish and game will not dehydrate when frozen.

7. Cool all cooked and baked dishes thoroughly before packing and freezing.

8. Garnish re-heated food before serving, not before freezing.

9. Pack and label all pre-cooked foods carefully and note the number of portions. Soups can be frozen in square containers, removed when solid and then packed in polythene bags; casseroles can be frozen in their cooking dishes, turned out and packed in polythene bags to be returned to their dishes for thawing and re-heating.

10. Do not freeze whole roast joints or cold meat without a sauce, as the results are often apt to be disappointingly dry.

FREEZING FRESH FOOD

Only good-quality fresh meat should be frozen, and the best results are obtained when the meat has been fully hung before freezing. Cut the meat into convenient sizes, such as joints and chops. Remove as much bone as possible so that the meat will take up less space in the freezer. The bones can be used to make stock.

Meat to be used in stews and casseroles can be cut into cubes and packed in rigid containers.

Remove excess fat, as it can become rancid if exposed to oxygen. For the same reason, pack meat carefully in airtight wrappings. Pad sharp corners or bones with foil or thin self-adhesive plastic wrap, to prevent them from perforating the packaging. Pack in foil. Overwrap with heavy-duty polythene, excluding as much air as possible.

Weigh the meat before freezing, and label it with weight, description and date. Cutlets, chops, steaks and hamburgers should be interleaved with waxed paper or thin polythene, so that they can be easily separated.

Allow meat to thaw slowly in its wrapping in a cool place or in the refrigerator. If it is needed in a hurry, the thawing can be speeded up by placing the meat, in its wrapping, in cold water; part of the flavour is, however, lost. Small cuts of meat such as chops and steaks can be cooked from the frozen state, but it is advisable to cook them over lower heat than usual.

FREEZING PREPARED AND PRE-COOKED DISHES

Meat dishes (2 months)	Cook for a slightly shorter time than usual to allow for re-heating. Do not season heavily. Make sure meat is completely immersed in gravy or sauce. It is better to add potatoes, rice, noodles, garlic and celery at time of serving. Pack in rigid foil containers; or freeze in foil-lined casserole, remove and pack in polythene bags	Turn frozen food out of container into saucepan to re-heat. Pre-formed foil-lined dishes may be re-heated in oven in original casserole for 1 hour at 400°F (200°C, mark 6), reducing heat if necessary to 350°F (180°C, mark 4) for last 40 min.
Meat loaves, pâtés, terrines (1 month)	Make in usual way, taking care not to season or spice heavily. When cold, remove from tins or moulds and wrap in polythene to freeze	Thaw in wrapping for 6–8 hours, or overnight in refrigerator

FREEZING UNCOOKED MEAT

Meat (storage time in brackets)	Preparation and Packaging	Thawing
Joints (beef 8 months; lamb, pork and veal 6 months)	Wrap in heavy-duty polythene bags, seal well and label. May be overwrapped with stockinet	Thaw thoroughly before cooking, preferably in a refrigerator. Allow 5 hours per lb. (450 g) in a refrigerator, 2 hours per lb. (450 g) at room temperature
Cutlets, chops, hamburgers, steaks and cubed meat (3 months)	Pack in suitable quantities. Separate cutlets, chops, hamburgers and steaks with waxed paper. Pack in polythene bags or rigid containers	These small cuts can be cooked frozen over gentle heat
Minced meat and sausage meat (3 months)	Pack in small quantities in bags or rigid containers	Thaw in a cool place for 1½ hours or in a refrigerator for 3 hours
Offal and sausages (1–3 months)	Clean and trim offal. Pack in small quantities in polythene bags	Thaw in a cool place for 1½ hours or in a refrigerator for 3 hours

A to Z of Cookery Terms

A

à point Of meat, medium cooked

arrowroot Starch made by grinding the root of an American plant of the same name. Used for thickening sauces

aspic Clear jelly made from the cooked juices of meat, chicken or fish

au gratin Cooked food, covered with a sauce, sprinkled with crumbs or grated cheese, dotted with butter and browned under the grill

B

barding Covering lean meat, game and poultry with thin slices of pork fat or bacon to prevent the flesh drying out during roasting

basting Moistening meat or poultry with pan juices during roasting by using a spoon or bulb baster

beating Mixing food to introduce air, to make it lighter and fluffier, using a wooden spoon, hand whisk or electric mixer

binding Adding eggs, cream or melted fat to a dry mixture to hold it together

blanching Boiling briefly 1. To loosen the skin from nuts, fruit and vegetables. 2. To set the colour of food and to kill enzymes prior to freezing. 3. To remove strong or bitter flavours

blanquette Veal, poultry or rabbit stew in a creamy sauce

blending Combining ingredients with a spoon, beater or liquidiser to achieve a uniform mixture

boiling Cooking in liquid at a temperature of 212°F (100°C)

bouquet garni A bunch of herbs, including parsley, thyme, marjoram, bay, etc., tied with string; or a ready-made mixture of herbs in a muslin bag. Used for flavouring soups and stews

bourguignonne In the style of Burgundy, e.g. cooked with red wine

braising Browning in hot fat and then cooking slowly, in a covered pot, with vegetables and a little liquid

browning Searing the outer surface of meat to seal in the juices

C

carbonnade Beef stew made with beer

casserole 1. Cooking pot, complete with lid, made of ovenproof or flameproof earthenware, glass or metal. 2. Also, a slow-cooked stew of meat, fish or vegetables

cassoulet Stew of haricot beans, pork, lamb, goose or duck, sausage, vegetables and herbs

chasseur Cooked with mushrooms, shallots and white wine

chilling Cooling food, without freezing it, in the refrigerator

chine Of pork; a pair of loins left undivided

chining Separating the backbone from the ribs in a joint of meat to make carving easier

chorizo Smoked pork sausage

clarified butter Butter cleared of water and impurities by slow melting and filtering

cocotte Small ovenproof, earthenware, porcelain or metal dish, used for baking individual dishes, mousses or soufflés

colander Perforated metal or plastic basket used for draining away liquids

creole Of Caribbean cookery; prepared with pimentoes, tomatoes, okra, rice and spicy sauces

crêpe Thin pancake

curdle To cause fresh milk or a sauce to separate into solids and liquids by overheating or by adding acid

cure To preserve fish or meat by drying, salting or smoking

D

daube Stew of braised meat and vegetables

déglacer To dilute pan juices by adding wine, stock or cream to make gravy

devilling Preparing meat, poultry or fish with highly seasoned ingredients, for grilling or roasting

dice To cut into small cubes

dough Mixture of flour, water, milk and/or egg, sometimes enriched with fat, which is firm enough to knead, roll and shape

dressing 1. Sauce for a salad. 2. Stuffing for meat or poultry

dripping Fat which drips from meat, poultry or game during roasting

dumplings Small balls made of dough, forcemeat or potato mixture, which are steamed or poached. Used to garnish soups and stews.

E

en croûte Encased in pastry

entrée 1. Third course in a formal meal, following the fish course. 2. Main dish, sauced and garnished

escalope Thin slice of meat which is beaten flat and shallow-fried

F

fines herbes Mixture of finely chopped fresh parsley, chervil, tarragon and chives

folding in Enveloping one ingredient or mixture in another, using a large metal spoon or spatula

freezing Solidifying or preserving food by chilling and storing it at 32°F (0°C)

fricadelles Meat balls, made with minced pork and veal, spices, breadcrumbs, cream and egg; poached in stock or shallow-fried

G

garnishing Enhancing a dish with edible decorations

gelatine Transparent protein, made from animal bones and tissue, which melts in hot liquid and forms a jelly when cold

ghee Clarified butter made from the milk of the water buffalo

glace de viande Meat glaze or residue in the bottom of a pan after roasting or frying meat. Or concentrated meat stock

glaze A glossy finish given to food by brushing with beaten egg, milk, sugar syrup or jelly after cooking

goulash Beef and onion stew flavoured with paprika and tomato

gratiné See au gratin

gravy 1. Juices exuded by roasted meat and poultry. 2. A sauce made from these juices by boiling with stock or wine, and sometimes thickened with flour

H

haggis Savoury Scottish pudding, consisting of chopped offal, suet, onions and oatmeal, which is boiled in the stomach lining of a sheep

hanging Suspending meat or game in a cool, dry place until it is tender

hash Dish of leftover chopped meat, potatoes or other vegetables, which are fried together

herbs Plants without a woody stem. Culinary herbs, which are available in fresh or dried form, include basil, bay leaf, chervil, marjoram, mint, oregano, parsley, rosemary, sage, savory, tarragon and thyme. Used for their aromatic properties

hors d'oeuvre Hot or cold appetisers served at the start of a meal

J

jardinière, à la Garnish of fresh, diced and cooked vegetables, arranged in separate groups

joint 1. Prime cut of meat for roasting. 2. To divide meat, game or poultry into individual pieces

jus Juices from roasting meat used as gravy

K

kebab Meat cubes marinated and grilled on a skewer

L

lard Natural or refined pork fat

larding Threading strips of fat through lean meat, using a special needle. This prevents the meat become dry during roasting

M

marinade Blend of oil, wine or vinegar, herbs and spices. Used to tenderise and add flavour to meat, game or fish

A to Z of Cookery Terms

marinate To steep in marinade
moussaka Near-Eastern dish of minced meat, aubergines and tomatoes, which is topped with cheese sauce or savoury custard

N

navarin Stew of lamb and vegetables

O

offal Edible internal organs of meat, poultry and game
osso buco Dish of marrow bones braised with tomato and wine

P

paprika Ground, sweet red pepper
par-boiling Boiling for a short time to cook food partially
pâté 1. Savoury mixture which is baked in a casserole or terrine, and served cold. 2. Savoury mixture baked in a pastry case and served hot or cold
paupiette Thin slice of meat rolled round a savoury filling
pickle To preserve meat or vegetables in brine or vinegar solution
pimento Sweet pepper
poaching Cooking food in simmering liquid, just below boiling point
provençale In the Provence style, e.g. cooked with garlic and tomatoes

R

ragoût Stew of meat and vegetables
reducing Concentrating a liquid by boiling and evaporation
rendering 1. Slowly cooking meat tissues and trimmings to obtain fat. 2. Clearing frying fat by heating it
rissole Small roll or patty made of cooked minced meat
roasting Cooking in the oven with radiant heat, or on a spit over or under an open flame
roux Mixture of fat and flour which, when cooked, is used as a base for savoury sauces

S

saignant Of meat; underdone
sauté To fry food rapidly in shallow, hot fat, tossing and turning it until evenly browned

scaloppine Small escalopes of veal
Schnitzel Veal slice; see escalope
scoring Cutting gashes or narrow grooves in the surface of food, e.g. in pork rind to produce crackling
searing Browning meat rapidly with fierce heat to seal in the juices
seasoned flour Flour flavoured with salt and pepper
simmering Cooking in liquid which is heated to just below boiling point
skimming Removing cream from the surface of milk, or fat or scum from broth or jam
smoking Curing food, such as bacon or fish, by exposing it to wood smoke for a considerable period of time
starch Carbohydrate obtained from cereal and potatoes
steaming Cooking food in the steam rising from boiling water
stewing Simmering food slowly in a covered pan or casserole
stuffing Savoury mixture of bread or rice, herbs, fruit or minced meat, used to fill poultry, fish, meat and vegetables
suet Fat around beef or lamb kidneys

T

terrine 1. Earthenware pot used for cooking and serving pâté. 2. Food cooked in a terrine
timbale 1. Cup-shaped earthenware or metal mould. 2. Dish prepared in such a mould

V

vinaigrette Mixture of oil, vinegar, salt and pepper, which is sometimes flavoured with herbs

W

whisk Looped wire utensil used to beat air into eggs, cream or batters
Wiener Schnitzel Veal slice cooked in the Viennese style, e.g. coated in egg and breadcrumbs, fried in butter and garnished with anchovies and capers

Y

yogurt Curdled milk which has been treated with harmless bacteria

Index

The Good Health Cookbooks

The Publishers wish to express their gratitude for major contributions by the following people:

Editor: URSULA WHYTE   Art Director: MICHAEL McGUINNESS   Designer: SANDRA DEON-CARDYN

Diet Consultant: MIRIAM POLUNIN   Home Economist: VALERIE BARRETT   Additional Photography: PHILIP DOWELL

The Publishers also wish to acknowledge the help of the following:

Gilly Abrahams for editorial help; Fred and Kathie Gill for proof reading; Mary-Anne Joy for help with calorie counting;
Terri Lamb for design assistance; Vicki Robinson for indexing; and Michelle Thompson for food preparation.
Additional photographic props were supplied by Graham and Green.

The Good Health Cookbooks are based on THE COOKERY YEAR, **to which the following made major contributions:**

Editorial Adviser: ELIZABETH POMEROY
Photographer: PHILIP DOWELL
Home Economist: JOY MACHELL

Writers:			**Artists:**
Ena Bruinsma	Elizabeth Pomeroy	Colour:	Black and white:
Margaret Coombes	Zena Skinner	Roy Coombs	David Baird
Derek Cooper	Katie Stewart	Pauline Ellison	Brian Delf
Margaret Costa	Marika Hanbury Tenison	Hargrave Hands	Gary Hincks
Denis Curtis	Silvino S. Trompetto, MBE,	Denys Ovenden	Richard Jacobs
Theodora FitzGibbon	Maître Chef des Cuisines,	Charles Pickard	Rodney Shackell
Nina Froud	Savoy Hotel	Josephine Ranken	Michael Woods
Jane Grigson	Suzanne Wakelin	Charles Raymond	Sidney Woods
Nesta Hollis	Kathie Webber	Rodney Shackell	Black and white photography:
Kenneth H. C. Lo	Harold Wilshaw	Faith Shannon, MBE	Michael Newton
		John Wilson	

Typesetting: Tradespools Ltd, Frome   **Printing:** W. S. Cowell Ltd, Ipswich   **Binding:** Dorstel Press Ltd, Harlow